# CiTY·SMaRT™ GUIDEBOOK

# Denver

Second Edition

by Georgia Garnsey and Hilary Garnsey
Dining chapter by Kyle Wagner

John Muir Publications
Santa Fe, New Mexico

John Muir Publications, P. O. Box 613, Santa Fe, New Mexico 87504

Copyright © 1998, 1996 by John Muir Publications
Cover and maps © 1998 by John Muir Publications
All rights reserved.

Printed in the United States of America.
Second edition. First printing September 1998.

The COORS and COORS FIELD trademarks are used
under license from Coors Brewing Company.

Many of the images in this book have been provided by the Denver Metro
Convention & Visitors Bureau and appear with the credit DMC & VB.

ISBN: 1-56261-420-7
ISSN: 1088-3606

Editors: Dianna Delling, Pamela Emsden
Graphics Editor: Tom Gaukel
Production: Nikki Rooker
Design: Janine Lehmann
Cover Design: Suzanne Rush
Maps: Julie Felton
Typesetter: Kathleen Sparkes, White Hart Designs
Printer: Publishers Press
Front Cover Photo: © Jack Olson—16th St. Mall
Back Cover Photo: © Jack Olson—Coors Field

Distributed to the book trade by
Publishers Group West
Berkeley, California

*While every effort has been made to provide accurate, up-to-date information, the author and publisher accept no responsibility for loss, injury, or inconvenience sustained by any person using this book.*

# CONTENTS

**How to Use This Book** v

## 1 Welcome to Denver 1
A Brief History of Denver 1 • Denver Time Line 6 • Denver and the Future 9 • Recommended Reading 10 • The People of Denver 11 • The City's Weather 13 • Calendar of Events 14 • Business and Economy 16 • Cost of Living 18 • Dressing in Denver 18

## 2 Getting Around Denver 19
Finding Your Way Around 20 • Public Transportation 20 • Driving in Denver 26 • Biking in Denver 27 • Denver International Airport 28 • Other Airports 32 • Train Services 32 • Interstate and Regional Bus Service 34

## 3 Where to Stay 35
Downtown Denver 37 • Central Denver 47 • East Denver 51• South Denver 57 • West Denver 58 • North Denver 60

## 4 Where to Eat 61
Downtown Denver 64 • Central Denver 72 • East Denver 84 • South Denver 86 • West Denver 90 • North Denver 93

## 5 Sights and Attractions 95
Downtown Denver 97 • Central Denver 108 • East Denver 113 • West Denver 114 • North Denver 118

## 6 Kids' Stuff 119
Animals and the Great Outdoors 119 • Museums and Libraries 122 • Puppets and Theater 125 • Theme Parks 127 • Stores for Kids 127• Restaurants Kids Love 129

## 7 Museums and Galleries 130
Art Museums 130 • Science and History Museums 132 • Art Galleries 135

## 8 Parks and Gardens 139

## 9 Shopping 147
Shopping Areas 147 • Specialty Stores and Markets 148 • Shopping Malls and Centers 163

## 10 Sports and Recreation 165
Bicycling 165 • Boating 166 • Bowling 168 • Camping/Backpacking 168 • Day Hikes 168 • Fishing 170 • Fitness Clubs 172 • Golf 173 • Horseback Riding 174 • Hunting 175 • In-line Skating 175 • Kayaking 175 • Scuba Diving 176 • Skating 176 • Downhill Skiing 177 • Cross-country Skiing 179 • Sledding 180 • Tennis 180• Spectator Sports 180

## 11 Performing Arts — 184
Theater 184 • Classical Music and Opera 188 • Dance 189 • Concert Venues 190

## 12 Nightlife — 194
Dance Clubs 194 • Jazz Clubs 196 • Blues Clubs 198 • Other Music Clubs 198 • Country and Western Clubs 200 • Pubs and Bars 201 • Comedy Clubs 204 • Dinner Theater 204 • Movie Houses 205

## 13 Day Trips From Denver — 207
Boreas Pass Scenic Drive 207 • Boulder 209 • Rafting at Buena Vista 211 • Central City 212 • Colorado Springs 213 • Estes Park and Rocky Mountain National Park 215 • Georgetown 216 • Rocky Mountain Arsenal National Wildlife Area 218 • Roxborough State Park 219

### Appendix: City•Smart Basics — 221

### Index — 225

## MAP CONTENTS

**Greater Denver Zones** vi

**2 Getting Around the City**
RTD Light Rail — 21
Airport — 29

**3 Where to Stay**
Downtown Denver — 36
Central Denver — 46
Greater Denver — 52–53

**4 Where to Eat**
Downtown Denver — 66
Central Denver — 73
Greater Denver — 82–83

**5 Sights and Attractions**
Downtown Denver — 96
Central Denver — 109
Greater Denver — 116-117

**13 Day Trips**
Denver Region — 208

# HOW TO USE THIS BOOK

Whether you're a visitor, a new resident, or a native of the Mile High City, you'll find *City•Smart Guidebook: Denver* indispensable. Written by Denver residents Georgia and Hilary Garnsey, with a dining chapter by Kyle Wagner, food writer at Denver's news and arts weekly, *Westword*, this book gives you an insider's view of the best Denver has to offer.

This book presents Denver and the greater metro Denver area in six geographic zones. The zone divisions are listed at the bottom of this page and are shown on the map on the following pages. Look for a zone designation in each listing. You'll also find maps of downtown, central, and greater Denver in chapters 3, 4, and 5 to help you locate the accommodations, restaurants, and sights in those chapters.

*Sample listing:*
**COLORADO HISTORY MUSEUM**
**1399 Broadway, Denver**
**303/866-3682**                    **DD**

## Greater Denver Zones

### DD—Downtown Denver
Bounded by Pennsylvania Street on the east, Ninth Avenue on the south, Osage on the west, and extending north to the intersection of Blake Street and Broadway. Includes the 16th Street Mall, the Civic Center, and the State Capitol building.

### CD—Central Denver
Bounded by I-70 on the north, Colorado Boulevard on the east, West Florida and East Louisiana Avenues on the south, and Federal Boulevard on the west. Includes Cherry Creek and City Park.

### ED—East Denver
Bordered by Colorado Boulevard on the west; includes Denver International Airport and Aurora

### SD—South Denver
Bordered by West Florida and East Louisiana Avenues on the north; includes Englewood and Littleton

### WD—West Denver
Bordered by Federal Boulevard on the east; includes Golden, Wheat Ridge, Arvada, and Lakewood

### ND—North Denver
Bordered by I-70 on the south; includes Thornton, Westminster, and Boulder (Boulder is not covered extensively in this book; however, the authors have included several sights, restaurants, and accommodations in the Boulder area and have also recommended a day trip to the area.)

# GREATER DENVER

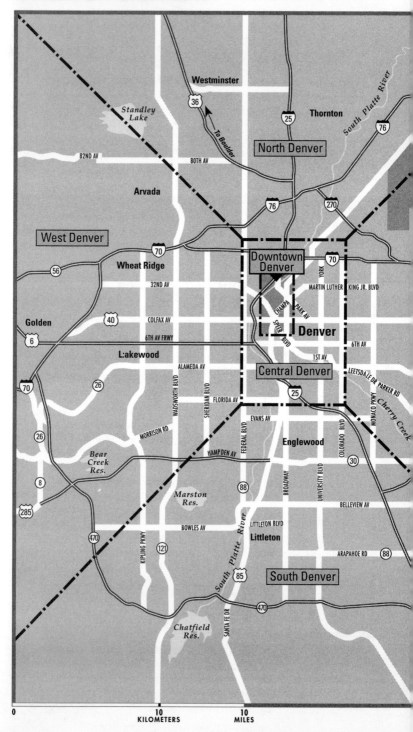

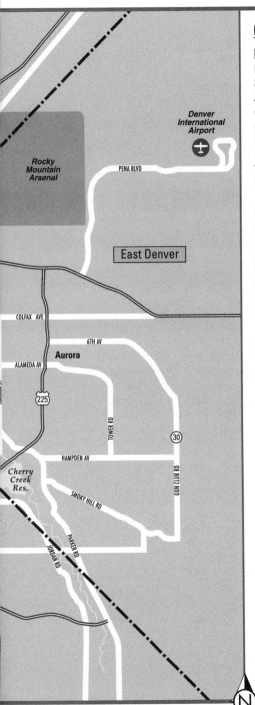

## Greater Denver Zones

### DD—Downtown Denver
Bounded by Pennsylvania Street on the east, Ninth Avenue on the south, Osage on the west, and extending north to the intersection of Blake Street and Broadway. Includes the 16th Street Mall, the Civic Center, and the State Capitol building.

### CD—Central Denver
Bounded by I-70 on the north, Colorado Boulevard on the east, West Florida and East Louisiana Avenues on the south, and Federal Boulevard on the west. Includes Cherry Creek and City Park.

### ED—East Denver
Bordered by Colorado Boulevard on the west; includes Denver International Airport and Aurora

### SD—South Denver
Bordered by West Florida and East Louisiana Avenues on the north; includes Englewood and Littleton

### WD—West Denver
Bordered by Federal Boulevard on the east; includes Golden, Wheat Ridge, Arvada, and Lakewood

### ND—North Denver
Bordered by I-70 on the south; includes Thornton, Westminster, and Boulder

# 1
# WELCOME TO DENVER

Denver's birth was almost accidental. It was settled by people who came for gold that the city didn't have, and decided to stay anyway. The city grew by improvisation. It became a place that supplied other places—an outpost of civilization for the gold miners, scouts, cowboys, adventurers, and rogues who roamed the mountains and the wide open spaces in between.

From such inauspicious beginnings, the fortunes of Denver have ebbed and flowed with nearly the same frequency as the sudden and unpredictable changes in the city's weather. Just as there can be beautiful "spring" days in January and snowstorms in June, the city has known wild prosperity one day and destitution the next. Perhaps this perverse changeability can account for the open-minded, laid-back, and friendly character of the city. Denverites are philosophic survivors, and Denver is a city that is coming into its own.

## A Brief History of Denver

### The Early Days
Denver's history dates from 1858, when a band of Cherokee Indians and some farmers from Georgia set up camp at the confluence of Cherry Creek and the South Platte River. Disappointed by the sparse gold in Cherry Creek, most of the party moved on, but a few stayed. Auraria and St. Charles sprang up as the first two settlements. St. Charles became Denver City when General William Larimer jumped the claim and renamed the site after the governor of Kansas Territory, General James W. Denver.

When Auraria and Denver City were consolidated in 1860, Denver was officially born.

The only trees growing in this dusty, sunny place were the cottonwoods and chokecherries that crowded the banks of the Platte River and Cherry Creek. During Denver's early years, a devastating flood and a fire destroyed its jumble of buildings, shops, and homes. When the Union Pacific Railroad chose Cheyenne, Wyoming, for its coast-to-coast connection, it seemed that the Rocky Mountains looming west of Denver would block the city's growth.

Denver, 1859

The city grew only because its people were stubborn. City officials and businessmen formed their own railway company and established a Cheyenne route that linked them to the transcontinental line. Residents built more durable houses out of brick made from the area's clay soil. During the late 1800s, prospering from the gold strikes in Colorado, they built houses in every Victorian style of the times—from Neoclassical to Mediterranean, Spanish, Tudor, Renaissance, Colonial, and back again.

Early Denverites were not fazed by the arid landscape. The "City Ditch" was built and filled with water from a foothills stream south of town. The City Ditch ran through Denver's parks, and residents diverted water into channels that ran down many streets. Denver became a place of maples and oaks and lindens and forsythia bushes reminiscent of every tree and plant that folks remembered from wherever they had come.

Robert Speer, early Denver mayor

Some came to Denver to cure their tubercular lungs in the clear, pure mountain air and sunlight. Many of those cured, such as Robert Speer, Denver's mayor from 1904 to 1912 and from 1916 to 1918, stayed and made invaluable contributions to the place where they had regained their health. Speer envi-

*Biking in turn-of-the-century Denver*

sioned a grand plan to transform a haphazard cow town into a "City Beautiful." He wielded the power of his well-oiled (and sometimes corrupt) political machine and a strong mayoral government system. The results included a master plan calling for parks, parkways, and a park-like Civic Center graced by beautiful government buildings and monuments.

Since the Panic of 1893 and the resulting repeal of the Silver Purchase Act, Denver's fortunes have risen and fallen with its dependence on the region's natural resources, first gold and silver, and later oil and gas. Residents have been dazed by the throngs who have flocked to the area for the boom periods, only to leave during the inevitable busts.

## Twentieth Century Denver

The 20-year administration of Mayor Benjamin Stapleton (1923–31, 1935–47) spanned from the prosperity of the 1920s through the early Depression years to Denver's rebuilding during the New Deal era and World War II. His reputation was marred by his involvement with Colorado's Ku Klux Klan, which he later disavowed, but Stapleton's first terms saw a continuation of major public works projects, most conspicuously the City and County Building at the Civic Center and the municipal airport. Called "Stapleton's Folly" by skeptics at its inception, the airport was later named after Stapleton.

New Deal projects provided critical employment and helped build the city's infrastructure during and following the years of the Depression. Vestiges of the New Deal include Red Rocks Amphitheater, the Capitol Annex building, and the old Police Building on Champa Street.

During World War II, the Denver area established itself as one of the country's highest per capita employers of federal workers, including those employed at Lowry Air Force Base, Rocky Mountain Arsenal, Buckley Field, and Denver Ordinance Plant (now the Denver Federal Center). The Denver area also prospered as a center of food production and light manufacturing.

The post-war period brought a boom to the city and its suburbs stimulated by the influx of new families seeking the economic opportunity and healthy lifestyle that the area offered. The leadership style of energetic young lawyer Quigg Newton appealed to those riding the wave of new prosperity. Newton served as Denver's mayor from 1947 to 1955. During the years of Newton's administration, the Denver area continued its growth as the dominant economic, cultural, and governmental center of the Rocky Mountain region. Denver repealed its turn-of-the-century 12-story building height limit, and opened the possibility for a real downtown skyline. In 1955, the city became a national retailing pioneer, with the opening of the Cherry Creek Shopping Center.

In the late 1950s and the 1960s, Denver's suburbs experienced unprecedented growth, while the downtown area matured. In 1958, downtown saw the completion of the I. M. Pei–designed Courthouse Square Project (the Hilton Hotel and the May D & F building) and arguably its first "skyscraper," the 28-story First National Bank Building. The same year, the Denver Urban Renewal Authority (DURA) was created to foster federally assisted downtown redevelopment. The new Denver Technological Center planted the seeds for a southeastern suburban commercial center in 1962, while the opening of Dillon Reservoir and Roberts Tunnel established a source of water for Denver's foreseeable growth. Alarmed at the loss of its historical riches, the city and its citizen preservationists launched the Denver Landmark Preservation Commission and Historic Denver, Inc., in 1967 and 1970.

*Denver Performing Arts Complex*

The 1974 Poundstone Amendment to the State Constitution limited Denver's ability to annex new land and solidify its tax base. Even so, from the early 1970s through the mid-1980s, the Denver area—stimulated by the growth of energy-related business resulting from the Arab oil embargo—continued its staggering growth. Largely financed with Canadian capital, office buildings sprang up in both downtown and the burgeoning suburban business parks located along the south I-25 corridor. The first new buildings were

## Top Ten Denver Favorites
### by former representative Pat Schroeder

1. Mountain panorama
2. City park system
3. Priority given to historic preservation projects such as the Mayan Theater
4. Support of the arts through the Scientific and Cultural Facilities Tax
5. Tattered Cover bookstore
6. City's progressiveness concerning disabled accessibility
7. 16th Street Mall
8. Caramel apples at the Chocolate Foundry
9. Denver Buffalo Company
10. Denver Public Library system

the Denver Center for the Performing Arts (DCPA), Boettcher Concert Hall (1978), and Helen Bonfils Theater (1980). The 16th Street Mall (1982) was developed to connect upper downtown to re-emerging lower downtown ("LoDo") with shuttle bus service and a landscaped, granite pedestrian mall. Later, the Platte River Greenway Project brought the first new life to the Platte River Valley with the construction of parks and trails along the river's banks.

Campaigning with the slogan "Imagine a Great City," Federico Peña became Denver's first Hispanic mayor in 1983. At the same time, however, the bottom fell out of the energy market and almost overnight the Denver area plunged into a sharp recession. Office and residential markets plummeted, and in spite of the current economic recovery, no new office building has been constructed in downtown Denver since 1985. Notwithstanding the economic slowdown, the Peña years included the completion of the DCPA complex and the Platte River Greenway Project, the construction of the new Colorado Convention Center, and the beginnings of Denver International Airport (DIA). Denver area cultural institutions received a boost in 1988 when the city approved a 0.1 percent sales tax increase to benefit the area's artistic and scientific establishments. In 1989, the Denver Symphony Orchestra dissolved and DSO musicians formed the very successful Colorado Symphony Orchestra.

Wellington Webb literally walked the city in 1991 to be elected Denver's first African American mayor. Inspired by the "City Beautiful" theme of the Speer administration, Mayor Webb committed to supporting the arts and historical preservation. He dubbed Denver the "Athens of the West."

# DENVER TIME LINE

| | |
|---|---|
| 1851 | Treaty of Fort Laramie gives Cheyenne and Arapaho Indians title to the eventual site of Denver. |
| 1858 | The towns of Auraria and St. Charles are founded. General William Larimer renames St. Charles Denver City after Kansas Territory Governor James W. Denver. |
| 1859 | William Byers founds the *Rocky Mountain News*. |
| 1860 | Auraria and Denver City merge into one town, named Denver. |
| 1861 | Treaty of Fort Wise hands over legal possession of Indian land to the U.S. government. |
| 1863–64 | Fires and a flood wreak havoc on the young city. |
| 1866 | Union Pacific Railroad takes its transcontinental line through Cheyenne, Wyoming, bypassing Denver. |
| 1867 | Smith's Ditch is completed to supply Denver with water. |
| 1869 | Denver Pacific Railroad & Telegraph Co. connects with the transcontinental railroad. The Kansas Pacific completes its line to Denver. |
| 1880 | Horace Tabor builds the Tabor block at 16th and Larimer. |
| 1893 | The repeal of the Silver Purchase Act eliminates silver as the monetary standard, plunging Denver into a severe depression. |
| 1895 | Frederick Bonfils and Harry Tammen found the *Denver Post*. |
| 1904–12 | Robert Speer serves as mayor. |
| 1910 | Coors Brewery opens in Golden. |
| 1916–18 | Speer, mayor again, launches the "City Beautiful" movement. |
| 1923–47 | Ben Stapleton, endorsed by the KKK, serves as mayor. |
| 1929 | Stapleton Airport is built near downtown Denver. |
| 1934 | Denver & Rio Grande RR develops a line to the Pacific Coast. |
| 1935 | A flood disaster provides impetus to widen Cherry Creek and the Platte River. |
| 1942 | Rocky Mountain Arsenal opens; begins manufacturing bombs. |
| 1945 | Post-war boom launches Denver's new growth. |
| 1952 | The 12-story building height limit is repealed. |
| 1953 | Rocky Flats plutonium weapons plant opens. |
| 1955 | Cherry Creek shopping center opens. Drought pushes Denver Water Board to draw "blue lines" beyond which water is withheld from suburbs until additional sources are found. |
| 1958 | Courthouse Square Project is completed. Valley Highway opens through the city center. Denver Urban Renewal Authority is formed. |

| | |
|---|---|
| Denver Technology Center opens in southeast Denver. | **1962** |
| Dana and John Crawford form the Larimer Square Association. | **1963** |
| Completion of Dillon Reservoir and the Roberts Tunnel relieves Denver's water problems and erases the "blue lines." | **1964** |
| Voters approve Skyline urban design plan, a DURA project. Many old buildings are razed to make way for new structures. | **1967** |
| Denver Landmark Commission is established. Structures and buildings given landmark status are protected against development. | **1967** |
| Bill McNichols serves as mayor. The Mountain View Ordinance institutes height limits for new buildings. | **1968–83** |
| Historic Denver is formed. | **1970** |
| Voters oppose bringing the Winter Olympics to Colorado. | **1972** |
| Arab oil embargo catapults Denver into a center for U.S. oil industry and research on alternative energy sources. | **1973** |
| Denver experiences a building boom of office parks and projects. | **1976–82** |
| 16th St. Mall opens. Energy companies flee Denver as oil and gas prices plummet. | **1982** |
| Federico Peña becomes Denver's first Hispanic mayor. State Senator Joe Shoemaker spearheads construction of the Platte River Greenway. | **1983** |
| Denver voters approve a 0.1 percent cultural facilities tax. | **1988** |
| Colorado Convention Center opens. | **1990** |
| Wellington Webb becomes Denver's first African American mayor. | **1991** |
| Coors Field opens in LoDo. Elitch Gardens Amusement Park moves to Platte Valley. Denver International Airport opens. Major additions and renovations to the Denver Public Library are completed. | **1995** |
| Delegations from around the world attend the Denver Summit of the Eight to discuss global economic issues. | **1997** |
| Denver Pavilions, a giant fashion and entertainment center, opens downtown. | **1998** |
| The Pepsi Center, home to Nuggets basketball and Avalanche soccer, opens, as does Colorado Ocean Journey, the newest large-scale aquarium in the country. | **1999** |

## Denver Today

Stimulated by massive public works projects, Denver has substantially rebounded in the 1990s. After countless delays and national lampooning, DIA opened in 1995—the same year that the Denver Public Library completed its renovations and additions. These projects created jobs and boosted the economy. The closing of Stapleton International Airport in northeast Denver and the finalization of the Stapleton Redevelopment Plan has created opportunities for inner city parks, schools, businesses, housing, museums, and shops. Redevelopment of historic lower downtown, beginning with the Central Platte River Valley, has stirred more excitement and growth. At a former industrial site, the Ferris wheels and giant swings of Elitch Gardens dominate the lower downtown landscape. The 100-year-old amusement park relocated its entire operation to a vacant 67-acre plot in the Central Platte Valley—becoming the only amusement park in the world to make such a move to an urban area.

Where trains once screeched through the Platte Valley to Union Station, Coors Field is now home to the Colorado Rockies. Brewpubs and restaurants have sprouted outside the stadium like prairie grass. Another unlikely candidate for life on the plains—Denver's first aquarium—is also slated to open in the Central Platte River Valley along with a projected new sports complex for the Denver Nuggets and the Colorado Avalanche.

The current boom is reportedly leveling off, but unlike in 1893 and again in 1970, the economy is now more diversified. Ideally situated between Canada and Mexico, Denver has benefited from the NAFTA trade agreements and emerged as a regional, and potentially international, trade hub. Cable television was born in Denver when Bill Daniels moved his operations from Casper, Wyoming, in the early 1950s. Today, Denver is the

*Denver skyline over City Park*

As of September 1, 1998, all calls in the 303 area code require 10-digit dialing.

telecommunications capital of the country, housing industry powerhouses TCI, Jones Intercable, and American Television & Communications Corp.

## Denver and the Future

Those streaming to Denver during this latest boom just might stay. Not only do they find economic opportunity, bright sunlight, abundant recreational activities, and an environment suited to a stubborn and independent will, but also thriving cultural communities and diverse neighborhoods offering living styles from urban to suburban to "in-the-wilds."

Currently, there are more than 2 million residents in Metropolitan Denver. They have taken advantage of the sweeping plains and spread out in every direction. But the development of the suburbs has created new issues for Metro Denver, namely how the growth will be managed and who will be responsible for what.

The other issues facing the Denver area are equally daunting. There is little water on the plains. Creation of the Dillon Reservoir in 1962 doubled the city's water supplies, but increasing growth underlines the need for new policy—and new sources.

Pollution has plagued Denver for much of its history. Indians who first camped along the shores of Cherry Creek noticed that smoke from their campfires tended to hover and collect in one place. Today, Denver—situated in a bowl like the area encompassing Mexico City—struggles with the pollution from increased traffic and industry. The new light-rail system extending from South Broadway to Five Points is a welcome attempt at solving Denver's traffic and pollution problems, but it is not certain there will be funding to expand the system to Metro Denver's four corners.

Since the early 1970s, court-ordered busing had been used as a way to integrate Denver's schools. But in 1994 Denver Federal District Court put an end to the project. Now, new neighborhood school boundaries are being drawn and quality education must be provided in what will be a less integrated school environment.

Denver faces other critical issues. Historic preservation must be balanced with plans to maintain the city's economic resurgence. Contamination at Rocky Flats defense plant poses severe health risks. At present, there is no permanent solution for ridding the area of its hazardous wastes. DIA has created anxiety as well as jobs. Will Denver's gamble on building

> **TRIVIA**
>
> ## Movies Filmed in Denver, Once Called the Hollywood of the Rockies
>
> - *The Glenn Miller Story*, 1953
> - *The Silent Witness*, 1962
> - Disney's *Little Britches*, 1963
> - *The Happy Ending*, 1969
> - *Vanishing Point*, 1970
> - *Endangered Species*, 1978
> - *Every Which Way But Loose*, 1978
> - Perry Mason movies
> - *Die Hard II*, 1990
> - *Things to Do in Denver When You're Dead*, 1995

the modern facility pay off and strengthen the city's position as a major transportation hub? And what about Downtown Denver? Will it survive as the metro area's financial, cultural, and recreational center, or will many of these institutions disperse to the suburbs?

There are sobering problems to face, but the city has energy, new ideas, and new dreams. Young people are moving here, and natives are returning to their homes. At night, the lower downtown area teems with activity from Coors Field at the east end to the nightclubs and restaurants around Larimer Street. Newspapers such as the *New York Times* and the *Wall Street Journal* have Denver offices now.

Why does Denver keep reinventing itself? In its early years, there was no real medical evidence supporting the claim of Denver's curative climate just as the area had no real supply of gold and no native ecology that jibed with the lush parks that sprang up on the prairie. Something took root at the joining of the Platte and Cherry Creek—a spirit of independence, inventiveness, and toughness that thrived on the open, sunny plains, and refused to let go.

## Recommended Reading

Following is a list of books about Denver's history recommended by area historians, architects, artists, and preservationists.

*Denver: The City Beautiful*, by Thomas J. Noel and Barbara S. Norgren

*History of Denver*, by Jerome C. Smiley

*The Queen City: A History of Denver*, by Lyle W. Dorsett & Michael McCarthy

*Rediscovering Northwest Denver: Its History, Its People, Its Landmarks*, by Ruth Eloise Wiberg

*Richthofen's Montclair: A Pioneer Denver Suburb*, by Thomas J. Noel

*Places Around the Bases: A Historic Tour of the Coors Field Neighborhood*, by Dianne Bakke and Jackie Davis

*Denver Going Modern*, by Don D. Etter

*Denver in Slices*, by Louisa Ward Arps (out of print, but available at the Denver Public Library)

*Historic Denver: The Architects and the Architecture*, 1858–1893, by Richard R. Brettell (out of print, available at the Denver Public Library)

*Cherry Creek Gothic*, by Sandra Dallas

*Robert Walter Speer and Benjamin Barr Lindsay: The Progressive Dilemma in Municipal Government*, by Walter Wood Garnsey, Jr. (Western History Department, Denver Public Library)

*The Denver Zoo: A Centennial History*, by Carolyn and Don Etter

## The People of Denver

A mixture of ethnic groups makes up the diverse Denver community. During the last decade, the Metro Denver minority population grew by 31.2 percent.

The Hispanic community, which represents 12 percent of the population, is the largest minority group in Metro Denver. Migrant workers from Mexico first came to Denver to work on surrounding farms at the turn of the century. Today, the strong Hispanic influence is evident in the large number of bilingual classrooms, billboards, Spanish-language radio stations, and authentic Mexican and Central American restaurants throughout the metro area. The local Hispanic community hosts the annual Cinco de Mayo celebration in downtown Denver. The Hispanic Chamber of Commerce supports local businesses, and the Fraternidad Hispana, El Centro Su Teatro, and Museo de las Americas all organize Latino cultural and educational events. *El Semenario* and *El Sol* are Spanish newspapers focusing on the Hispanic community. Former mayor Federico Peña, most recently President Clinton's secretary of energy, was elected the city's first Hispanic mayor in 1983. A large portion of the Hispanic community lives in west and northwest Denver.

The African American community makes up more than 5 percent of the Metro Denver population. A majority of the community lives in the north Park Hill, west City Park, and Five Points neighborhoods. Since his first election in 1991, Mayor Wellington Webb, the city's first black mayor, has

# Ten Ways to Enjoy Denver's Latino Culture and Community

1. Check out some of Denver's fine Latino public art, including the Mayan Numerals Mural at the Crusade for Justice Building; Neighborhood Epic by Martha Keating and Bob Luna on 20th Street, and A Life in Harmony With All Creation by Maria Aguilar at the 15th Street viaduct.
2. Visit La Gente Exhibition at the Colorado History Museum.
3. Visit the Museo de las Americas, Colorado's Latino Arts and History Museum.
4. Visit two 32nd Avenue gems: Galeria Mexicana (art gallery) and Cultural Legacy (bookstore)
5. Lunch at Sabor Latino, also on 32nd Avenue. Try Pastel de Choclo (Peru) and/or Arepas (Columbia/Venezuela).
6. Shop at Old San Juan Groceries (664 Perioria Street, Aurora) to find the ingredients of your favorite Latino meals.
7. Try a free salsa lesson at Los Cabos II (1512 Curtis St.). Or pay for a group lesson with Jal "El Rumbero" Monreno (303/333-636) or Nilsa (303/685-9005).
8. Contact the Chicano Humanities and Arts Council (CHAC) at 303/477-7733 or Artes del Pueblo (303/293-8251), organizations that preserve and promote the Chicano/Latino culture, for information on their current programs and exhibitions.
9. Enjoy the rhythmic sounds of Tico Tico, Denver's finest Latin jazz band. Call 303/666-1954 to find out about shows.
10. On Sundays, tune your radio to KUVO 89.3 FM for Canción Mexicana (9 a.m.–1 p.m.) and the Latin Musicians Show. (1 p.m.–3 p.m.).

brought attention to the economic, political, and social issues important to the black community. Jo Bunton Keal, director of Eulipions, Inc., and Cleo Parker Robinson, director of the Cleo Parker Robinson Dance Ensemble, feature African American dance and theater productions through their prominent organizations. The Colorado Black Chamber of Commerce is another important community resource. Many black-owned businesses are thriving in the Welton Street development area and throughout Denver. The community features its outstanding artists every year in the outdoor Black Arts Festival in City Park.

The Asian community represents just over 2 percent of the Metro Denver population. Historically, Japanese make up the largest part of the metro area's Asian community. While other major cities were interning Japanese people in prison camps during WWII, Colorado Governor Ralph Carr welcomed the Japanese to Denver. Downtown Sakura Square, an important resource center for the Japanese community, has a bust commemorating Governor Carr. The square hosts the Cherry Blossom Festival every summer. Chinese, Vietnamese, and a small group of Hmong sponsored by missionary groups live in small pockets in the Denver and Boulder areas.

Although Native Americans such as the Cheyenne and Arapaho lived throughout the plains area that is now Metro Denver long before other ethnic groups, today they make up less than 1 percent of the metro population. The Natural History Museum and Denver Art Museum both document the history of the region's American Indians in permanent exhibits. Groups such as the Denver Indian Center and the American Indian Women's Resource Center sponsor powwows, conferences, and cultural events for the community throughout the year. The annual Colorado Indian Market displays traditional dances, crafts, and other presentations in downtown's Currigan Hall in December.

Denver has one of the largest gay populations in the country, behind San Francisco and New York. Some believe that the passage of controversial Amendment 2—which denied gays special treatment, or access to equal rights, depending on your point of view—actually encouraged members of the gay community to relocate to Denver. Much of the gay community lives in the Capitol Hill area near Cheesman Park.

## The City's Weather

Each of the seasons is played out perfectly in the Denver area. Winter brings cold, arctic-like frosts and fills the city streets with snow. Like clockwork, just when most people have had their fill of the cold, spring comes and gradually turns the browns to an emerald green. Random spring snow showers occasionally storm through town, but they're usually followed by days of bright sunshine. Summer comes suddenly in June when hot, dry heat sizzles the city. But visitors can count on the daily late afternoon rain showers to bring cool respite to long hot days. For many, fall is the perfect season. Cool, crisp breezes fill the air, and the city and mountain trees turn to brilliant colors.

Denver weather is basically mild. Contrary to its reputation for cold, harsh winters, the city actually averages 300 days of sun a year. Even at the height of winter, warm fronts bring mild weather and sunshine to the metro area. "Erratic" characterizes Denver weather, but long-time Denverites are used to it. A slight shrug of the shoulders and a "this is typical Colorado" usually follow the onset of a summer hail storm or winter hot spell. Come to the city prepared for anything weather-wise. Bring a light sweater and rain coat in the summer, and a warm jacket and boots during the potentially cold winter months. The weather can, and will, surprise you.

## Denver's Weather

| | Average Daily High / Low Temperatures (degrees Fahrenheit) | Average Monthly Precipitation (in inches) |
|---|---|---|
| January | 44 / 16 | .61 |
| February | 46 / 19 | .67 |
| March | 50 / 24 | 1.21 |
| April | 61 / 34 | 1.93 |
| May | 70 / 44 | 2.64 |
| June | 80 / 52 | 1.93 |
| July | 87 / 59 | 1.78 |
| August | 85 / 57 | 1.29 |
| September | 78 / 48 | 1.13 |
| October | 67 / 37 | 1.13 |
| November | 53 / 12 | .76 |
| December | 46 / 19 | .43 |

Source: U.S. Department of Commerce, National Oceanic and Atmospheric Administration.

## A City for All Seasons

Colorado's winter ski conditions are legendary. But every season has its own appeal in Denver. In spring, the parks and parkways turn green, while skiers enjoy the last of the season and kayakers take advantage of spring run-off in the mountain streams. Summer is the peak time for outdoor recreation in Denver—most locals tune their bikes, weatherproof their hiking boots, and take off for the hills. Popular summer activities include biking, hiking, running, climbing, fishing, boating, camping, and in some cases, skiing. Colorado competes with the likes of Vermont, Maine, and Massachusetts to claim the most beautiful autumn in the country. In mid-September, trees lining parkways and parks throughout Metro Denver turn brilliant shades of auburn. Drive to the mountains to watch the aspen groves changing to beautiful red, orange, and gold hues. Any of the mountain passes—Boreas, Hoosier, Loveland, or Vail, to name a view—make for beautiful, scenic fall drives.

## Calendar of Events

**JANUARY**
National Western Stockshow, Rodeo and Horse Show; Denver Coliseum
Martin Luther King Jr. Celebration

**FEBRUARY**
Buffalo Bill's Birthday Celebration; Buffalo Bill Memorial Museum

**MARCH**
Denver March Pow Wow; Denver Coliseum
St. Patrick's Day Parade; Downtown Denver

**APRIL**
Easter Sunrise Service; Red Rocks

**MAY**
Cinco de Mayo Celebration; Civic Center Park
Bolder Boulder 5K and 10K race; Boulder
Springthing; Old South Pearl Street

**JUNE**
Capitol Hill People's Fair; Memorial Day weekend at Civic Center Park
City Park Jazz; City Park Bandstand
*The Denver Post* "Ride the Rockies"
Renaissance Festival; weekends at Larkspur
Juneteenth; Five Points and Montbello
Greek Marketplace; Greek Orthodox Cathedral in Denver

**JULY**
Cherry Creek Arts Festival
Colorado Indian Market
Denver Black Arts Festival
Denver Municipal Band; Washington Park and City Park
Mile High Nationals; Bandimere Speedway
Buffalo Bill Days; Golden

**AUGUST**
LoDo Music Festival; Lower Downtown Denver
Cherry Blossom Festival; Sakura Square
Chili Harvest Festival; Botanic Gardens
Sprint International Golf Tournament; Castle Pines Golf Club

**SEPTEMBER**
A Taste of Colorado; Labor Day weekend at Civic Center Park
Labor Day Parade; Downtown Denver
Oktoberfest; Larimer Square

**OCTOBER**
Denver International Film Festival; Downtown Denver
Memorial Pow Wow; Denver Indian Center

**NOVEMBER**
Holiday Tree Lighting; Larimer Square

**DECEMBER**
Blossoms of Light; Botanic Gardens
Festival of Arts; 16th Street Mall
First Night Colorado; New Year's Eve
Luminarias de Santa Fe; Santa Fe Drive
Parade of Lights; Downtown Denver
Victorian House Tour; Castle Marne Inn, 1572 Race St.
Wild Lights; Denver Zoo
Winterfest; weekends at Larimer Square

## Business and Economy

Following an eight-year boom, growth in Metro Denver subsided to a more sustainable level in 1996. Immigration decreased significantly and many of the city's major public works projects, like Coors Field, the Denver International Airport, and the Denver Public Library, came to an end—but only to be replaced by others. Despite the slow-down, the area economy is still prospering.

Since prospectors first converged on Denver in the 1800s hoping to discover gold, the city has been based on the availability of natural resources and a "boom or bust" economy. The Denver business community seems to have learned its lesson after a drop in 1980 oil prices plummeted the city into a major recession.

Today, Denver ranks as the second most diversified economy in the

---

**TRIVIA**

### Ten Denver Inventions

1. Ice cream soda
2. Cheeseburger
3. The "Denver Boot," used to lock the wheels of habitual parking offenders
4. Shredded wheat
5. Water Pik
6. Ice target gun
7. De-icing equipment
8. Electric street trolley
9. Apple 'n' Spice doughnut
10. Cafeterias

**TIP:** Denver sits a mile (5,280 feet) above sea level. Many people visiting Denver—and especially the nearby mountains—feel the altitude. The body adjusts within a few days, but in the interim drink more water than usual to keep hydrated, cut down on activities for the first day, and stay away from alcohol—it affects the body more at higher altitudes.

country. In place of natural resources like oil and gas, 80 percent of the Denver economy is based on manufacturing, services, government, and trade. Numerous high-tech companies such as Lockheed Martin and StorageTek now call Denver home, as do such major telecommunications companies such as MCI, Sprint, AT&T, and US West. With the exception of Washington, D.C., Metro Denver has the largest concentration of federal workers in the country. Most of the federal employees work in offices in Golden and the massive Jefferson County Government Center.

Denver's location near the center of the U.S., the international airport, and accessibility to markets in Japan, Europe, Mexico, and Canada make it a profitable and convenient area for national and international trade. In fact, *World Trade* magazine named Denver one of the top ten cities for international business in 1994. Nearly 1,300 Colorado companies are involved in the export business, primarily exporting computer and machinery equipment, food and agricultural products, and photographic and medical goods.

Metro Denver is a hub for big businesses. There are nearly 300 employers in the city that each employ at least 250 workers. The city's top employers are US West, AT&T, Health One, United Airlines, and King Soopers.

*Sculpture at 17th and Lawrence Streets*

United Airlines controls the majority of flights into and out of Denver International Airport, and employs more than 8,000 people in Metro Denver.

## Cost of Living

According to a national cost of living index, living in Denver is relatively inexpensive compared to other major cities across the country. The cost of living in Denver falls right in the middle of the 17 surveyed cities, and between Portland, Oregon, and Miami. Here's what you'll pay for some typical goods and services:

| | |
|---:|:---|
| 5-mile taxi ride: | $8.50 |
| hotel double room: | $75 |
| average dinner: | $10–$15 |
| movie admission: | $6 |
| daily newspaper: | 25¢ |
| 8 oz. tube of brand-name toothpaste: | $2.80 |
| hot dog from a downtown vendor: | $1 |

## Dressing in Denver

"Anything goes" is the general rule in Denver, where locals are not quick to jump on the East or West Coast fashion bandwagons. Urban cowboys, yuppies, alternative artists, students, a wide range of ethnic groups, and rugged mountain types all bring their own fashion ideas to the diverse Denver community. An evening at the opera will attract everything from blue jeans and cowboy boots to sophisticated sequined dresses. Only a handful of upscale restaurants and country clubs require men to wear ties. Other establishments, such as the Trail Dust Steak House, shun ties to the point of cutting them off. Local professionals stick to the conservative suit look until Fridays, which many offices have declared a casual dress day. The only thing that matters as far as city dressing goes is dressing for the weather and being prepared for quick and random weather changes. This means always take a heavy coat out during winter, and bring at least a light sweater any other time of the year. Although Denverites don shorts during warm winter spells, the only dependable shorts-wearing weather runs May through September—but snow in June is not unheard of.

DMC & VB

# 2
# GETTING AROUND DENVER

The Metro Denver area consists of six counties: Denver, Adams, Arapahoe, Boulder, Douglas, and Jefferson. Denver, the state capital, is the hub of metro commercial and cultural activity, although business parks and some cultural centers are now sprouting in surrounding counties. Sheridan and Quebec Avenues bound Denver to the west and east, while I-70 and Evans Avenue roughly serve as the north and south boundaries.

East Metro Denver encompasses parts of Adams and Arapahoe Counties, and the cities of Aurora and Commerce City. The Denver International Airport, which opened in east Denver in 1995, has brought new development to the area.

Littleton and Greenwood Village, two cities on Denver's southern outskirts, are in the narrow central arm of Arapahoe County. The rest of the county branches east into Aurora and Byers. The Denver Technological Center and Inverness Park both attract much business activity to the area.

Douglas County, the fastest growing county in the area, stretches due south of Denver. Highlands Ranch and Castle Rock, with Parker to the east and Sedalia to the west, are all important Douglas County towns. Sprawling farming communities such as Parker and Larkspur make Douglas the most sparsely populated county of the six, but with plenty of room to grow.

Most of Jefferson County, with its urban, suburban, and foothills communities, is in west and southwest Metro Denver. Lakewood, Wheat Ridge, Morrison, and Golden are in west Metro Denver. The Adolph Coors Company, Lockheed Martin, and the Denver Federal Center provide numerous job opportunities in the county, projected to be the most populated by 1998.

Boulder County is not covered in this book, aside from day trips and a few sights and restaurants. The area requires a book of its own.

# Finding Your Way Around

## Streets

A standard grid layout makes Denver streets easy to navigate and street maps easy to use. Most of the streets and boulevards run north-south, while the numbered avenues head east-west. The only glitch is downtown Denver. The first platting of the city in 1859 established the streets on parallel lines with the confluence of the Platte River and Cherry Creek—the point where Denver was originally founded. However, as the city expanded in all directions, city planners decided a strictly east-west/north-south grid was more practical for the growing urban sprawl. As a result, downtown Denver on a map looks like a square tipped off-center in relation to the rest of the city. Downtown, the numbered streets run toward the Platte River and the named streets parallel the river. Also, nearly all downtown streets are one-way. Visitors should note that 14th Street downtown is *not* a continuation of east/west traveling 14th Avenue. Each follows the different grid. When all else fails, the Front Range provides the perfect compass heading—the mountains are always west.

## Highways

The city of Denver is boxed in by the state's major interstates. **Interstate 70**, the major east-west interstate, runs along the north side of the city. I-70 east goes toward the Denver International Airport Exit, and continues through the eastern plains into Kansas. I-70 west serves as the major highway through the Colorado Rocky Mountains and into Utah—providing access to the Front Range, Summit County, Eagle County, and Aspen ski areas. From downtown Denver, take I-25 north to the I-70 turn-offs. **Interstate 25** is the state's primary north-south artery, traveling north to Wyoming and south to New Mexico. The interstate passes just west of downtown Denver, making it an easy tributary into the city center through the Speer Boulevard South Exit. I-25 south is the route to Colorado Springs, Pueblo, and Trinidad, while I-25 north travels past Fort Collins and Greeley to Wyoming. **C-470** is one of the newest additions to the Colorado interstate system. C-470 runs east-west along the south end of the metro area. The interstate junctions with I-70 near Morrison and runs east into Aurora, crossing I-25. C-470 west is a tollway. **Interstate 225** connects I-25 and I-70 via Aurora. I-225 provides a shortcut to the Denver International Airport for travelers coming from south Metro Denver. I-225 junctions with I-70 near the Smith Road and Peoria Street intersection.

## Public Transportation

Despite the need to cut down on Metro Denver's smog and traffic congestion problems, public transportation is underused by Denver commuters

# RTD LIGHT RAIL

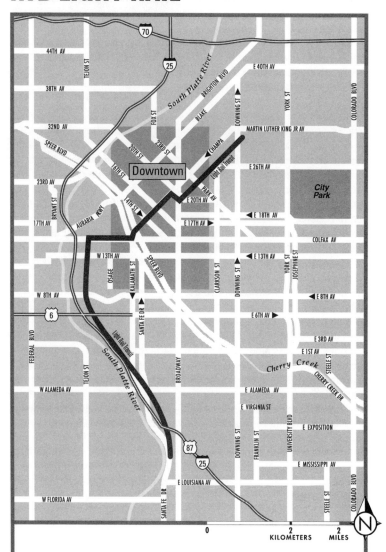

### RTD Light Rail

Denver's light rail system runs north-south from I-25 and Broadway to 30th and Downing in Denver's Five Points area. The 5.3-mile line stops at 14 stations between the two turnaround points—including seven stops in the heart of downtown Denver.

and travelers. Some say it takes too long, others can't separate themselves from their cars. But while the bus system demands some patience (it *will* take more time than driving), it makes up for it in worry-free commuting and convenience. Rapid growth has congested the metro area and severely limited parking options, especially in LoDo, making public transportation a helpful option. Bus rides like the No. 15 on Colfax also provide consistent people-watching entertainment.

## Bus Service

The Regional Transportation District, or the RTD, offers bus service throughout the Metro Denver. With the help of free transfer tickets and careful pre-planning, the RTD can bring you within walking distance of most areas around the city. RTD fares are $1.25 at peak hours (6–9 a.m. and 4–6 p.m.) and 75¢ all other times. Bus riders pay the fare upon boarding the front of the bus. Monthly passes are also available. Bus stops, marked by red RTD signs, are conveniently located every three or four blocks within each route. Hours: Most city buses run 5 a.m.–11 p.m., although some buses run later and others 24 hours a day.

Important Denver area bus routes are the No. 15, which runs 24 hours east-west on Colfax Avenue; the No. 40, which travels north-south on Colorado Boulevard; the No. 6, which travels east-west from Aurora to downtown Denver; the No. 20, which connects east Denver to downtown via 23rd and 17th Avenues; and the No. 12, which runs from the Auraria campus downtown south on Downing Street to Washington Park. The No. 10 line goes from the Platte Valley area east to 12th Avenue, Cheesman Park, the University of Colorado Health Sciences Center, and into Aurora. RTD provides service to all the surrounding counties including an express bus to Boulder.

Call RTD's automated information center at 303/299-6000 to speak to a customer service representative or select from the automated menu. Tell the representative your location and destination, and he or she can direct you to the most convenient bus line. Over 90 percent of all RTD buses are wheelchair accessible. The Regional Transit District also helps businesses with the EcoPass, Commuter Check, and Guaranteed Ride Home Programs.

## RTD 16th Street Mall Bus

The 16th Street Mall bus is the gem of Denver's public transportation system. The mall bus provides free transportation up and down the 16th Street Mall in downtown Denver from the Civic Center Station at Broadway to the Market Street Station. The bus stops located at the far corner of every mall street make the mall bus the easiest way to access downtown. The busy mall is closed to all other vehicular traffic, so pedestrians and the mall bus have free rein over the terrain. Major 16th Street Mall destinations are the Tabor Center on the corner of 16th and Larimer, Larimer Square at 15th and Larimer, and the Paramount Theatre on 16th and Glenarm. Many downtown

*Tabor Center, 16th Street Mall*

workers park in cheaper parking lots outside the city center and ride the mall bus to office buildings. Hours: 5:30 a.m.–12:45 a.m.

## RTD Light Rail

When RTD started light rail construction in the early 1990s, the company planned to extend the rail system to the new Denver International Airport to give passengers a convenient and inexpensive transportation option. Although RTD still hopes to fulfill this plan, a lack of funds and support have derailed progress indefinitely. In 1996, the Clinton Administration earmarked funds to help RTD extend the southbound line. Currently light rail runs north-south from I-25 and Broadway to 30th and Downing in Denver's Five Points area. The 5.3-mile line stops at 14 stations between the two turnaround points—including seven stops in the heart of downtown Denver. The light rail tallied a few fatal and minor accidents in its first months of operation. Drivers, bikers, and pedestrians not used to the rail system looked the wrong way or didn't look at all and ended up in dangerous collisions. People have since learned the new rules of the road, and no serious accidents have occurred of late. Be sure to take the light rail warning and approach signals seriously. When a rail car is approaching, a flashing red light signals traffic to stop.

A good way for south Denver commuters to avoid downtown congestion is to park their cars at the I-25 and Broadway station and ride the light rail into the city center. While entrepreneurs and the city have developed the areas around the Five Points stations, some parts are still relatively untrafficked and light rail riders should take precautions at night.

Light rail operates daily from 4:30 a.m. until 1:30 am. The day trains generally run at 10-minute intervals until 11 p.m., when trains run at 30-minute intervals. Light rail fares are $1 during peak hours (6–9 a.m., 4–6 p.m.) and

*RTD Light Rail*

50¢ at all other times. Purchase tickets at vending machines located at each light rail station. Call 303/299-6000 for schedule information.

## RTD Cultural Connection Trolley

The Cultural Connection Trolley, which runs from the end of May through Labor Day weekend, is a great way for visitors to see the city's major cultural attractions. A $3 pass allows passengers unlimited access to the trolley between 9:30 a.m. and 6:20 p.m. The trolley runs from downtown Denver (including stops at the Denver Art Museum, the Denver Performing Arts Complex, and the Colorado History Museum) to northeast Denver's City Park area (which provides access to the Denver Zoo, the Natural History Museum, and the IMAX Theatre). In between stops include the Denver Botanic Gardens, the Colorado State Capitol, and the Cathedral of the Immaculate Conception. The trolley runs every 30 minutes, and it is suggested that passengers wave to the trolley drivers to indicate they want a ride. Purchase day passes and pick up maps at any RTD station, the Ticket Bus on 16th and Curtis Streets, the Denver Visitor's Bureau, or directly from the trolley driver.

## SkyRide

The RTD SkyRide is the most affordable means of public transportation to Denver International Airport. Five different bus lines provide service to the airport from Boulder, downtown Denver, Stapleton, Adams County, and Littleton. One-way fares range from $4 to $8, with discounts available for advance purchase round-trip tickets. The buses have under-coach storage

## Denver by Light Rail

*Billie Bramhall, former Deputy Director of Planning under former mayor Federico Peña, 1983–1991, suggests taking the light rail as a way to see the city and entertain out-of-town guests. Park your car at either the 30th and Downing Station lot or the I-25 Broadway Station and ride the length of the line and back. The round trip (without side trips) takes about 25 minutes.*

*Starting at 30th and Broadway, you will see the Black American West Museum and Heritage Center across the street. A tour of the museum followed by lunch at Tosh's Hacienda a block away would be a great way to begin, or end, your excursion.*

*The train will take you past the old Rossonian Hotel, where most of the twentieth-century jazz greats played. Speeding through downtown you will catch sight of Coors Field Stadium and the Ice House to one side and the Church of the Holy Ghost with a modern skyscraper wrapped around it to the other. You will pass the Equitable Building and the old marble U.S. Post Office, recently remodeled as the Byron White Courthouse, with Gladys Fisher's stone bighorn sheep standing guard outside. The Colorado Convention Center on 14th Street is another sight along the way.*

*The train continues through the Auraria Campus with views of St. Cajetan's Church and the Tivoli Brewery and the arches of the Denver Center for the Performing Arts complex in the distance. Enjoy the mountain vistas as you pass through the western outskirts of downtown. Get off at the 11th and Osage Station for lunch at the Buckhorn Exchange, then continue on to the final stop, where Aspen artist Herbert Bayer's bright yellow sculpture presides.*

for large luggage and overhead storage space for smaller bags. Call RTD at 303/299-6000 for more information.

### Taxi Service

While taxis are abundant in the metro area, visitors need to remember that Denver is no New York City. Rarely will you see people furiously flagging down taxis from busy street corners. The more common method of taxi

> **TRIVIA**
>
> The Denver transportation system was "born" in a building on the corner of 17th and Wynkoop Streets, where the Denver City Railroad Company kept its horses in stables and which now houses Sostanza. The company established a Horse Car Service in 1883 to transport people around the downtown area in horse-pulled trolleys. The trolleys, which ran from 7th and Larimer Streets to 27th and Champa Streets, helped create the first Denver suburbs by giving the city's affluent a way to commute further away from downtown. Electric trolley cars replaced the horse-powered transport in 1890.

grabbing is to call the taxi company operators to order a pick-up. In response to sky-high fares, the city approved a $35 flat rate for cab rides to the Denver International Airport in February 1996.

The larger companies serving Greater Denver with 24-hour service are: **Yellow Cab**—303/777-7777; **Metro Taxi**—303/333-3333; **Zone Cab** 303/444-8888; **Freedom Cab**—303/292-8900; and **American Cab**—303/321 5555.

### Shuttle Services
Several local shuttle companies provide door-to-door service to and from the Denver International Airport for about $15 one way. Call **Denver Airport Shuttle**, 303/342-5454, or **Express Shuttle and Limo**, 303/751-7246.

## Driving in Denver

Thousands of newcomers have moved to Metro Denver since the mid-1980s. As a result, the traffic situation has changed dramatically. Traffic on Colorado Boulevard, a major south-north throughway, is incessant, and most city trip times have generally increased. On Denver streets as well as outlying highways and interstates, traffic is worst during peak rush hour periods of 7 to 9 a.m. and 4 to 6 p.m. Commuters from the foothills and suburbs usually sit through hours of bumper-to-bumper traffic each work day.

Beware of I-70 east in the early morning hours, and I-70 west during the evening rush hour. Both I-25 north and south are packed with cars during the morning and evening rush hours. There are few alternate routes into Denver from the outlying areas, so the best bet is to avoid rush hour altogether or use public transportation and spend the wait reading the newspaper.

Metro Denver has three roads with carpool lanes: I-25 north, U.S. 36 south from Boulder, and Santa Fe Drive south of downtown. Two or more drivers make a carpool, which greatly decreases trip time.

## Driving Tips
Denver visitors and newcomers are often stymied by local driving and road rules, so here are a few regulations (written and unwritten) to heed. Drivers can legally make a turn onto a one-way street on a red light—provided no pedestrians are in the crosswalk, of course. U-turns are permitted unless there is a sign indicating otherwise. Pedestrians do not have the "California" right-of-way on city streets unless the walk symbol is flashing. However, many downtown Denver intersections are regulated by the "Barnes Dance," named after a Denver engineer. Before the traffic light turns green for vehicles, a pedestrian signal gives walkers the go-ahead to cross the street in any direction, including diagonally. The moral of this tip is, don't be too quick with the gas pedal when you notice the opposite light has finally turned red—you'll have a few more minutes to wait.

## Parking Tips
Rather than driving into the heart of bustling downtown, consider parking in a less expensive outlying lot and taking the light rail or mall bus to your destination. Also, take the parking meters seriously—especially downtown. The meter readers appear out of nowhere the second your meter time is up, and those $15 violations really add up.

# Biking in Denver

Denver has one of the most advanced bike trail systems in the country. However, bikers still need patience to battle the city's urban sprawl and bike-ignorant drivers. The best advice is to ride on the designated bike- and

*Denver City Railroad Horse Car Service*

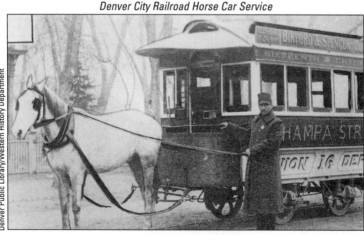

GETTING AROUND THE CITY

pedestrian-only paths, or stick to the parkways and side streets. The rule of the road: assume drivers do not see you and ride defensively.

However, the city's bike paths do make biking a feasible mode of transportation within Denver proper. The **Cherry Creek Trail** parallel to Speer Boulevard, often called a bike interstate, provides easy access to downtown Denver. You can access the path from ramps located every three or four blocks along Speer and First Avenue near the Denver Country Club. The Larimer Street ramp off the bike trail makes a good disembarkment point into the city center and Auraria Campus. Once downtown, bikers should always stay on the right side of the road and watch for cars turning right onto one-way streets. They tend to "overlook" bikers. Other easy routes into downtown are via 9th, 12th, 16th, and 22nd Avenues. Seventh Avenue Parkway is a quiet street with another established bike route. Seventh, 9th, and 12th Avenues all run into the Cherry Creek path at Speer Boulevard.

The city parks and many side streets also make for pleasurable biking. Denver Parks and Recreation, located near 15th and Platte Street, will hand out free maps of Metro Denver bike trails. All local Boulder RTD buses are equipped with external bike racks for commuters who want to bike to work once they reach the city. The city tentatively plans to build a bike path to the Denver International Airport.

## Denver International Airport

After numerous missteps and baggage system glitches, the Denver International Airport made its debut at the foot of the grassy eastern plains in February 1995. From an artistic perspective, the final product was definitely worth the embarrassingly long and expensive wait. Approaching the air-

*Denver International Airport*

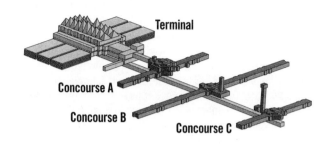

port from Peña Boulevard, the cloud-like teflon-coated roof structure seems to sway gently in the open air. DIA looks like a fairy-tale castle rather than one of the largest airports in the world. Inside the buildings, both the east and west sides of the terminal are packed with art works by local and national artists. Natural light streams in from the roof, providing excellent conditions for art viewing in the main Jeppesen Terminal atrium. A south-facing massive glass wall provides a view (weather permitting) of the Rocky Mountains.

While DIA took an initial beating in the local, national, and international media, the airport has won recent praise for its handling of large holiday crowds. It is about $50 more expensive to fly out of DIA than other international airports. The average passenger fee into and out of Denver is a whopping $18.30—a fact mostly due to the $3.2 billion construction tab, well above the original $1.4 billion estimate. Getting to and from the airport also involves at least 25 minutes of travel time to most city destinations—a fact loathsome to some travelers but welcomed by the heavily populated Stapleton area communities who finally escaped the constant roar of overhead jets.

### Getting to DIA

DIA is located 24 miles northeast of downtown Denver. From central or west Denver, follow I-70 east to the Peña Boulevard Exit. Peña Boulevard runs about 10 miles straight into DIA, so as long as you stay on the road you can't miss the airport. Traveling from the south part of the metro area, take I-25 north to I-225. I-225 junctions with I-70 east just past Smith Road. Again, take I-70 east to the Peña Boulevard Exit.

### Getting around DIA

The DIA toll plaza, located about 2 miles from the airport terminal, marks the airport entrance point. Because of the distance to the airport and the

> **TIP**
>
> Peña Boulevard is the number one speed trap in the city, so plan your airport trip ahead and watch your speed.

airport size, visitors have 70 free minutes to complete drop-offs or pick-ups before they pay a fee. After the first 70 minutes, however, drivers face a minimum $4 gate fee. The main Jeppesen Terminal, named after aviation pioneer Elrey Jeppesen, is divided into east and west terminals. Signs line the airport road directing travelers to the appropriate terminal. The road seems to fork suddenly, so be sure to heed the signs' warnings early. United Airlines, which handles 70 percent of the airport's traffic, takes up most of the west terminal, while Continental, Delta, and America West Airlines are on the east side. Separate covered parking garages, with a total of about 13,000 spaces, serve each terminal. Again, large airport signs direct travelers to the appropriate garage. Passenger drop-off and ticketing take place on Level 6, and baggage claim is on Level 5.

Underground subway trains transport passengers and friends to all concourses. Passengers first pass through security in the atrium-area, and then proceed down to the subways. Flight information monitors are located in front of the security checkpoint. If you forget to check your concourse on the monitor, signs inside the trains list each airline under either an A, B, or C concourse heading. Trains usually pass by every five minutes during peak traveling times, and it takes about that same time to

## Major Airlines Serving DIA

American Airlines: 800/433-7300
Continental Airlines: 800/523-FARE
Delta Airlines: 800/221-1212
Frontier Airlines: 303/371-7000
Mesa Airlines: 800/637-2247
Mexicana Airlines: 800/531-7921
Northwest Airlines: 800/225-2525
Trans World Airlines: 800/221-2000
United Airlines: 800/241-6522
USAir: 800/428-4322

reach the farthest concourse. Passengers traveling to Concourse A can make the five-minute walk to or from the terminal through a glass-enclosed bridge. DIA is long and skinny, so some passengers will have a long trek to the last gate. Moving walkways in the concourses aid the trek.

## Culture for Travelers: Airport Art

*The mayor's Office of Art, Culture and Film went to great lengths to commission local artists to fill the airport's terminals with works of art. Passengers with a layover should pick up the airport art guide at any of the information booths. The following is a list of the impressive pieces.*

### Jeppesen Terminal
- *Cactus and palm tree garden/ Denver Botanic Gardens*
- *Line of 140 suspended colored metal airplanes/ Patty Ortiz*
- *Exhibit of Native American photographs and paintings/ 11 tribes*
- *In Peace and Harmony with Nature (mural)/ Leo Tanguma*
- America, Why I Love Her *(mural)/ Gary Sweeney*

### Subway Tunnel
- *Kinetic light air curtain of 5,280 metal propellers in the subway tunnel/ Antonette Rosato and William Maxwell*
- *Deep Time/Deep Space/ Lori Schwendinger*

### Concourses
- *60-foot-high titanium arch sculpture in Concourse A/ David Griggs*
- *Floor mosaics of moving human figures on Concourse A terrazzo floors/ Darrell Anderson and Barb McKee*
- *Multicolored neon light arches in Concourse B/ Alice Adams*
- *Embedded bronze and cast-stone designs in Concourse B floors/ Carolyn Braaksma and Mark Villareal*
- *Indoor garden landscape with latticework walls in Concourse C/ Michael Singer*

## Downtown's Grand Dame: Union Station

*More than 100 years after its construction, Union Station still presides over lower downtown like a grand dame from behind its terra cotta front facade and bright red marquee. Union Station, originally Union Depot, was built in 1881 after the smaller downtown Denver depots agreed to consolidate all in-coming and outgoing train traffic through the one station. By the turn of the century 100 passenger trains passed through the busy station daily. Since the original construction, Union Station has undergone numerous superficial face lifts. An 1894 electrical fire destroyed the entire central part of the historical building, leaving intact only the north and south wings. Two Denver architects, Aaron Gove and Thomas Walsh, redesigned the existing central waiting room in 1914. A 64-foot-high ceiling and two-story-high windows fill the grand room with seemingly endless space and sprays of early morning and late afternoon sunlight. Passengers and visitors should admire the room from one of the ten huge oak benches lining the waiting area.*

## Other Airports

Some travelers are taking advantage of lower airport costs at the Colorado Springs Airport. It takes about 90 minutes to reach the airport from Denver, so gas and parking costs limit the savings, but for most it's the principle of the thing. Local shuttle services take passengers to the Colorado Springs Airport for about $25. All of the major airlines fly out of Colorado Springs. Call the Colorado Springs Airport Administration for information: 719/550-1900.

## Train Services

### AMTRAK

All Denver Amtrak train travel goes through historic Union Station. The Amtrak provides daily train service to Chicago, Denver, and Salt Lake City. The Amtrak *Desert Wind* travels from Chicago, through Denver, Salt Lake City, and Nevada, ending in Los Angeles. The *Desert Wind* arrives in Denver at 8:25 a.m. and departs Denver at 9 p.m. Tuesday, Friday, and Sunday. The

Union Station is perfectly located for downtown exploring and dining. The Wynkoop Brewery, Colorado's oldest brewpub, has great food, a huge selection of house-brewed beers, and more than 20 pool tables upstairs. As you walk out of Union Station, turn left and walk down the sidewalk to the corner. Cross Wynkoop Street; the brewery is right on the corner. Walker's, located in the north wing of Union Station, is a new lower downtown restaurant and sports bar. From the large windows on the west wall, diners can watch the large trains slowly rolling in and out of Union Station. The 16th Street Mall is within walking distance. Walk directly out of Union Station and continue down 17th Street. Turn right at Market Street, and left on 16th on to the pedestrian mall.

Amtrak **Pioneer** runs from Chicago to Seattle with a stop in Denver. The *Pioneer* arrives in Denver at 8:25 and 9:45 a.m. and departs at 6:05 and 9 p.m. Monday, Wednesday, and Friday. The Amtrak **California Zephyr** runs from Chicago to San Francisco with a stop in Denver. The *Zephyr* arrives in Denver at 8:25 and 9:10 a.m. and departs Denver at 7:50 and 9 p.m. Monday, Wednesday, Thursday, and Saturday. For reservations and information, call 800/USA-RAIL or the Union Station office at 303/534-2812. Union Station passenger services, baggage room, and package express service can also be reached at: 303/534-2812. All trains have first-class sleeping cars, lounge cars with panoramic windows and night movies, and full service dining cars. Lockers line the southern wall, and a snack bar operates during the station's open hours, Monday to Friday 7 a.m. to 1 a.m.

## Ski Train

Continuing a Denver tradition that dates to 1940, the orange and silver Rio Grande ski train still takes skiers and sightseers alike to the Winter Park Ski Area Saturdays and Sundays from mid-December to late March.

For sightseers, the ski train affords beautiful views of the Front Range and Rocky Mountains. The train leaves Denver's Union Station at 7:15 a.m., winds its way past the Flatirons, through the historic 6-mile Moffat Tunnel and over the Continental Divide, and arrives at the base of the Winter Park Ski Area at 9:15 a.m. An added bonus for skiers is the après-ski experience. Ski Train passengers can rest their ski-weary legs and avoid the I-70 traffic jams as the train makes it way back to Denver. The train leaves the ski area at 4:15 p.m. and arrives in Denver at 6:15 p.m. Pour La France provides food and beverage service in cafe lounge cars and snack bars.

Coach-class tickets are $35 and club car tickets (including continental breakfast buffet, private bar, and après-ski snacks) are $50. Discounted lift tickets are available aboard the train. Call 303/296-I-SKI for more information.

## Interstate and Regional Bus Service

The main bus terminal spans the entire north side of 19th and Curtis Streets on the north side of downtown Denver. The Greyhound and TNM and O Coaches (Texas, New Mexico, and Oklahoma) bus lines operate from the terminal with numerous daily bus departures to anywhere in the country. Greyhound fare and schedule information, 800/231-2222. Suburban Greyhound: Aurora, 15179 E. Colfax Avenue, 303/340-0501.

The large concrete terminal is user- and layover-friendly. Passengers will find 24-hour lockers, a gift and snack shop, video games, and a large central seating area to wile away the hours. Ticket reservation and customer service counters are on the station's north wall. The terminal is open from 6 a.m. to midnight. Taxis pick up regularly outside the main south doors on 19th Street. The terminal sits in a reasonably well-trafficked part of downtown, but take normal big-city precautions at night. Several homeless shelters and raucous bars lie within walking distance of the terminal.

Other bus lines: According to local youth hostel owners, a lot of young travelers are coming to Denver on "alternative," and cheaper, bus lines such as Turismos Rapidos, 2147 Broadway, 303/292-0333; and El Paso-Los Angeles Limousine Express (service to El Paso, Texas; Juarez, Chihuahua, and Torreón, Mexico; and other destinations), 838 Park Avenue West, 303/293-2244.

Michael Lewis

# 3
# WHERE TO STAY

The first hotel in the settlement that became Denver was the Eldorado, a log cabin with an American flag (made from the proprietess's petticoat) flying from the squat log tower on its roof. Discovered under the siding of an old house in 1939, the structure was moved from its lower downtown site to the May Bonfils Stanton estate on Wadsworth Boulevard, where it still stands.

The prosperity of the late 1800s spawned other and grander Denver hotels where Buffalo Bill Cody drank everyone under the table and traveling royalty like the Russian Romanov, Grand Duke Alexis, dazzled Denver's would-be duchesses far into the night. The most prominent survivors of this era are the lower downtown's Oxford Hotel and the Brown Palace Hotel in the upper downtown area.

Today, Denver offers a variety of hotels, motels, and bed and breakfasts in many different metropolitan locations—from downtown to the Denver Tech Center—and in communities closer to the mountains. Some radiate the lore of the past; others offer every up-to-date luxury; and there are even those that strive to offer all the comforts of home.

*Price rating symbols:*
$ Under $50
$$ $50 to $75
$$$ $75 to $125
$$$$ $125 and up

# DOWNTOWN DENVER

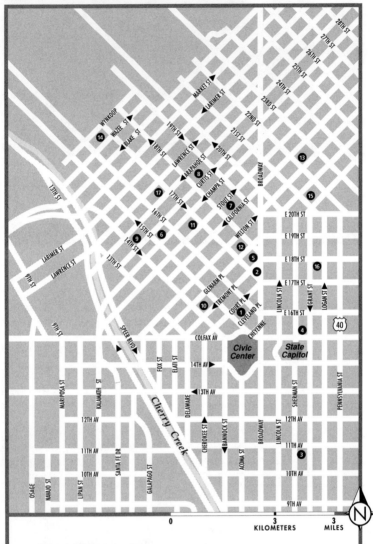

## Lodging in Downtown Denver

1. Adam's Mark Hotel
2. Brown Palace Hotel
3. The Burnsley
4. The Cambridge
5. Comfort Inn Downtown Denver
6. Courtyard by Marriott
7. Denver Mariott-City Center
8. Embassy Suites Hotel & Athletic Club at Denver Place
9. Executive Tower Hotel
10. Holiday Inn Denver Downtown
11. Holtze Executive Place
12. Hyatt Regency Denver
13. Melbourne Hotel and Hostel
14. Oxford Hotel
15. Queen Anne Bed and Breakfast Inn
16. Warwick Hotel-Denver
17. Westin Hotel Tabor Center Denver

## DOWNTOWN DENVER

### Hotels and Motels

Most of these downtown hotels are within walking distance of the 16th Street Mall. The mile-long mall is a pleasant, tree-lined expanse running through the center of all the downtown areas. The 16th Street Mall bus ferries passengers up and down the street at regular intervals day and night, making the entire area readily accessible wherever you are.

**ADAM'S MARK HOTEL**
1550 Court Pl.
Denver, CO 80202
303/893-3333
$$$–$$$$ DD
A newcomer to Denver, Adam's Mark aims to be the premier hotel of the Midwest. From the airy, spacious lobby to the green and rose rooms, everything here is strictly first class. Amenities include the concierge level Concorde Club, a state-of-the-art health club, a variety of restaurants, and luxurious "extras" in the guest rooms. In addition to full catering and convention service, Adam's Mark boasts the state's largest ballroom, along with banquet and exhibit space and 22 meeting rooms.

**BROWN PALACE HOTEL**
321 17th St.
Denver, CO 80202
303/297-3111
$$$$ DD
Anchored like the ship of state in upper downtown, the Brown Palace is a well-loved Denver institution. The wedge-shaped sandstone and gran-

---

## Legend and Lore: The Brown Palace

*There are hundreds of stories and anecdotes about the Brown Palace. Old-timers fuel the rumor that a tunnel ran from the Brown Palace to a house of ill repute in the Navarre Building across the street. Tracks underneath the Navarre do lead to a brick wall, but that is all the proof there is.*

*Several rooms at the Brown have interesting histories. During Prohibition, a group of Spanish-American war veterans smuggled liquor into Room 929 for a private reunion. Federal agents got wind of the bash and not only raided the room, but locked it off for a year. Room 629 was where the "Unsinkable" Molly Brown always stayed and where she took her singing lessons as well. Although guests in neighboring rooms complained of Molly's screeching howls, hotel employees were too afraid of the imposing lady—and too fond of her—to ask her to stop.*

# Top Ten Interesting Facts about the Brown Palace Hotel

### by Corinne Hunt
### Author of *The Brown Palace Story*

Julie Kanellos conducts popular tours of the Brown Palace every Wednesday and Saturday at 2 p.m.

1. The Brown Palace Hotel has been open every minute of every day since it opened on August 12, 1892.

2. The hotel still uses its original artesian wells. The wells are exactly as deep as the 53-story Republic Building across the street is high: 720 feet.

3. Two of the cast iron panels, depicting dancing ladies, on the railings circling the hotel's eight-story atrium are upside down. A mistake or a practical joke? No one knows.

4. The Beatles stayed at the Brown. Before their visit in 1964, young girls vied for housekeeping positions. The Beatles Suite commemorates the stay of the famous guests.

5. The Eisenhower Suite is where Ike and Mamie stayed, sometimes for months at a time. The dent in the fireplace molding caused by one of Ike's stray golf balls is still there.

6. During World War II, visiting soldiers from the Tenth Mountain Division tried rappelling from the hotel balconies.

7. At a time when dogs were no longer allowed in the hotel, a wealthy man arranged for meals on hotel china and covered with silver domes to be served to his dog on the sidewalk. After dining, the dog slept in a rented limousine along with the driver.

8. Following the advice of his veterinarian, a wealthy fox terrier from Philadelphia, heir to part of his owner's fortune, visited Denver to breathe Rocky Mountain air and cure his consumption. Accompanied by an entourage that included a nursemaid, the dog rented a seven-room suite at the Brown.

9. Cowboy star Monty Montana not only used to ride his horse, Rex, into the Brown Palace lobby, but often roped the general manager as well. Sometimes Monty and Rex mounted the grand staircase to attend meetings of the Rodeo Cowboy Association.

10. The 26 medallions carved into the sandstone between the seventh-floor windows of the Brown represent wild animals native to Colorado.

*Brown Palace Hotel*

ite building, designed in 1892 by prominent Denver architect Frank E. Edbrooke, was erected on a triangular patch of pasture land owned by early settler Henry Brown. Now beginning its second century of business, the hotel proudly maintains the look and feel of its Victorian origins. Black-caped doormen usher guests into the marble and onyx atrium/lobby, where afternoon tea and cocktails are served daily to the strains of harp music. The nine stories of guest rooms all look out on the open space. Every room is furnished with period antiques. The ground-floor restaurants and common areas are filled with artifacts reflecting the Brown's long and illustrious history. A $9.5 million restoration project has brought hallway and room renovation, climate controls in guest rooms, and a long-awaited cigar lounge in the new Churchill Bar.

**THE BURNSLEY**
**1000 Grant St.**
**Denver, CO 80203**
**303/830-1000**
**$$$**                                    **DD**

The Burnsley, once a jazz and entertainment establishment owned by Kirk Douglas and Ella Fitzgerald, has the cozy elegance of a home away from home. An all-suite hotel, it is a good choice for the traveler booking an extended stay. Located a short distance from downtown, all suites have balconies with mountain views. Japanese screens and tasteful furnishings accent the spacious living rooms. Suites also include kitchens, dining areas, and bedrooms with king-sized beds.

**THE CAMBRIDGE**
**1560 Sherman St.**
**Denver, CO 80203**
**303/831-1252**
**$$$**                                    **DD**

Another all-suite hotel, the Cambridge appeals to the extended-stay business traveler as well as romantics in search of a weekend getaway. Tucked into a street a half-block from the capitol and close to the 16th Street Mall, the Cambridge radiates the charm and luxury of a fine European hotel. Each suite is uniquely decorated and meticulously maintained. The staff is committed to catering to each guest's needs.

**COMFORT INN DOWNTOWN DENVER**
**401 17th St.**
**Denver, CO 80202**
**303/296-0400**
**$$$**                                    **DD**

Billing itself as the only economy facility downtown, Comfort Inn Downtown is a bit shabby, but many people rave about this place. Guests can

*Denver Marriott-City Center*

as well. With Starbuck's around the corner and jazzy Rialto's Café next door, it's hard to say what more you could ask for. Ask for rooms facing Curtis St. or the Mall, where Joslin's original wall-size windows provide splashes of high-country light and spectacular views.

**DENVER MARRIOTT-CITY CENTER**
1701 California St.
Denver, CO 80202
303/297-1300
$$$$      DD

You know you're in Colorado when you enter this newly remodeled Marriott. Designs of columbine and Indian paintbrush accent the carpets in the lobby and halls. Artwork commissioned by Colorado artists on Colorado themes lines the walls. Bustling and friendly, this very pretty hotel offers every convenience for the business traveler and tourist alike. The light rail stops on both sides of the building, making it doubly easy for guests to get around downtown.

cross a covered walkway bridge and find themselves at the Brown Palace next door. The Brown's restaurants and catering facilities service both hotels. The friendly and cheerful service is another bonus at the bustling Comfort Inn Downtown.

**COURTYARD BY MARRIOTT**
934 16th St.
Denver, CO 80202
303/571-1114
$$      DD

Housed in the century-old Joslin's Department Store building, this new hotel is a sparkling addition to downtown Denver. The sweet scents from a candle shop greet guests who enter from the bustling Sixteenth Street Pedestrian Mall, while a fountain and views of the mountains provide welcome from the west drive-through entrance. A large atrium dominates the spacious lobby where Joslin's original tin-painted ceilings have been immaculately restored. The original ceilings extend into the tasteful guest rooms

**EMBASSY SUITES HOTEL & ATHLETIC CLUB AT DENVER PLACE**
1881 Curtis St.
Denver, CO 80202
303/297-8888
$$$$      DD

Located between Coors Field and the 16th Street Mall, Embassy Suites is also next door to the old white marble Post Office. The top ten floors of this 29-floor hotel contain one- and two-bedroom apartments reserved for relocating corporate executives. The remaining two-room suites are all comfortable and well appointed. Complimentary breakfast and cocktails are served daily. The adjoining health club charges a fee, but offers every state-of-the-art piece of exercise equipment you can imagine

**EXECUTIVE TOWER HOTEL**
**1405 Curtis St.**
**Denver, CO 80202**
**303/571-0300**
**$$$**                                          **DD**

Union-owned, the Executive Tower attracts government and union groups, but deserves wider attention. The staff here is extremely friendly and helpful. The hotel is well situated across the street from the Denver Center for the Performing Arts and a few blocks from the Convention Center. True, the lobby sports a confusing mix of Parisian and Wild West themes, and the guest rooms have a traditional, out-of-the-Fifties look, but the sweeping mountain views from the west-side rooms (especially those on the corners) make up for these drawbacks.

**HOLIDAY INN DENVER DOWNTOWN**
**1450 Glenarm Pl.**
**Denver, CO 80202**
**303/573-1450**
**$$–$$$**                                 **DD**

A glassed-in high-rise on the edge of upper downtown, the Holiday Inn is the closest hotel to the Convention

---

## The Windsor: A Vanished Denver Landmark

*Many hotels flourished in the area bordering Union Station during the late 1800s in Denver, but most are gone now. The most famous of the now-demolished structures was the Windsor Hotel, located on the corner of 18th and Larimer. Designed to resemble Windsor Castle, the hotel featured grand staircases, a gold-plated bathtub, and a tunnel that led to Roman baths in the Barclay Building across the street.*

*The countless stories told about the Windsor indicate that it was a very colorful—and accommodating—place. Harry Tammen was a bartender at the hotel (and later a co-owner of the* Denver Post*) where famous patrons such as Buffalo Bill used to hang out. The legendary frontiersman was limited to ten drinks a day—but allowed to drink shots out of a beer glass. When Baby Doe Tabor stayed at the Windsor, Silver King H. A. W. Tabor would hire bellhops at a silver dollar a bucket to fill his beloved's tub, even though the hotel had its own running water. It is said that Oscar Wilde insisted on a change of wallpapers in his Windsor suite every time his mood changed.*

Center. Guest rooms, available in varying price ranges, are comfortable and clean. A bank of windows in the small exercise room provides wonderful mountain views, and the activity of the 16th Street Mall can be seen as you swim laps in the rooftop pool. Free parking in the covered garage is another plus.

**HOLTZE EXECUTIVE PLACE**
818 17th St.
Denver, CO 80202
303/607-9000
$$$–$$$$  DD

Entering the lobby of the new Holtze is like sinking into a lush and very stylish cave off of Main Street. Tucked between two old buildings in the center of downtown, the interiors are dark, but beautifully designed and elegantly decorated. A variety of accommodations are available, from suites to guest rooms. Meeting spaces vary from the casual to the more formal and structured.

## The Elegant Oxford Hotel

*The Oxford's architect, Frank E. Edbrooke, wrapped the hotel around a light well, ensuring that rooms would receive lots of clear, bright Rocky Mountain light and air. The Edbrooke-designed Brown Palace also made use of the area's light. Guest rooms at the Brown surround a glass-domed atrium. Other noteworthy facts about the Oxford:*

- *Built during the years of Colorado's silver bonanza, the Oxford boasted every convenience. The hotel had its own Western Union office, barber shop, pharmacy, library, saloon, and stables.*
- *In 1912 the Oxford added an annex, designed by Edbrooke's apprentice, Montana Fallis, to accommodate increasing business. Advertisements hawked "absolutely modern" rooms at $1, $1.50, and $2 a day.*
- *Designed in the Thirties as an art deco showcase, the Oxford's Cruise Room bar features handcarved panels that celebrate the end of Prohibition.*
- *The Oxford's lobby was a favorite hang-out for newspapermen such as Ernie Pyle and Gene Fowler.*
- *During renovation of the Oxford in 1980, Edbrooke's original blueprints for the hotel were found, allowing designers to faithfully reproduce features of the old hotel. Art deco panels surfaced in the basement. Other artifacts were discovered above false ceilings and behind closets.*

*Queen Anne Bed & Breakfast Inn*

**HYATT REGENCY DENVER**
**1750 Welton St.**
**Denver, CO 80202**
**303/295-1234**
**$$$$**      **DD**

The Hyatt Regency is a sophisticated, attractive hotel in the middle of downtown. Small lounge groupings create intimate spaces in the wood-paneled lobby. Blue faux-finished walls and oriental-red doors give the halls a distinctive look, and the rooms are spacious and elegantly furnished. On the fourth floor, tennis courts and a swimming pool overlook historic Trinity Church.

**OXFORD HOTEL**
**1600 17th St.**
**Denver, CO 80202**
**303/628-5400**
**$$$$**      **DD**

The Oxford Hotel, designed by architect Frank Edbrooke, who designed the Brown Palace a year later, was built in 1891 as a first-class accommodation near Union Station. Located in the lively LoDo section of downtown, it is a smaller, lighter, friendlier version of its first cousin down the way. French and English antiques grace the rooms and public areas. Restaurants and the Oxford Club, an outstanding fitness club, spa, and salon are located on the street level. (Ask for a corner room; with four floor-to-ceiling windows, these are especially lovely.) The Oxford has also added a Grand Ballroom that overlooks Union Station. There is an overhang level for a band, and the hardwood flooring hails from the old Celebrity Bowling Alley. Meeting rooms fill the lower levels.

**WARWICK HOTEL DENVER**
**1776 Grant St.**
**Denver, CO 80203**
**303/861-2000**
**$$$$**      **DD**

The Warwick is a European-style hotel with both guest rooms and suites available. Since the Warwick was originally designed as an apartment building, rooms are more spacious here than in any other

## The Westin's Colorful History

*The Westin Hotel Tabor Center relishes its ties with namesake H. A. W. (Horace) Tabor. The hotel sponsors pilgrimages to Riverside Cemetery where Tabor and his wife, Augusta, are buried, and even helped local historians restore Augusta's crumbling tombstone. Along with the Daughters of the American Revolution, the Westin stages high teas in Augusta Tabor's honor. The teas take place in the hotel's four-star Augusta restaurant. Thanks to events like these, the Tabors' incredible story—intertwined with so much of Denver's own history and reminiscent of other Denver tales—continues to be told.*

*Having made his fortune in the silver mines of Leadville, Horace Tabor came to Denver with his strait-laced wife, Augusta, and made his mark as a prominent developer, cultural scion, and eventually U.S. Senator. Responsible not only for the "skyscraper" built where the Westin and Tabor Center now stand, Tabor also built the Tabor Grand Opera House (described by Denver newspaperman Eugene Field as "modified Egyptian Moresque"). Sarah Bernhardt was one of the many luminaries who performed there. Tabor also supported many of the area's hotels with his opulent lifestyle and extravagant upkeep of his auburn-haired mistress, Baby Doe.*

*Horace finally divorced Augusta and married Baby Doe. The new Mr. and Mrs. Tabor continued to scandalize and delight Denver society until the crash of the silver market in 1893. Plunged into poverty, the couple remained devoted to each other. When Horace died, Baby Doe and her two daughters, Lillie and Silver Dollar, returned to the Tabor's Matchless Mine in Leadville. Baby Doe died at the cabin—old, penniless, and alone. When the townsfolk who found her removed the cap she had always worn around Leadville, her still-beautiful auburn hair spilled out.*

*In the end, it was Augusta who ended up with her fortune (from the divorce settlement) intact.*

downtown hotel. Most rooms have wet bars, refrigerators, dining tables, and private balconies. Banquet and meeting facilities are available for the smaller-meetings market. The Warwick staff prides itself on treating guests "like family."

**WESTIN HOTEL TABOR CENTER DENVER**
1672 Lawrence St.
Denver, CO 80202
303/572-9100
$$$$ DD

The Westin is in the Tabor Shopping Center, on the site where silver king Horace Tabor built the first "skyscraper" (six stories high!) in Denver. From the sweeping grey marble lobby to the luxurious rooms featuring every amenity, the Westin is a delight. The hotel offers fine dining, a wide range of recreational facilities, meeting spaces, and specialty shops nearby. Sixteen rooms are specially equipped for handicapped use. There are special programs for children, weekend shopper packages, and unique activities offered throughout the year. Contact the Westin about unique packages for the Colorado Ballet, Colorado Symphony, Central City Opera, and Best of Broadway series at the DCPA. The Westin also offers one-day ski packages to Winter Park on the Ski Train.

## Bed and Breakfasts

**QUEEN ANNE BED AND BREAKFAST INN**
2147–51 Tremont Pl.
Denver, CO 80205
303/296-6666
$$$ DD

The Queen Anne, the closest B&B to

---

# A Happy Haven:
# The Melbourne Hotel and Hostel

*The idea for the Melbourne Hotel and Hostel was born the day Leonard Schmitt met "Big John" at the Greyhound bus depot near Leonard's Five Points' warehouse property. Leonard, a former airline pilot, was retired and trying to figure out what to do with his property and his life. As he has done every day for years, Big John was volunteering his services to debarking bus passengers—giving directions and advice about where to go in the city. The two men started talking.*

*Big John thought Leonard's warehouse would be a perfect place to house travelers to Denver. He envisioned a hostel similar to those he'd encountered in Europe. Leonard had never heard of a hostel, but he liked the idea. Now, Big John's portrait hangs in the community kitchen of the Melbourne Hotel and Hostel, where Leonard's global village of young people, families, and travelers gather to chat and cook and pass the time of day.*

# CENTRAL DENVER

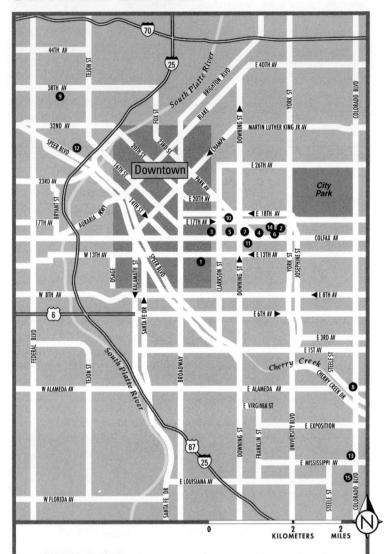

## Lodging in Central Denver

1. Capitol Hill Mansion
2. Castle Marne
3. Denver International Youth Hostel
4. Franklin House Bed & Breakfast
5. Haus Berlin Bed & Breakfast
6. The Holiday Chalet
7. Hostel of the Rocky Mountains
8. Landmark Hotel
9. Lumber Baron Inn
10. Merritt House Bed & Breakfast Inn
11. Ramada Limited Capitol Hill
12. Residence Inn by Marriott
13. Sheraton Four Points Cherry Creek
14. Victoria Oaks Inn
15. Wynham Garden Hotel

downtown, is housed in two neighboring Victorians that border a small park. The older of the homes was built by Frank Edbrooke in 1879 for the brother of H. A. W. Tabor's first wife, Augusta. Joan Baez prefers the Rooftop Suite, named for its rooftop spa overlooking the mountains and downtown, when she visits Denver. The Remington Suite with leaded glass windows, private hot tub, and entry to the garden is another great choice.

### Hostels

**MELBOURNE HOTEL AND HOSTEL**
607 22nd St.
Denver, CO 80205
303/292-6386
$ DD

Once you figure out that the office for the Melbourne is in the laundromat next door, you are in for a treat. Owner Leonard Schmitt will greet you with great warmth and enthusiasm. He will even fill you in on world events, gleaned from the many foreign travelers who frequent his hotel. Entering the hotel has the feel of walking onto the set of *Casablanca*. All rooms face a long, wide hallway where giant ceiling fans whir. Rooms are clean, basic, and well ventilated, thanks to open-grill security doors. There is a community kitchen, and a house mother presides over the women's dorm.

## CENTRAL DENVER

### Hotels and Motels

**LANDMARK HOTEL**
455 S. Colorado Blvd.
Denver, CO 80222
303/388-5561
$$ CD

This Best Western hotel, very near the Cherry Creek Shopping Center, is always busy. The guest rooms are sunny and clean. There are an indoor pool and Jacuzzi, a full-service restaurant and sports bar, as well as seven meeting rooms and a ballroom.

---

## The Lumber Baron Inn: A Labor of Love

*Maureen Keller's mother cried when she saw the crumbling old mansion that her daughter and new husband planned to buy. The couple had planned on teaching careers before spotting the derelict structure in the Highlands neighborhood of North Denver. Inspired to start the B&B they had always dreamed of, Maureen and Walter not only bought the home but moved in as well. The mansion had only one working toilet, the original 1890s electrical wiring, water from an outdoor hose only, and no heat. Despite the hardships, the Kellers carried out much of the renovation work themselves and brought lumber baron John Mouat's Victorian estate back to life.*

**WHERE TO STAY**

### LUMBER BARON INN
2555 W. 37th Ave.
Denver, CO 80211-2865
303/477-8205
$$$ CD

The Lumber Baron Inn is the realized dream of two Colorado College graduates. Thanks to a hefty bank loan and help from the mayor's Office of Economic Development, the 1890 Queen Anne mansion and many of its original furnishings have been impeccably restored. The large honeymoon suite has a canopy bed and a Jacuzzi in the bay area. Every room is decorated with unique fabrics and furnishings. The lovely yard and garden are perfect for weddings and receptions. The third-floor ballroom is a great place for a party.

### RAMADA LIMITED CAPITOL HILL
1150 East Colfax Ave.
Denver, CO 80218
303/831-7700
$$ CD

A cheerful surprise on what some call "the longest commercial strip in the U.S.," the Ramada Limited Capitol Hill offers a laid-back alternative to the large, corporate hotels in central downtown. The cream and rose lobby leads to a lounge, a restaurant, and even an espresso bar/antique shop. Guest rooms are simple, clean, and sunny. Parking lot; free shuttle service to downtown.

### RESIDENCE INN BY MARRIOTT
2777 Zuni St.
Denver, CO 80218
303/458-5318
$$–$$$ CD

With an air of cheerful efficiency and great views of Elitch Amusement Park and downtown, the all-suite Residence Inn by Marriott provides a pleasant retreat for the extended-stay visitor to Denver. The many amenities make up for the busy traffic outside this gated hotel. The suites, with mauve carpets, fireplaces, and fully equipped kitchens, are inviting and immaculate. Guests are shuttled downtown by van.

### SHERATON FOUR POINTS CHERRY CREEK
600 S. Colorado Blvd.
Denver, CO 80222
303/757-3341
$$ CD

The busy Cherry Creek Inn caters to small corporate groups and vacationers. It is within walking distance of the Cherry Creek Shopping Center and close to downtown. There is free parking. The single and double guest rooms are clean and offer basic amenities. Guests receive free passes to the nearby Bally's Health Club, and there is a jogging path nearby. Ask for a room with views of the mountains.

### WYNDHAM GARDEN HOTEL
1475 S. Colorado Blvd.
Denver, CO 80222
303/757-8797
$$ CD

Don't panic when you realize an Amoco station fronts this hotel. For a moderately priced hotel within spitting distance of the Cherry Creek Shopping Center and 15 minutes max from downtown Denver, this Wyndham Garden is just fine. The lobby sports a cozy bar and dining area, and the rooms are tastefully decorated. Be sure to ask for rooms facing the mountains to the west. An added plus is the Skyline Ballroom, a rooftop multipurpose room offering beautiful views of the Rockies and the Denver skyline.

## Bed and Breakfasts

A handful of bed and breakfasts located in the historic districts bordering downtown Denver offer attractive alternatives to the larger hotels. All of these B&Bs—depending on your stamina and perhaps your desire to help cut down on smog—are within walking distance of downtown.

### CAPITOL HILL MANSION
1207 Pennsylvania St.
Denver, CO 80203
303/839-5221
$$$–$$$$  CD

Just a ten-minute walk from downtown, the Capitol Hill Mansion is a beautiful sandstone structure graced with balconies, turrets, and a sweeping front porch. The interior is equally spectacular, with original carved oak woodwork, grand staircase, and beveled windows. Rooms are named after Colorado wildflowers and feature fireplaces, Victorian furniture, murals, and original artwork by Colorado artists. Several rooms have whirlpool baths. Guests feel safe in this quiet residential neighborhood.

### CASTLE MARNE—A LUXURY INN
1572 Race St.
Denver, CO 80206
303/331-0621
$$$–$$$$  CD

Featured in magazines such as *Bride's*, *Honeymoon*, and *Gourmet*, Castle Marne truly offers every luxury. The nine guest rooms, each with private bath, are individually decorated to evoke the romance of the Victorian era. Several rooms feature hot tubs for two on private balconies. Prices include gourmet breakfast and afternoon tea with Marne-blend coffee and homemade breads and muffins.

*Castle Marne*

### FRANKLIN HOUSE BED AND BREAKFAST
1620 Franklin St.
Denver, CO 80218
303/331-9106
$–$$  CD

Standing on the front porch of this 1890 home, you get a great view—across several vacant lots—of downtown Denver. The Franklin House is not impeccably restored like its neighboring B&Bs, but it is cheap, clean, and down-to-earth—styled after European B&Bs. Breakfast is served every day in the kitchen under a smiling portrait of Butch Cassidy. The front hall can be smoky.

### HAUS BERLIN BED AND BREAKFAST
1651 Emerson St.
Denver, CO 80218
303/837-9527
$$$  CD

Another stately Victorian on a quiet tree-lined street, Haus Berlin's interior reflects more the tastes of its well-traveled owners than the era in which it was built. The common areas, three guest rooms, and the third-floor suite are decorated in French, Mediterranean, and Mexican styles. Co-owner Dennis Brown is quick to give his German-born wife, Christiana, credit for the beauty of the rooms. The gourmet breakfasts of homemade delicacies are thanks to Christiana as well.

**THE HOLIDAY CHALET**
1820 E. Colfax Ave.
Denver, CO 80218
303/321-9975
$$ CD
Once a premier neighborhood in early Denver, East Colfax is now a busy commercial strip. The Holiday Chalet is housed in one of the few Victorian homes standing as a reminder of the bygone era. The home was built in 1896 and purchased in 1912 by the present owner's grandfather. Each of the ten guest rooms is decorated with a different "Victorian eclectic" look. There are lots of lacy curtains, and flowered spreads and carpets. Breakfast is self-serve and there is a pleasant patio. Street-side rooms are a bit noisy.

**MERRITT HOUSE BED AND BREAKFAST INN**
941 East 17th Ave.
Denver, CO 80218
303/861-5230
$$$ CD
When the power fails in nearby neighborhoods, homeowners hotfoot it to Merritt House until their own lights go on again. Brown Palace architect Frank Edbrooke not only designed this home, he also lived next door. This beautiful Victorian has been lovingly restored by the owners, who claim lots of repeat customers. The ten guest rooms feature antiques, skylights, Jacuzzis, and more. The main floor restaurant serves breakfast.

**VICTORIA OAKS INN**
1575 Race St.
Denver, CO 80206
303/355-1818
$$ CD
Many unusual features distinguish this inn—from the hanging staircase leading to the upper stories to the ornate brass chandelier dropping to the living room/lobby below. Second-floor bedrooms feature original engraved ceilings, leaded bay windows, and oriental rugs. Third-floor bedrooms are attic-style. Rates include continental breakfast, maid service, and TV in the lounge.

## Hostels

**DENVER INTERNATIONAL YOUTH HOSTEL**
638 E. 16th Ave.
Denver, CO 80203
303/832-9996
$ CD
Travelers will check into the Denver International Youth Hostel for the company—not the aesthetics of the place. Owner Richard Mitchell, who has run the hotel for 28 years, loves to chat. He offers his guests basic, clean dorm rooms equipped with bunk beds, a kitchen, and a bathroom with shower. Mitchell has also assembled a homey basement lounge, with encyclopedias, games, and a TV, where guests can congregate. The Colfax neighborhood is not safe, so guests should not walk alone at night. Also, check valuables in the office safe! Office hours: 8–10 a.m. and 5–10:30 p.m.

**HOSTEL OF THE ROCKY MOUNTAINS**

1530 Downing St.
Denver, CO 80218
303/861-7777
$ CD

Across the street from a post office and Smiley's Laundromat, the Hostel of the Rocky Mountains is also near downtown. The owner describes the hostel as a cross between a pension and a guest-house, modeled after hostels he discovered while traveling in Europe. The hall is a bit smoky, but the rooms are clean and spacious. Each room is limited to a few people and includes a bath, TV, and private locked entrance. The hostel also offers a community kitchen.

## EAST DENVER

### Hotels and Motels

*Stranded by the now-defunct Stapleton Airport, East Metro Denver hotels along the commercial strip between DIA and downtown have rallied to provide convenient, economical accommodations for business travelers and conventioneers. This corridor is 20 minutes from DIA and near I-70, I-25, and I-225. Hotels in the direction of DIA are popping up at a frantic pace on I-70 exits.*

**BEST WESTERN
EXECUTIVE HOTEL**
4411 Peoria St.
Denver, CO 80239
303/373-5730
$$–$$$ ED

There is an informal, art deco feel to this upbeat, busy hotel. Scattered couches surround the lobby's fireplace, while jazz music and noisy chatter emanate from the Cockpit Grille. The rooms are clean and all overlook the pool. The Park and Fly program allows you to park your car in a supervised lot for two weeks at no extra charge.

**COMFORT INN-AIRPORT**
16921 E. 32nd Ave.
Aurora, CO 80011
303/367-5000
$$ ED

The hotel offers all the basics, including continental breakfast, non-smoking guest rooms, meeting rooms, an exercise room, and an indoor pool and spa. There are wheelchair-accessible rooms as well. However, a dark lobby and guests grumbling about airport shuttle service are negatives at this Comfort Inn

**COURTYARD
BY MARRIOTT**
7415 East 41st Ave.
Denver, CO 80216
303/333-3303
$$–$$$ ED

Well suited to small business groups, the Courtyard provides a very classy and pleasant refuge. There are inviting areas for informal chats or deal-making in the lobby, the two meeting rooms are well equipped, and the pastel guest rooms overlook a pretty

Worried about jet lag, lost luggage, or a missed connection? Relax. DIA can help you out...with a massage. Stop by A Massage Inc. (303/342-7485) on the sixth level of the main terminal. Prices start at $20.

# GREATER DENVER

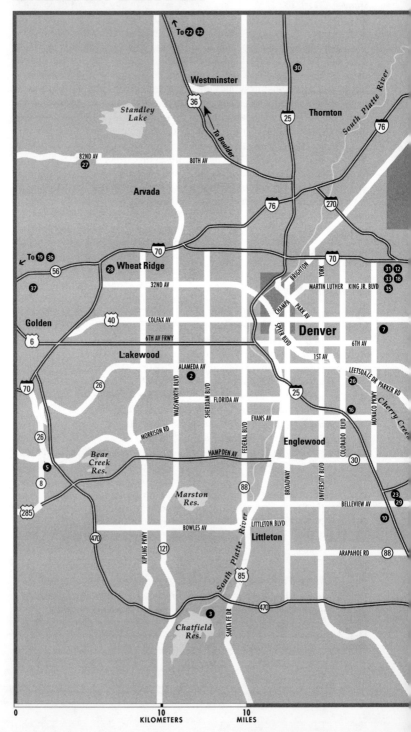

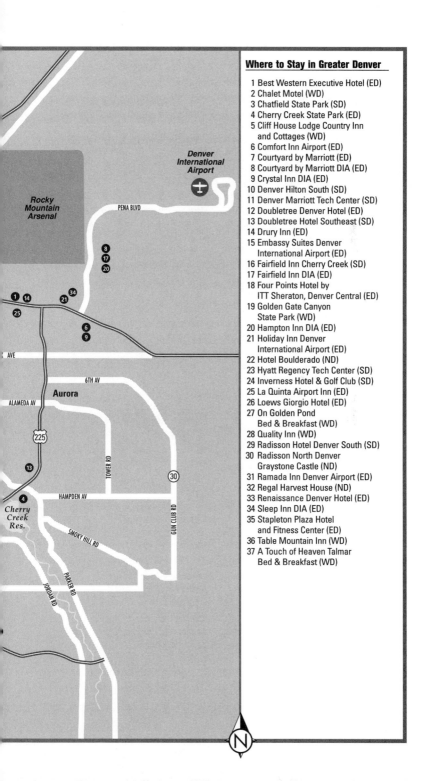

## Where to Stay in Greater Denver

1. Best Western Executive Hotel (ED)
2. Chalet Motel (WD)
3. Chatfield State Park (SD)
4. Cherry Creek State Park (ED)
5. Cliff House Lodge Country Inn and Cottages (WD)
6. Comfort Inn Airport (ED)
7. Courtyard by Marriott (ED)
8. Courtyard by Marriott DIA (ED)
9. Crystal Inn DIA (ED)
10. Denver Hilton South (SD)
11. Denver Marriott Tech Center (SD)
12. Doubletree Denver Hotel (ED)
13. Doubletree Hotel Southeast (SD)
14. Drury Inn (ED)
15. Embassy Suites Denver International Airport (ED)
16. Fairfield Inn Cherry Creek (SD)
17. Fairfield Inn DIA (ED)
18. Four Points Hotel by ITT Sheraton, Denver Central (ED)
19. Golden Gate Canyon State Park (WD)
20. Hampton Inn DIA (ED)
21. Holiday Inn Denver International Airport (ED)
22. Hotel Boulderado (ND)
23. Hyatt Regency Tech Center (SD)
24. Inverness Hotel & Golf Club (SD)
25. La Quinta Airport Inn (ED)
26. Loews Giorgio Hotel (ED)
27. On Golden Pond Bed & Breakfast (WD)
28. Quality Inn (WD)
29. Radisson Hotel Denver South (SD)
30. Radisson North Denver Graystone Castle (ND)
31. Ramada Inn Denver Airport (ED)
32. Regal Harvest House (ND)
33. Renaissance Denver Hotel (ED)
34. Sleep Inn DIA (ED)
35. Stapleton Plaza Hotel and Fitness Center (ED)
36. Table Mountain Inn (WD)
37. A Touch of Heaven Talmar Bed & Breakfast (WD)

garden and gazebo. There are also a glassed-in pool area, restaurant (for breakfast and snacks), exercise room, and sauna.

**COURTYARD BY MARRIOTT DIA**
6901 Tower Rd.
Denver, CO 80249
303/371-0300
$$-$$$ ED

A clear winner on the airport hotel scene, this Courtyard welcomes guests with its style, cheerful efficiency, and lots of nice touches. The lobby is bright and spacious, with an inviting lounge where guests can relax by the stone fireplace and sip microbrews. A full service restaurant is open for breakfast, lunch, and dinner—a real plus since eateries are sparse in this part of town. Decorated in pretty mauves and greens, the rooms have large work desks, telephones with data ports, and balconies. There are also meeting rooms, a boardroom for 12, an indoor swimming pool, an exercise room, and free shuttle to the airport.

**CRYSTAL INN DIA**
3300 North Ouray St.
(I-70 Exit 285)
Aurora, CO 80011
303/340-3800
$$-$$$ ED

Very new and cheerful, Crystal Inn offers excellent customer service and great amenities. A free hot buffet breakfast is offered every morning, and the Crystal Bistro serves gourmet evening meals. Off the indoor pool and whirlpool spa area is a patio with a barbecue grill. Rooms are large, with microwave ovens, small refrigerators, three phones, data ports, and second phone lines. There are even special buttons on one phone for ordering pizza or Chinese food delivered to your room. A low divider creates a separate space for a pull-out sleeper in each bedroom area. With four large meeting rooms, catering services, and audio-visual equipment, the Crystal is a good value for business travelers.

**DOUBLETREE DENVER HOTEL**
3203 Quebec St.
Denver, CO 80207
321-3333
$$$ ED

With a fire in the fireplace, a baby grand piano to the side, and plants everywhere, the lobby of the Doubletree is inviting. An air of friendly efficiency pervades in this bustling hotel on the corner of Quebec and Martin Luther King Boulevard. Rooms are bright and pretty, furnished with armoires, desks, and marble counters in the bathrooms. Amenities include a pool, spa, restaurant, lounges, and plenty of meeting space.

**DRURY INN**
4400 E. Peoria St.
Denver, CO 80239
303/373-1983
$$ ED

Competitor to the La Quinta on the other side of I-70, the Drury Inn offers guest rooms as well as six king deluxe rooms. Three small meeting rooms are available. A complimentary breakfast and a cocktail hour are offered to guests.

**EMBASSY SUITES DENVER INTERNATIONAL AIRPORT**
4444 Havana
Denver, CO 80239
303/375-0400
$$$ ED

A Spanish grotto greets guests entering Embassy Suites DIA. The staff is very conscious of maintaining a high-quality environment here. Impeccable rooms feature small kitchens. Amenities include complete health club facilities, a restaurant and lounge, executive meeting suites, and a grand ballroom. Special packages include those titled Family Night at the Movies and Kidnap Your Husband—gambling and ski packages are available, too.

**FAIRFIELD INN DIA**
6851 Tower Rd.
Denver, CO 80249
303/576-9640
$$ ED

This hotel offers the usual Fairfield features and amenities—complimentray breakfast, indoor pool, fax and copier service, and guest rooms with desks and computer data ports. But there is a bare look to the lobby and the rooms and the service is slow and indifferent. Airport access is a draw, however.

**FOUR POINTS HOTEL
BY ITT SHERATON,
DENVER CENTRAL**
3535 Quebec St.
Denver, CO 80207
303/333-7711
$$–$$$ ED

This Sheraton is a mid-size hotel. Aside from a few ceiling tiles sagging here and there, rooms are pleasant and clean. Floors three through eight are newly recarpeted. Other features include a Junior Olympic swimming pool, grassy backyard for volleyball and horseshoes, full-service restaurant, and ample meeting space.

**HAMPTON INN DIA**
6290 Tower Rd.
Denver, CO 80249
303/371-0200
$$-$$$ ED

A surprising landmark—the silver-domed Moonlight Diner—signals travelers to the Hampton Inn DIA. The hotel is very pleasant and tastefully decorated with sofas scattered through the large lobby, a fireplace, and a TV area tucked into a corner. Rooms are fresh and pretty. There are double mirrors in the bathrooms, hair dryers, coffeemakers, and a free in-room movie channel. More amenities include complimentary continental breakfast, free local phone calls, and airport van service. Kids eighteen and under stay free.

**HOLIDAY INN DENVER
INTERNATIONAL AIRPORT
HOTEL AND
CONFERENCE CENTER**
15500 East 40th Ave.
Denver, CO 80239
303/371-9494
$$$–$$$$ ED

The Holiday Inn DIA Hotel has a variety of meeting and conference spaces and a ballroom. Amenities include pool, spa, weight room, restaurant, lounge, nightclub, hair salon, free parking, and airport shuttle service.

**LA QUINTA AIRPORT INN**
3975 Peoria Way
Denver, CO 80239-3334
303/371-5640
$$ ED

White, bright, clean, and cheerful, the La Quinta Airport Inn offers special promotions that give you free nights for extended visits (from three to 11 days). There is an outdoor heated pool. A complimentary continental breakfast is served daily.

**LOEWS-GIORGIO HOTEL**
4150 E. Mississippi Ave.

Denver, CO 80222
303/782-9300
$$$$ ED

Entering the Loews-Giorgio, one of three four-star, four-diamond hotels in Denver, is like stepping into a luxurious Italian villa. Original artwork, frescoes, and marbleized faux finishes adorn the lobby. Guest rooms feature antique furniture, armoires, brass doorstops, bathroom commodes—even real plants. "Whatever it takes" is the staff's personal service motto. Pets are even allowed at this very civilized stop-over!

**RAMADA INN
DENVER AIRPORT**
3737 Quebec St.
Denver, CO 80207
303/388-6161
$$ ED

From the modest peach and green lobby to the clean, pastel guest rooms, the Ramada Inn Denver Airport is a comfortable retreat. The staff is friendly and helpful. The Inn offers meeting space, in-room coffee, and passes to nearby exercise facilities.

**RENAISSANCE
DENVER HOTEL**
3801 Quebec St.
Denver, CO 80207
303/399-7500
$$$–$$$$ ED

Deluxe accommodations are offered in this pyramid-shaped hotel. Uniformed doormen welcome guests into a spacious and sunny lobby complete with waterfall. The blue and green rooms are pretty, with light oak furniture and balconies. There are a restaurant and lounge, as well as Jacuzzis, pools, health club, detached three-story parking garage, and three club level floors with extra amenities. The employee-to-room ratio is high, and the service is excellent.

**SLEEP INN DIA**
15900 East 40th Ave.
Aurora, CO 80011
303/373-5906
$$

Behind the Holiday Inn and surrounded by hotel construction projects, Sleep Inn DIA welcomes guests with a nicely landscaped entrance, friendly service, and clean, comfortable surroundings. There is a coffee shop, an indoor pool and outdoor patio, airport shuttle service, and free continental breakfast. Business travelers will appreciate extra-long desks in the rooms, along with desk and bedside modem ports.

**STAPLETON PLAZA
HOTEL AND FITNESS CENTER**
3333 Quebec St.
Denver, CO 80207
303/321-3500
$$$ ED

All rooms at the Stapleton Plaza face the 11-story atrium/lobby where you can get everything from a fine meal to a shoeshine or a new haircut. The nicely decorated rooms have private balconies. The extensive fitness center features racquetball courts, outdoor running courts, weight equipment, and more. The convention service staff is on hand to tailor the meeting spaces to specific needs.

## Camping

**CHERRY CREEK STATE PARK**
4201 S. Parker Rd.
Aurora, CO 80014
303/690-1166
$ ED

Camping sites are located on the east side of the 880-acre reservoir. Sandy beaches and picnic areas line the shore. Activities at the 3,915-acre park include boating, swimming, hiking, horseback riding, and biking. Shower and laundry facilities and limited electrical hook-ups are available. Reserve campsites in advance by calling 470-1144 or 800/678-CAMP. A park pass is required.

## SOUTH DENVER

### Hotels and Motels

*Hotels in South Metro Denver are off I-25 in and around the Denver Tech Center, or on Colorado Boulevard, between the Cherry Creek Shopping Center and the I-25 turn-off.*

**DENVER HILTON SOUTH**
**7801 East Orchard Rd.**
**Englewood, CO 80111-2508**
**303/779-6161**
**$$–$$$$** SD

The color schemes are dramatic at the beautiful Denver Hilton South. There are purple rugs and turquoise chairs in the spacious lobby, while hot coral chairs accent the rooms. Hilton hotels are known for their impeccably clean rooms, and the Denver Hilton is no exception. All rooms have balconies. There is a restaurant and a lounge on the premises, and convention facilities are available.

**DENVER MARRIOTT**
**TECH CENTER**
**4900 S. Syracuse St.**
**Englewood, CO 80237**
**303/779-1100**
**$$$** SD

The lobby of the Denver Marriott Tech Center is dark, crowded, and sprawling. All the convention and meeting space, health club facilities, restaurants, lounges, and shops are located on the ground floor. It's like a teeming city with the kind of indifferent service you might expect. The guest rooms are adequate. There are suites available.

**DOUBLETREE HOTEL (SOUTHEAST)**
**13696 E. Iliff Place at I-225**
**Aurora, CO 80014**
**303/337-2800**
**$$$** SD

The six-story Doubletree Hotel, 15 minutes from DIA and adjacent to the Denver Tech Center, hovers over this busy commercial area. Hotel guests may golf, swim, and play tennis—for a fee—at the HeatherRidge Country Club across the street. There are an indoor pool and whirlpool off the hotel lobby. The guest rooms have specially designed windows that afford good mountain views and let in lots of natural light, but request rooms farthest from the noise of freeway traffic.

**FAIRFIELD INN CHERRY CREEK**
**1680 S. Colorado Blvd.**
**Denver, CO 80222**
**303/691-2223**
**$$** SD

For an economical version of the Marriott, this Fairfield Inn off I-25 is a stand-out. Employee awards for excellence are proudly displayed in the very pleasing lobby. West-side rooms have views of the mountains from Pikes Peak to Longs Peak. Ask for #703 for a special treat.

**HYATT REGENCY TECH CENTER**
**7800 East Tufts Ave.**
**Denver, CO 80237**
**303/779-1234**
**$$$$** SD

From the glamorous lobby to the rooftop Centennial Restaurant, the Hyatt Regency Tech Center is a deluxe hotel. It offers gorgeous panoramas of the mountains and city as well as amenities such as tennis courts, health club facilities, and a covered garage. Extensive meeting spaces are available. The deluxe suites on the eleventh floor concierge level are especially lovely.

**INVERNESS HOTEL AND GOLF CLUB**
**200 Inverness Dr. West**
**Englewood, CO 80112**
**303/799-5800**
**$$$$** SD

Located in the Inverness Business Park, this beautiful, sunny hotel is flanked by a par 70 championship golf course. There are tennis courts, outdoor and indoor swimming pools, jogging trails, and full health club facilities. Dining choices range from four-star to casual. The state-of-the-art conference center contains meeting rooms, boardrooms, and auditoriums.

**RADISSON HOTEL DENVER SOUTH**
**I-25 and Arapahoe Rd.**
**Englewood, CO 80112**
**303/799-6200**
**$$$** SD

The Radisson Hotel Denver South is a big, bustling convention hotel just off I-25. While it does offer every business convenience, this property lacks the charm and hospitality of some of the other hotels located in the area.

## Camping

**CHATFIELD STATE PARK**
**11500 N. Roxborough Park Rd.**
**Littleton, CO 80125**
**303/791-7275** SD

Chatfield State Park is a 5,600-acre recreation area with a 1,450-acre dammed lake. Park visitors can choose from activities including fishing, hiking, horseback riding, sailing, and boating. More than 180 bird species, including great blue herons, can be seen at Chatfield. Beavers, muskrats, mule deer, and coyotes also call this place home.

Visitors may stay 14 days in any 45 day period at any of the three campgrounds. Sites, which can be reserved in advance, offer water faucets, fire rings, and grills. Camping permits and park passes can be purchased from park headquarters, which is located on the southeast side of the lake.

# WEST DENVER

## Hotels and Motels

**CHALET MOTEL**
**6051 W. Alameda Ave.**
**Lakewood, CO 80226**
**303/237-7775**
**$** WD

The AAA-rated Chalet Motel offers units with kitchenettes, waterbeds, and at-door parking. Non-smoking rooms are available. The Chalet is near the Villa Italia Shopping Mall and a 45-minute drive from the Loveland Ski Area.

**QUALITY INN**
**12100 W. 44th Ave.**
**Wheat Ridge, CO 80033**
**303/467-2400**
**$-$$** WD

Immediately off I-70 at the foothills of the Rockies and bordered by a 150-acre park with three lakes, this recently renovated Quality Inn offers guest rooms and suites, and a restaurant/lounge. There is a free casino shuttle. Ask for a room with mountain/lake views and bring your fishing rod! Ski areas are nearby as well.

**TABLE MOUNTAIN INN**
1310 Washington Ave.
Golden, CO 80401
303/277-9898
$$$                                    WD

The Table Mountain Inn is an all-suite hotel nestled between North and South Table Mountains and the Rocky Mountain Front Range. It is also in the heart of Golden's downtown historic district and within walking distance of the Coors Brewery. With its deluxe rooms, elegant Southwestern decor, and award-winning restaurant, the Inn is a great choice for vacationers and business travelers alike. Guests receive free passes to the nearby Golden Recreation Center, a superb facility.

## Bed and Breakfasts

**A TOUCH OF HEAVEN TALMAR BED AND BREAKFAST**
16720 W. 63rd Pl.
Golden, CO 80403
303/279-4133
$–$$$                                  WD

Talmar is a one-woman spectacular. Designed, built, and managed by owner Kathy Bury on a 2-acre estate where her Arabian horses roam, this unique B&B is lovingly maintained. The Royal Suite, complete with baby grand piano, Jacuzzi, and deck, is sheer elegance, while the upstairs guest rooms, built around an indoor cottonwood tree, offer cozy country comforts. Gourmet breakfasts, fresh flowers, outdoor picnic area, and riding privileges round out A Touch of Heaven. Cash or check only.

**CLIFF HOUSE LODGE COUNTRY INN AND COTTAGES**
121 Stone St.
Morrison, CO 80465
303/697-9732
$$$–$$$$                                WD

A perfect spot for honeymooners or for anniversaries or special occasions, the Cliff House Lodge is located in a quaint mountain town within walking distance of restaurants, bars, and shopping (mostly antiques). Scenic Red Rocks Park and cliffs bearing the fossilized tracks of dinosaurs are also close by. Each cottage has its own private indoor or outdoor hot tub. Breakfast is delivered every morning to your room. Ask for the room overlooking the 1800s dinosaur excavation.

**ON GOLDEN POND BED AND BREAKFAST**
7831 Eldridge
Arvada, CO 80005
303/424-2296
$$–$$$                                  WD

Locals looking for a getaway and travelers from all over the world come to stay at On Golden Pond. The secluded bed and breakfast is on a 10-acre site—horses, peacocks, and chickens mill about—but it's only a short distance from downtown and an hour's drive from many ski areas. Jacuzzis, hot tubs, and swimming pool complete the picture of this relaxing country retreat

## Camping

**GOLDEN GATE CANYON STATE PARK**
3873 Highway 46
Golden, CO 80403

**303/642-3856**
**$**                                          **WD**

Golden Gate Canyon State Park is about an hour's drive from Denver. To reach the park, take Highway 6 west to Highway 93. Drive north 1 mile to Golden Gate Canyon Road. Turn left and continue for 15 miles through the canyon to the park.

Reverend's Ridge Campground accommodates trailers, campers, and tents. Flush toilets, hot showers, and laundry facilities are available.

Aspen Meadow Campground provides 35 campsites for tents only. Facilities include water pumps, vault toilets, and fire rings.

Four backcountry shelters, each sleeping up to six people, are available inside the park. There are also 23 backcountry tent sites where no fires are allowed. Obtain permits at the visitors center.

## NORTH DENVER

### Hotels and Motels

**HOTEL BOULDERADO**
2115 13th Street
Boulder, CO 80302
303/442-4344 or 800/433-4344
**$$$–$$$$**                         **ND**

The Hotel Boulderado opened on New Year's Day, 1909. The early Boulderites envisioned a "hotel beautiful" that would belie the beauty of their community and stimulate interest in the area. The fortunes of the city and the hotel have been intertwined ever since. The luxurious accommodations (with telephones, full baths and light fixtures in many rooms) attracted guests like Theodore Roosevelt, Ethel Barrymore, Douglas Fairbanks, Jr., and Bat Masterson.

Today this beautifully restored and maintained hotel offers three bars, three restaurants, a few rumors of ghosts, and an extensive array of services and amenities.

**RADISSON NORTH DENVER GRAYSTONE CASTLE**
83 E. 120th Ave.
Thornton, CO 80233
303/451-1002
**$$$–$$$$**                         **ND**

Located halfway between Denver and Boulder off I-25, the Radisson Graystone Castle has an appearance halfway between bizarre and camp. Inside, many amenities are offered in a relaxed atmosphere. Offered are free airport shuttle, complimentary breakfast and cocktail hour, meeting/banquet facilities, indoor pool, hot tub and sauna, and a concierge floor.

**REGAL HARVEST HOUSE**
1345 28th St.
Boulder, CO 80302-6899
303/443-3850 or 800/545-6285
**$$$–$$$$**                         **ND**

Located five minutes from the University of Colorado campus at the base of the Rocky Mountains, Regal Harvest House offers an ideal base for enjoying and exploring the unique Boulder community. The hotel is situated on 16 acres with lovely gardens, indoor and outdoor heated pools, 15 tennis courts, basketball and volleyball courts, bike paths, exercise facilities, and two whirlpools. The restaurant, lounge, and meeting and banquet rooms make this hotel a good choice for vacationers as well as conventioneers.

Brasserie Z

# 4
# WHERE TO EAT

If you still think of Denver as a cow town, think again. The 1990s witnessed an unprecedented migration into the Mile High City—and along with the newcomers have come the new restaurants. What a variety of restaurants Denver has! Many reflect the American origins of the chefs and owners: California, Texas, New Mexico, New York, and points elsewhere. The influx has meant a dining bonanza for the city, whose residents have had their fill of the steakhouses and pseudo-Western eateries that dominated for decades.

Metro area restaurants are taking advantage of technology as well as tastebuds. The decreasing costs of transporting seafood means this landlocked city can enjoy fish as fresh as that found along the coasts. Also, the realization that Colorado has many unusual ingredients growing right in its own back yard has spiced up Rocky Mountain cuisine. And while Denver has always had its share of celebrity chefs, now there are more of them than ever.

Add to this mix a few other Denver dining attributes, such as the "Rocky Mountain formal" dress code followed by the majority of eateries. Only a handful require jacket and tie; the rest expect that anything goes, from well-worn cowboy boots and jeans to, well, brand new cowboy boots and jeans. And although the attire of 21- to 35-year-olds seems to dominate in some of Denver's brewpubs—Colorado has the largest number of microbreweries per capita in the United States—diners of all ages benefit from the wide variety of handcrafted beers to be had.

This chapter begins with a list of restaurants organized by the type of food each offers. For details about each restaurant, see pages 64–94 —dining spots are listed alphabetically within each geographic zone. Dollar-sign symbols indicate how much you can expect to spend per person for a meal (entree and dessert) at each restaurant. All restaurants are wheelchair-accessible unless otherwise noted.

*Champion Brewery*

Duffy's Shamrock Tavern (DD) p. 68
Dumitri's (ED) p. 82
The Egg-Ception Eatery (ED) p. 84
The Eggshell (CD) p. 76
The Egg Shell &
   Incredibles Cafe (DD) p. 68
Fratelli's (SD) p. 87
Hot Cakes (CD) p. 77
New York Deli News (SD) p.86
Pour La France! (CD, ND) pp. 80, 92
Sunrise Sunset (WD) p. 92
Zaidy's (CD) p. 81

### Brewpubs

Broadway Pub (CD) p. 74
Champion Brewing
   Company (DD) p. 65
Columbine Mill Brewery
   & Pizza Company (SD) p. 86
Denver ChopHouse
   & Brewery (DD) p. 67
Sandlot Brewery (DD) p. 71
Walnut Brewery (ND) p. 94
Wynkoop Brewing
   Company (DD) p. 72

*Price rating symbols:*
$   Under $10/person
$$   $11 to $20
$$$   $21 and up

### American/Contemporary

Aubergine Cafe (CD) p. 74
Bistro Adde Brewster (CD) p. 74
Brasserie Z (DD) p. 64
Coos Bay Bistro (SD) p. 87
Dandelion (ND) p. 93
Denver ChopHouse &
   Brewery (DD) p. 67
Hugh's New American
   Bistro (CD) p. 77
Mel's Bar & Grill (CD) p. 78
Papillon (CD) p. 79
Strings (CD) p. 80
Today's Gourmet/
   Highlands Garden Cafe (WD) p. 92

### Breakfasts

Annie's Cafe (CD) p. 72
Dozens (DD) p. 68

### Burgers

Cherry Cricket (CD) p. 75
Grand Slam Sports
   Cafe (SD, WD) pp. 87, 91
My Brother's Bar (CD) p. 78
Paul's Place (CD, SD) pp. 80, 89

### Chinese

China Jade (CD) p. 75
Empress Seafood (CD) p. 76
Imperial Seafood
   Restaurant (CD) p. 77
La Chine (SD) p. 88

### Delis/Sandwiches

Cucina Leone (CD) p. 76
Maria's Bakery & Deli (CD) p. 78

The Market at Larimer
   Square (DD) p. 69
New York Deli News (SD) p. 88
Zaidy's (CD) p. 81

## Diners

Annie's Cafe (CD) p. 72
Duffy's Shamrock Tavern (DD) p. 68
Rocky Mountain Diner (DD) p. 71

## Fine Dining

Cliff Young's (CD) p. 76
Flagstaff House (ND) p. 93
Palace Arms at the
   Brown Palace Hotel (DD) p. 70
Tante Louise (ED) p. 83

## French

La Coupole Cafe (DD) p. 69
Le Central (CD) p. 77
The Normandy/Chez
   Michelle (CD) p. 79
Pour La France!
   (CD, ND) pp. 80, 93
Tante Louise (ED) p. 85

## Greek

Central 1 (CD) p. 75
Dumitri's (ED) p. 84
Yanni's (ED) p. 86

## Indian

Gandhi (SD) p. 87
India's (SD) p. 88

## Italian

Al Fresco (DD, ND) pp. 64, 93
Barolo Grill (CD) p. 74
Caffe Antica Roma (ND) p. 93
Carmine's on Penn (CD) p. 75
Fratelli's (SD) p. 85
Pasta's (SD) p. 89

Tuscany at the Loews-
   Giorgio Hotel (CD) p. 81

## Japanese

Kobe-An (WD) p. 91
L'Auberge Zen (ED) p. 84
Mori Japanese
   Restaurant (DD) p. 70
Sonoda's (DD, ED) pp. 71, 85
Sushi Den (DD) p. 80
Sushi Tazu (CD) p. 81

## Kids Extra-Welcome

Annie's Cafe (CD) p. 72
Cedars (CD) p. 75
Emil-Lene's Sirloin House (ED) p. 84
Gandhi (SD) p. 87
Grand Slam Sports
   Cafe (SD, WD) pp. 87, 91
Healthy Habits
   (CD, SD, ND) pp. 76, 88, 93
La Cueva (ED) p. 84
Paul's Place (CD, SD) pp. 80, 89
Taste of Thailand (SD) p. 89

## Late-Night Spots

Duffy's Shamrock Tavern (DD) p. 68
Jerusalem Restaurant (SD) p. 88
My Brother's Bar (CD) p. 78
Wazee Supper Club (DD) p. 71

## Mexican

El Taco de Mexico (DD) p. 68
La Cueva (ED) p. 84
Tosh's Hacienda (CD, SD) pp. 81, 90
Z-Teca Mexican Grill (CD) p. 81

## Middle Eastern

Cedars (CD) p. 75
Fettoush (DD) p. 68
Jerusalem Restaurant (SD) p. 88

## Pizza

Cappuccino's Italian
  Ristorante & Cafe (WD) p. 88
Papa's Pizza (CD) p. 79
Pasquini's Pizzeria (CD) p. 79
Wazee Supper Club (DD) p. 71

## Seafood

Cherry Crest Seafood
  Market & Restaurant (SD) p. 86
Fresh Fish Company (SD) p. 87
Jax Fish House (DD, ND) p. 69
McCormick's Fish House
  & Bar (DD) p. 70
240 Union (WD) p. 92

## Southwestern

J. Beatty's (DD) p. 68
Table Mountain Inn (WD) p. 92
Zolo Grill (ND) p. 94

## Steakhouses

Beacon Grill (DD) p. 65
Brook's Steak House (SD) p. 86
Buckhorn Exchange (CD) p. 74
Cadillac Ranch (DD) p. 65
Denver Buffalo
  Company (DD) p. 65
Emil-Lene's Sirloin House (ED) p. 84
The Fort (WD) p. 90
Luke's—A Steak Place (WD) p. 92
Morton's of Chicago (DD) p. 70
The Palm (DD) p. 71

## Thai

Chao-Praya Thai (ED) p. 81
J's Noodles (CD) p. 77
Taste of Thailand (SD) p. 89
Thai Landing (ED) p. 85

## Vegetarian

Healthy Habits
  (CD, SD, ND) pp. 76, 88, 93
Mediterranean
  Health Cafe (CD) p. 78
Rudi's (ND) p. 94

## Vietnamese

New Orient (ED) p. 85
New Saigon (CD) p. 78
Tay-Do (ED) p. 85

# DOWNTOWN DENVER

**AL FRESCO**
**1020 15th St., Denver**
**303/534-0404**
**$$–$$$**                    **DD**
Upscale Italian food in an upscale setting is the most accurate way to describe Al Fresco. Don't pass up the lightly fried calamari and the creamy minestrone, which is as rich as rich gets, and someone in your party should order the incredible seafood risotto. The wine list is varied and well priced. Reservations recommended. Lunch and dinner.

**BEACON GRILL**
**303 16th St., Denver**
**303/592-4745**
**$$–$$$**                    **DD**
Beef is what's for lunch and dinner at Beacon Grill, a sleek, wood-lined establishment that overlooks the 16th Street Mall. Start off with Beacon's sound Caesar salad and then order a filet or a burger—it's all char-grilled from lean Limousin cattle. In nice weather, the outdoor patio dotted with umbrella-topped tables gives diners a view of the city and the stars. Reservations recommended. Lunch and dinner; closed Sundays.

*Buckhorn Exchange*

**BRASSERIE Z**
**815 17th St., Denver**
**303/293-2322**
**$$**   **DD**

Nationally known chef Kevin Taylor closed down his popular Zenith to open "Brass Z." The restaurant is more like something you'd find in San Francisco than Denver, but the lush, eye-catching decor and breezy American-influenced brasserie fare have made it one of the most popular spots in town. The deep-fried artichoke appetizer and any of the pasta dishes are can't-misses. For many, the burger is the best in town. The most appealing aspect of Brass Z, though, is that it looks like a million bucks but prices are surprisingly reasonable. The happy hour is tops. Reservations recommended. Lunch and dinner.

**CADILLAC RANCH**
**1400 Larimer St., Denver**
**303/820-2288**
**$$–$$$**   **DD**

Sit among blow-up photos of James Dean on the set of *Giant* and sample an eclectic menu that pulls from Tex-Mex, Asian, and American cuisines. Red meat rules at the Ranch, but the Rocky Mountain trout and the rotisserie chicken are also highlights, as is the buffalo green chile. The outdoor patio affords one of the best views of the mountains to be had downtown. Reservations recommended. Lunch and dinner.

**CHAMPION BREWING CO.**
**1442 Larimer Square, Denver**
**303/534-5444**
**$**   **DD**

The food isn't necessarily the reason Champion is always bustling—there are the pool tables, the many televisions for sports viewing, and the young, hip crowd to take into account, too. The grub is bar food turned way up (fresh pretzels with green chile and garlic, chicken breast sandwich with pineapple jicama relish) and the microbrews are sound. Reservations recommended. Lunch and dinner. Call ahead for wheelchair access.

# DOWNTOWN DENVER

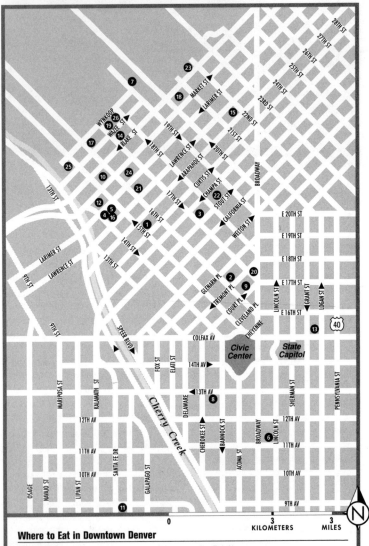

### Where to Eat in Downtown Denver

1. Al Fresco
2. Beacon Grill
3. Brasserie Z
4. Cadillac Ranch
5. Champion Brewing Co.
6. Denver Buffalo Company
7. Denver Chophouse & Brewery
8. Dozens
9. Duffy's Shamrock Tavern
10. The Egg Shell & Incredibles Cafe
11. El Taco de Mexico
12. Fettoush
13. J. Beatty's
14. Jax Fish House
15. La Coupole Cafe
16. The Market at Larimer Square
17. McCormick's Fish House & Bar
18. Mori Japanese Restaurant
19. Morton's of Chicago
20. Palace Arms at the Brown Palace Hotel
21. The Palm at Tabor Center
22. Rocky Mountain Diner
23. Sandlot Brewery
24. Sonoda's
25. Wazee Supper Club
26. Wynkoop Brewing Co.

**DENVER BUFFALO COMPANY**
1109 Lincoln St., Denver
303/832-0880
$$–$$$ DD

Buffalo is big in Denver but still expensive, so many locals look at the Buffalo Company as a once-in-a-while, but welcome, excursion. And once out-of-towners accept the idea that buffalo aren't extinct, they usually settle down to a stellar steak or "buff burger"—order it no hotter than medium, though, or it dries out—and applaud the clean flavor that comes with only 2 percent fat. The kitchen tries to make up for the high cost by adding a few nice touches, such as chile-studded muffins, and the attached general store is a great place to load up on Colorado-made goods (buffalo jerky, buffalo hides) for the folks back home. Reservations recommended. Lunch and dinner.

**DENVER CHOPHOUSE & BREWERY**
1735 19th St., Denver
303/296-0800
$$–$$$ DD

One of Denver's most attractive restaurants sits a baseball's throw away from Coors Field. The ChopHouse resides in the train station's former Head House, and the restaurant kept the train theme rolling with plush upholstery and old black-and-white photos of diners on Pullman cars. The famed dining car service is in effect here, too, as is the attention to quality food. Authentic pizza crusts are piled with toppings never seen in Napoli (try the bourbon-spiked beef or the Thai peanut sauce), and the pancetta-wrapped shrimp appetizers are killer. Order everything with the hand-mashed potatoes, and

## The Other Red Meat

*Buffalo, which many people try for the first time at the Denver Buffalo Company eatery, is 97 percent lean, which makes it a healthier "other red meat." A lot of folks still imagine that the animal is extinct, but there are nearly 100,000 buffalo roaming the United States. A large number of them are in Colorado, including those on the ranch owned by broadcasting magnate Ted Turner, as well as the Kiowa-based herd raised for the Denver Buffalo Company. Still, buffalo is more expensive than beef because the numbers remain well behind that of cattle, and each buffalo cow can produce only one offspring per year. The meat is usually described as tasting more refined and cleaner than beef. Be sure to order it cooked no hotter than medium—the low fat content means the longer it cooks, the drier it gets.*

wash it down with one of the excellent microbrews. On game days you won't be able to get near the place without having called weeks before. Reservations recommended. Lunch and dinner.

## DOZENS
**236 West 13th Ave., Denver**
**303/572-0066**
**$**                    **DD**

Lawyers and construction workers jockey for elbow room at Dozens, one of the most happening breakfast joints around. The typical offerings include omelettes and Belgian waffles as well as biscuits with gravy, but the huge, sticky-sweet cinnamon rolls are probably the most sought-after item on the menu. The staff goes easy on diners who aren't morning people, and the sunny, cheerful surroundings are easy on hangovers. Reservations not accepted. Dozens serves breakfast and lunch.

## DUFFY'S SHAMROCK TAVERN
**1635 Court Pl., Denver**
**303/534-4935**
**$**                    **DD**

Duffy's is the diner's diner, a comfortable throwback to fern bars and Harvey Wallbangers, where someone will prop you up against a wall if the going gets tough. Business people and the unemployed—and, really, anyone who enjoys a liquid lunch—sit in the well-worn booths and wolf down Southern fried chicken and other cholesterol-laden goodies. The kitchen stays open until 1:30 a.m., so Duffy's is the stop for the post-party party, or crawl in at dawn for the quintessential bacon-and-eggs breakfast. Reservations accepted. Breakfast, lunch and dinner.

## THE EGG SHELL & INCREDIBLES CAFE
**1520 Blake St., Denver**
**303/623-7555**
**$**                    **DD**

The Egg Shell & Incredibles is one of the few places to grab breakfast in lower downtown (LoDo), so there's usually a sizable crowd. The feather-light Swedish pancakes with lingonberry sauce are a favorite, as are the regular pancakes and the skillets. The exposed-brick, poster-lined decor fits in with the artsy (and artsy-wannabe) types who frequent the cafe. Reservations not accepted on weekends. Breakfast and lunch.

## EL TACO DE MEXICO
**714 Santa Fe Dr., Denver**
**303/623-3926**
**$**                    **DD**

Next to the word "dive" in the dictionary is a picture of El Taco de Mexico, but Denverites don't care, because this is where they go for the best burritos in town. Served with seasoned shredded pork and the most flavorful refried beans imaginable, the fare is forked over by people who speak no English, and there's no liquor license. But for under $4, diners walk out as stuffed as the tortillas. Reservations are not accepted. Lunch and dinner.

## FETTOUSH
**1448 Market St., Denver**
**303/820-2554**
**$$**                  **DD**

The sweetly char-broiled kabobs and ample portions for a small price are the reasons to pop into this snazzy, breezy Middle Eastern eatery two blocks from the Market Street bus station. On hot summer days, the rosewater-tinged lemon-

> ## TRIVIA
>
> Denver lays claim to the invention of the cheeseburger, a boast backed up by the application for trademark of the name Cheeseburger in 1935 by Louis Ballast, owner of Denver's first drive-through restaurant, the Humpty Dumpty Drive-In at 2776 North Speer Boulevard. Ballast said he came up with the cheeseburger at Humpty Dumpty while testing hamburger toppings. Humpty Dumpty closed its doors in the early 1970s, but the cheeseburger lives on.

ade can't be beat. Reservations recommended. Dinner only.

**J. BEATTY'S**
**321 East Colfax Ave., Denver**
**303/861-0726**
**$–$$** DD
Not only is J. Beatty's an excellent place to hook up with a Colorado legislator—the restaurant sits across the street from the capitol—but it also serves some excellent pork in the form of a massive BLT. But the Southwestern fare is solid, too, with plenty of spicy offerings. The Southwestern chicken is done well, and the cheese-filled lamb quesadilla with an apple-enhanced salsa is the choice of the cocktail crowd. Reservations recommended. Lunch and dinner; closed Saturdays and Sundays.

**JAX FISH HOUSE**
**1539 17th St., Denver**
**303/292-5767**
**$$–$$$** DD
Landlocked Denver can nonetheless get some of the freshest fish available, and you need look no further than Jax for proof. The second location of a popular Boulder eatery, Jax offers innovative seafood dishes and a well-priced oyster bar. Chile fans shouldn't pass up the habanero-enhanced oyster shooters, and both the lobster bisque and the chef's signature "filet mignon of tuna" are top-notch. Reservations recommended. Dinner only.

**LA COUPOLE CAFE**
**2191 Arapahoe St., Denver**
**303/297-2288**
**$$** DD
La Coupole is a jazzy French restaurant in an old hotel, complete with art-covered exposed-brick walls, hardwood floors, and an ivy-strewn wrought-iron-enclosed courtyard for summer dining. The neighborhood isn't as spiffy as the eatery's interior, but don't let that deter you, because the smartly executed modern French cooking and the suave setting—and the excellent prices—are worth the trip. Dessert is a must. Reservations recommended. Lunch and dinner; closed Mondays.

**THE MARKET AT LARIMER SQUARE**
**1445 Larimer Square, Denver**
**303/534-5140**
**$** DD
If you absolutely must be "seen" while in Denver, the Market on busy Larimer Square is a good place for it. In nice weather, the sidewalk can barely hold the customers and the wrought-iron tables; throughout the year it's a challenge to get past the

> **TRIVIA**
>
> The most famous meal in Colorado took place not in a restaurant, but at a camp in Ouray in the winter of 1873. The story, well-documented in the newspaper of the time and retold and debated many times since, is of Alfred Packer, a prospector who supposedly killed and ate his five companions when food ran out while they trekked through the snowy mountains. Packer was convicted of that crime and of killing five other men, but his sentence was later commuted.

doors. Once inside, stations overflow with trend-setters and trend-seekers trying to get a latté or a pastry; farther back in the narrow space is a soup-sandwich-salad set-up, along with a bakery, a hot-food line, and an ice cream bar. Reservations not accepted. Breakfast, lunch, and dinner. No wheelchair access.

### McCORMICK'S FISH HOUSE & BAR
1659 Wazee St., Denver
303/825-1107
$$$  DD

Unquestionably one of the best seafood restaurants in Denver, McCormick's, part of a Seattle chain, sits at the bottom of the Oxford Hotel in the heart of lower downtown. The elegant setting and impeccable service hark back to a more genteel time, and the daily selection of oysters—raw and cooked—is unparalleled. Weekend breakfast features Dungeness crab eggs Benedict in the main dining room. In the evening, stop by the art deco–styled Cruise Room bar for a nightcap. Reservations recommended. Lunch and dinner daily, breakfast weekends only.

### MORI JAPANESE RESTAURANT
2019 Market St., Denver
303/298-1864
$–$$  DD

The massive menu is a travel guide to Japan, and the food will make you feel as if you're already there. Buried in an old American Legion Post, Mori is fondly thought of by many Denverites as the best Japanese restaurant in town, as much for the low prices as for the delicious fare. The lunch and happy-hour sushi deals are considerable, and aficionados of Japanese cuisine will marvel at the number of options available here. Reservations for six or more only. Lunch and dinner; closed Sundays.

### MORTON'S OF CHICAGO
1710 Wynkoop St., Denver
303/825-3353
$$$  DD

This Denver link in the famous national steakhouse chain will cost you, but most locals agree that Morton's has the best beef anywhere. Side dishes and salads are extra, but the portions are sharing size, and the pricey wine list is well-rounded. Morton's is also the place for an impressive business meal. Reservations recommended. Dinner only.

### PALACE ARMS AT THE BROWN PALACE HOTEL
321 17th St., Denver
303/297-3111
$$$  DD

From the moment diners are escorted from the car at the valet station, the Palace Arms in the Brown Palace Hotel dazzles. The restaurant, the most formal of the 100-year-old hotel's four eateries, is replete with the same red leather upholstery, antique furniture, china, and silver that the rest of the hotel is garnished with, and it is one of the few Denver-area establishments that require jacket and tie. Wander through the building to savor the breathtaking decor, and try to stop by the lobby on Sundays for the lovely high tea. The Palace Arms itself is unobtrusively formal, and although tradition dictates the service, it does not carry over to the split-personality menu, which features such standards as beef Wellington listed next to seared ahi tuna. The duck à l'orange is magnificent. Sundays are also a good time to visit Ellyngton's down the hall for a blowout brunch buffet. Reservations recommended. Lunch and dinner.

### THE PALM AT THE TABOR CENTER
**1201 16th St., Denver**
**303/825-7256**
**$$$**  DD

Another national chain, The Palm is a steakhouse with an unusual atmosphere—the walls are covered with flattering caricatures of Denver celebrities and Palm regulars—and above-average beef. You'll pay less at lunch for the same meals served at dinner. Service can be stuffy, but this is a power place that attracts expense-account types. Reservations recommended. Lunch and dinner.

### ROCKY MOUNTAIN DINER
**800 18th St., Denver**
**303/293-8383**
**$–$$**  DD

The portions are huge, the aged-bourbon roster is huge, the staff's smiles are huge, and the prices are small at this fun Western diner. Meatloaf and chicken-fried steak are among the homey items the Diner cooks up, and even though each meal's accompanying sweet cornbread, steamed vegetables, and fried potatoes make it tough, room must be saved for their gigantic desserts (the chocolate cake is dynamite). Reservations accepted for dinner only. Lunch and dinner.

### SANDLOT BREWERY
**2161 Blake St., Denver**
**303/298-1587**
**$–$$**  DD

Attached to Coors Field and owned by Coors Brewing Co., Sandlot is almost impossible to squeeze into during a game, but when the Rockies are away, the fans do still play here, watching sporting events and drinking microbrews. The grub is one step above typical bar fare (try the way-hot wings) and the camaraderie among sports types is comforting. Reservations not accepted. Lunch and dinner.

### SONODA'S
**1620 Market St., Denver**
**303/595-9500**
**$$**  DD

Some of the most masterfully carved sushi and sashimi are available at Sonoda's, where the bright blue color scheme and plethora of fish tanks will make you think you're underwater. The rest of the Japanese fare is fair, but what sushi is what you get: fresh, fresh fish sliced right, and for the right price. Reservations accepted. Lunch and dinner. See also East Metro.

### WAZEE SUPPER CLUB
**1600 15th St., Denver**

> ## General Edward W. Wynkoop
>
> *Wynkoop Brewing Company and Wynkoop Street are named after Gen. Edward Wanshear Wynkoop (1836–1891), a pioneer and soldier who came to Colorado from the East to seek his fortune in Denver. Wynkoop worked several jobs, including sheriff of Arapahoe County and bartender for a place called the Criterion Saloon, but it was for his sympathies to American Indians—he believed, before it was fashionable, that things could be resolved without bloodshed—that he was best known, and which earned him friends and enemies in equal numbers. It is not known how he felt about microbrews.*

**303/623-9518**
**$** **DD**
Wazee makes pizzas with a one-of-a-kind crust; dusted with cornmeal, it pops up like the top of a flaky pie. And they put more on their pizzas than you'd think possible—so much topping you can hardly find the bottom. But you will, because once you get started on one of these, it's difficult to stop. They're the best thing about this wacky place, except for the fact that they serve it until 1 a.m. The burgers are tops, too, and the crowd runs the gamut. Reservations accepted. Lunch and dinner.

**WYNKOOP BREWING CO.**
**1634 18th St., Denver**
**303/297-2700**
**$–$$** **DD**
Wynkoop was Denver's first microbrewery, and it has remained one of its most beloved. The vittles can be hit-and-miss, but there's a beer for everyone among the seven or eight available at any given time, and only those looking for absolute quiet won't love the atmosphere. Head upstairs in the historic, built-in-1899 building for drinking and pool-playing, or stay down to take on upscale pub grub such as bangers and mash or turkey pot pie. The desserts look like they're on steroids, and non-drinkers should taste the house-made root beer. Reservations recommended. Lunch and dinner.

## CENTRAL DENVER

**ANNIE'S CAFE**
**4012 East 8th Ave., Denver**
**303/355-8197**
**$** **CD**
Kids are not only welcome at this fifties-style diner, they're catered to. And kids of all ages love Annie's old-fashioned milkshakes, great greasy burgers, and chicken-fried steak. The breakfasts are huge, and

# CENTRAL DENVER

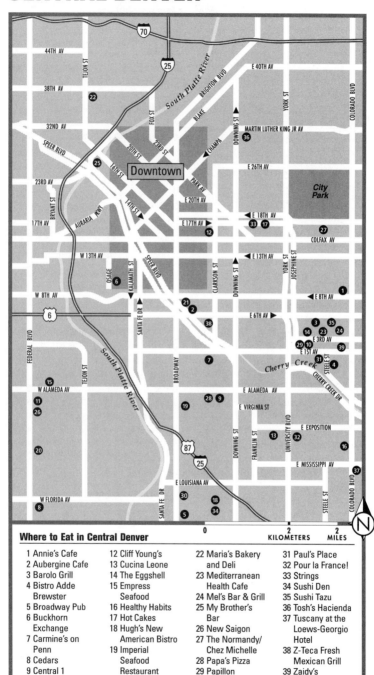

**Where to Eat in Central Denver**

1. Annie's Cafe
2. Aubergine Cafe
3. Barolo Grill
4. Bistro Adde Brewster
5. Broadway Pub
6. Buckhorn Exchange
7. Carmine's on Penn
8. Cedars
9. Central 1
10. Cherry Cricket
11. China Jade
12. Cliff Young's
13. Cucina Leone
14. The Eggshell
15. Empress Seafood
16. Healthy Habits
17. Hot Cakes
18. Hugh's New American Bistro
19. Imperial Seafood Restaurant
20. J's Noodles
21. Le Central
22. Maria's Bakery and Deli
23. Mediterranean Health Cafe
24. Mel's Bar & Grill
25. My Brother's Bar
26. New Saigon
27. The Normandy/Chez Michelle
28. Papa's Pizza
29. Papillon
30. Pasquini's Pizzeria
31. Paul's Place
32. Pour la France!
33. Strings
34. Sushi Den
35. Sushi Tazu
36. Tosh's Hacienda
37. Tuscany at the Loews-Georgio Hotel
38. Z-Teca Fresh Mexican Grill
39. Zaidy's

> ## TRIVIA
>
> The Buckhorn Exchange, a veritable shrine to the Old West, was founded in 1893 by a scout of Buffalo Bill's. It sports Colorado's "Liquor License No. 1" by the oak bar, built in 1858, and has been visited by many famous people, including Teddy Roosevelt. The walls of the Exchange are decorated with 500 stuffed animals—the formerly alive kind.

Annie's also makes decent Mexican chow. Don't be surprised if a waiter swings your toddler around the room while Elvis croons in the background. Reservations for six or more only. Breakfast, lunch, and dinner. No wheelchair access to restrooms.

### AUBERGINE CAFE
**225 East 7th Ave., Denver**
**303/832-4778**
**$–$$**            **CD**
Mediterranean-inspired contemporary American cuisine is served at Aubergine, a comfortable, homey cafe decorated with warm colors and quaint knickknacks. Choose from the regular "cafe" menu, which includes Aubergine's signature mussels in saffron broth, or go with something from the ever-changing list of specials based on the fresh ingredients available that day. As the name suggests, Aubergine also serves eggplant in several ways. Reservations recommended. Lunch and dinner; closed Mondays.

### BAROLO GRILL
**3030 East 6th Ave.**
**Denver**
**303/393-1040**
**$$–$$$**            **CD**
Everything about Barolo Grill is wonderful, from the California-kissed country-Italian cuisine to the enchanting decor to the well-priced, well-chosen wine list. Barolo is another place to be "seen," and sitting along the windows affords the perfect opportunity to see. The kitchen carries off appetizers to desserts with aplomb, and the duck in Barolo wine with olives is one of its signatures. Reservations recommended. Dinner only; closed Sundays, Mondays.

### BISTRO ADDE BREWSTER
**250 Steele St., Denver**
**303/388-1900**
**$$**            **CD**
The best gourmet burger in town can be had at the chic Bistro Adde Brewster in chichi Cherry Creek. Go for "small plates" of pasta or take on a full meal, but be sure to try the house-cured gravlax. And you'd better dress for success: this is one of the places to see and be seen. Reservations are recommended. Serving lunch and dinner; closed Sundays.

### BROADWAY PUB
**2441 Broadway, Denver**
**303/292-2555**
**$**            **CD**
A funky brewpub with an attitude but no signs of "concept," Broadway Pub is a hangout for downtown Denver's working-class types of all ages. Pumping tunes, serious munchy food, and made-on-the-premises microbrews, as well as beers from elsewhere, add up to fun for all. Res-

ervations not accepted. Lunch and dinner.

## BUCKHORN EXCHANGE
**1000 Osage Ave., Denver**
**303/534-9505**
**$$**  CD

More than 100 years old, the Buckhorn, which procured Colorado's first liquor license, takes diners back to the Old West. Jam-packed with memorabilia, animal heads, and rustic furnishings, the Buckhorn also continues one of Denver's die-hard traditions by carving up steaks night after night, and accompanies them with the simplest of fixin's, such as baked potatoes and steamed vegetables. The desserts are hearty and the prices reasonable. Don't be surprised if the tourists outnumber the locals, though. Reservations accepted for dinner only. Lunch and dinner.

## CARMINE'S ON PENN
**92 South Pennsylvania St., Denver**
**303/777-6443**
**$–$$**  CD

Modeled after the family-style trattorias in New York—and, ultimately, the originals in Italy—the noisy Carmine's makes eating a family affair. Each platter of pasta or meat, at an average cost of $15, feeds two or three people, and many dishes are based on the four basic food groups of Italian cooking: olive oil, garlic, basil, and tomatoes. The minestrone and the cannolis are top-notch, and the convivial setting makes for raucous reunions. Reservations recommended. Dinner only; closed Mondays. No wheelchair access to restrooms.

## CEDARS
**1550 South Federal Blvd., Denver**
**303/936-2980**
**$–$$**  CD

The emphasis is on Lebanese at this family-run Middle Eastern spot frequented for its spicy curries and exceptional baklava. The staff, mostly relatives of the owners, welcomes diners as if they were also family members, and the kitchen is usually willing to whip up special requests. Ask for the Lebanese chicken, dark meat roasted with beef, almonds, and pistachios. Reservations accepted. Lunch and dinner; closed Sundays.

## CENTRAL 1
**300 South Pearl St., Denver**
**303/778-6675**
**$**  CD

The small but cozy Central 1 is authentic Greek all the way. The Greek salad is a smart starter, as is the avgolemono (lemon soup). An order of the moussaka could feed two comfortably. You can't go wrong with the souvlaki or the gyros, either. Reservations for five or more only. Lunch and dinner; closed Sundays.

## CHERRY CRICKET
**2641 East 2nd Ave., Denver**
**303/322-7666**
**$**  CD

If tony Cherry Creek has a neighborhood hangout, the Cherry Cricket is it. Downstairs in a dimly lit restaurant/bar is where Denverites go for the best burger in town. Cooked on a special grill that uses lava rocks, the patty comes out flawless every time: gently charred outside, lean and juicy inside. Wash it down with one of their 120 beers (a quarter of them on tap) and get to know the locals. Reservations not accepted. Lunch and dinner.

## CHINA JADE
**375 South Federal Blvd., Denver**
**303/935-0033**
**$$** CD

Located in the Far East Center, China Jade has a reputation for being one of the most consistent Chinese restaurants around. Delectable dim sum and savvy seafood dishes are among the top choices here, and while the service can be spotty, it usually doesn't interfere with a pleasant dining experience. Reservations for eight or more only. Lunch and dinner.

## CLIFF YOUNG'S
**700 East 17th Ave., Denver**
**303/831-8900**
**$$$** CD

One of the premier special-occasion restaurants, Cliff Young's has the ability to make even a boring business dinner better by means of its attentive staff, soothingly formal decor, and beautiful food. In response to the market, this establishment offers a few dinner entrees for less than $20, but the majority are far above that. The virtues of the Caesar salad prepared tableside are well known. Reservations recommended. Dinner only.

## CUCINA LEONE
**763 South University Blvd., Denver**
**303/722-5466**
**$$** CD

Gourmet take-out is all the rage, and so is Cucina Leone. Morning, noon, and night, hungry patrons stop by to pick up a bite or an entire repast from the well-stocked display cases of freshly prepared items to feed the kids at home or to pack for a romantic picnic for two. Choose from several different main courses, such as the succulent roast chicken, and dozens of side dishes—and don't forget fresh breads, salads, and desserts, including decadent homemade ice cream. Everything's priced by the portion or by the pound, and while cost can add up fast, the quality cannot be beat. A new dining room means you can eat in too. Reservations are not accepted. Breakfast, lunch, and dinner.

## THE EGGSHELL
**300 Josephine St., Denver**
**303/322-1601**
**$** CD

Healthy breakfasts are an option at the super-friendly Eggshell, but the eggs Benedict and huevos rancheros are hard to turn down. Fortunately, the better-for-you stuff doesn't skimp on flavor, so go ahead and take on a stack of whole-wheat pancakes with wheat germ and fresh fruit compote. Reservations not accepted. Breakfast and lunch. Call ahead for wheelchair access.

## EMPRESS SEAFOOD
**2825 West Alameda Ave., Denver**
**303/922-2822**
**$$** CD

More than 40 kinds of dim sum can be had at this large Chinese restaurant just west of the city. If dim sum's not your cup of tea, stick with the specialties of the house, particularly the oyster pot and the roast pig. Kids love the roasted duck display, and the Empress loves kids. Reservations accepted. Lunch and dinner.

## HEALTHY HABITS
**865 South Colorado Blvd., Denver**
**303/733-2105**
**$** CD

Healthy Habits is one of Denver's favorite grazing sites, where one low price gains access to an all-you-can-eat feast from a variety of stations. There's a pizza-and-pasta bar, a soup set-up, a 60-item salad bar, a bakery section and, of course, dessert. As with any buffet, the quality wavers, but you can't beat the bargain. Reservations not accepted. Lunch and dinner. See also South Metro and North Metro.

### HOT CAKES
**1400 East 18th Ave., Denver**
**303/830-1909**
**$**   CD

The only things that sizzles more than the hotcakes at Hot Cakes is the staff, a collection of gum-snapping wisecrackers who aren't afraid to needle the doctors from the nearby hospitals—or anyone else who walks through the door. Along with the cheerful repartee, the servers dole out pancakes the size of hubcaps and omelettes that require forklifts to move. The whopping portions—the excellent sandwiches and salads are big, too—along with the casual diner atmosphere and the low prices make Hot Cakes a hot commodity. Reservations for seven or more only. Breakfast and lunch.

### HUGH'S NEW AMERICAN BISTRO
**1469 South Pearl St., Denver**
**303/744-1940**
**$$**   CD

What started as one of Denver's first vegetarian restaurants has transformed into a place where freshness and quality form the main agenda. There are still a few meatless dishes—polenta with roasted vegetables is one fine example—but the rest are prepared only with free-range, chemical-free animals. Instead of fat, the kitchen uses herbs and spices, some that get little attention outside their native countries and many indigenous to Colorado, to provide the flavor, and Hugh's also produces a unique and delicious tiramisu. Feast your eyes on the walls: they're painted using actual spices to achieve the soothing colors. Reservations recommended. Dinner only.

### IMPERIAL SEAFOOD RESTAURANT
**431 South Broadway, Denver**
**303/698-2800**
**$$**   CD

The vastness of Imperial is outdone only by the grandness of its decorating scheme. One of the more upscale Chinese restaurants, Imperial is known for spectacular spicy dishes and mediocre everything else. The once-stiff service has improved greatly over the years, but the prices have remained high for the quality of the food. Still, the opulent atmosphere and fiery sesame chicken, as well as the fried Dungeness crab and wisely chosen wine list, have kept it busy. Reservations for five or more only. Lunch and dinner.

### J's NOODLES
**945 South Federal Blvd., Denver**
**303/922-5495**
**$**   CD

No atmosphere to speak of, but the staff is friendly and the Thai food at J's is both cheap and delicious. One of the few places that loads up on the chiles the way it's done in Thailand, J's is also generous with portions and flavor. No credit cards. Reservations accepted. Lunch and dinner.

### LE CENTRAL
**112 East 8th Ave., Denver**
**303/863-8094**
**$–$$**      **CD**

Called "the affordable French restaurant," Le Central lives up to its billing. High-quality provincial French fare fills this quaint bistro with regulars daily, and the low prices make it easy to become a regular. Known for flexing its skill with mussels and inexpensive sit-down Sunday brunches—try to get out on the cute plant-filled porch if possible—as well as its overly generous portions, Le Central is value central. Reservations are recommended. Lunch and dinner. No wheelchair access to the restrooms.

### MARIA'S BAKERY AND DELI
**3705 Shoshone St., Denver**
**303/477-3372**
**$**      **CD**

In summer, Maria's garden overflows with herbs and flowers as well as diners soaking up the sun and the superb sandwiches. The rest of the year, it's takeout only at this self-server that caters to the connoisseur who doesn't mind paper plates and a limited selection. Everything, including the mayonnaise, is homemade, and the portions are way out of proportion to the tiny prices. No credit cards. Reservations not accepted. Lunch only; closed Saturdays, Sundays, Mondays. Wheelchair access on patio only.

### MEDITERRANEAN HEALTH CAFE
**2817 East 3rd Ave., Denver**
**303/399-2940**
**$**      **CD**

Fish is the only meat available at the Mediterranean, but it's in the minority. Most of the menu is devoted to such vegetarian pleasures as lasagne with roasted red peppers and pasta with meatless sauces. From the other side of the sea come above-average falafel sandwiches and hummus, baba ghanouj, and tabouleh. Lunchtime draws crowds, so get there early. Reservations not accepted. Lunch and dinner. No wheelchair access.

### MEL'S BAR & GRILL
**235 Fillmore St., Denver**
**303/333-3979**
**$$–$$$**      **CD**

Longtime Denver restaurateurs Mel and Janie Master have made Mel's one of the hottest restaurants in the city by cooking up consistently marvelous Mediterranean-influenced contemporary American food. The cozy, calming setting is enhanced by whimsical bric-a-brac, and if you can get into one of the comfy pillow-filled booths, you may never get out again. That's okay—it'll give you the chance to take in more of the menu: chewy, rustic breads, flawless risotto, succulent braised lamb shank, a rich bisque of lobster and butternut squash, and fresh-fruit tarts are just the beginning. Reservations recommended. Lunch and dinner.

### MY BROTHER'S BAR
**2376 15th St., Denver**
**303/455-9991**
**$**      **CD**

Situated at the corner of 15th and Platte, My Brother's Bar is a Denver institution, owned by the same family that runs Wazee Supper Club & Lounge. Classical music plays as the bar food arrives in paper-lined baskets, but the Beethoven-and-burgers combination hasn't scared anyone away in nearly 30 years. My Brother's Bar is one of the city's late-night spots, serving food until 1:30 a.m. Reservations are taken for parties of six or more only. Lunch and dinner.

### NEW SAIGON
**630 South Federal Blvd., Denver**
**303/936-4954**
**$**     **CD**

Year after year, New Saigon has been voted Denver's best Vietnamese restaurant, and after ten minutes in the place it won't be hard to figure out why. Consistently well-cooked dishes, low prices and an accommodating staff are the hallmarks of New Saigon, and the huge menu (40 fish choices alone) makes it tough to choose but easy to return. Reservations accepted. Lunch and dinner.

### THE NORMANDY/CHEZ MICHELLE
**1515 Madison St., Denver**
**303/321-3311**
**$$–$$$**     **CD**

Traditional French meets the modern at The Normandy, known for its chateaubriand that shares menu space with light, fruit-thickened sauces. Chez Michelle, a restaurant-within-a-restaurant, is more affordable and features even lighter French fare. Reservations recommended. Lunch and dinner at the Normandy, dinner only at Chez Michelle; both closed Mondays. No wheelchair access.

### PAPA'S PIZZA
**540 East Alameda Ave., Denver**
**303/722-4723**
**$**     **CD**

Fans of drippy cheese, extra sauce with lots of spicy zing, and super-thin crusts will find that Papa's knows best how to bring it all together. What makes this pizza extra-special is the outer ring of dough as thick as fists, which makes for easy handling, and the casual atmosphere and small menu make it easier to concentrate on the pies. Reservations not accepted. Lunch and dinner.

### PAPILLON
**250 Josephine St., Denver**
**303/333-7166**
**$$–$$$**     **CD**

When veteran Denver chef/restaurateur Radek Cerny decided to go solo, the result was Papillon, where Cerny's skills with Asian-influenced infused oils and vinegars and rich-tasting sauces are put to tasteful use on seafood and pasta. That's not to say there aren't a few temptations waiting: the sweetbreads are worth falling off the diet wagon for, and the desserts look like works of art. Papillon's setting is low-key but stylish—and so is the clientele. Reservations recommended. Lunch and dinner.

---

### TRIVIA

Denver once had a Chinatown, in what is now part of the recently renovated Historic District of Lower Downtown. Purportedly contained within the area referred to as LoDo—now home to art galleries and trendy restaurants—there were Chinese eateries and opium dens, along with about 300 residents. Around the turn of the century, one Denver newspaper claimed this area held "the fourth largest Chinese population in the United States."

## PASQUINI'S PIZZERIA
**1310 South Broadway, Denver**
**303/744-0917**
**$**                                                     **CD**

Pasquini's purveys great pizzas through thick and thin, the two ways their top-notch dough is offered. The football-size subs and the calzones are also must-haves, and although chaotic and noisy describes the scene during peak times, the staff is perpetually cheerful. Wine drinkers will appreciate the roster of ten wines for $10. Reservations not accepted. Lunch and dinner.

## PAUL'S PLACE
**3000 East 1st Ave., Denver**
**303/321-5801**
**$**                                                     **CD**

Paul's Place is about gourmet fast food, much healthier and better-tasting than anything you'll get at a major chain. Parents weary of the empty calories their children are subjected to elsewhere will be relieved by the low-fat hot dogs, lean burgers, and cholesterol-free mayonnaise sold at Paul's, and they can even rest assured that the onion rings and French fries are dipped in good-for-you oil. Don't get too carried away by the health of it, though, because Paul's also whips up incredible milkshakes. Reservations are not accepted. Lunch and dinner. See also South Denver.

## POUR LA FRANCE!
**730 South University Blvd., Denver**
**303/744-1888**
**$–$$**                                      **CD**

A local chain that originated in Aspen, the casual Pour La France! focuses on light French but steals a few tricks from elsewhere along the Mediterranean. The French-style pizzas are nicely done, and the tomato-Brie pie is divine, as are the desserts from Denver's estimable Blue Point Bakery. Reservations recommended. Breakfast, lunch, and dinner. See also North Metro.

## STRINGS
**1700 Humboldt St., Denver**
**303/831-7310**
**$$–$$$**                                  **CD**

Nationally respected restaurateur and philanthropist Noel Cunningham owns several Denver eateries, but none is better known than Strings. California meets Italy in these snappy digs, where both the food and the scene are so highly regarded that the cast parties from Broadway shows passing through are held here regularly. Strings has something for everyone, from light, simple fare such as broiled fish on pasta to full-fledged meals of veal and venison, and the wine list is exceptional. Reservations recommended. Lunch and dinner.

## SUSHI DEN
**1487 S. Pearl St., Denver**
**303/777-0826**

*Pour La France!*

Pour La France!

**$$–$$$**      **CD**

The locals' favorite sushi spot, Sushi Den is also a mecca for celebrities and travelers looking for the best quality sushi and a snazzy, hip decor. The sushi chefs are charming, and they know how to slice. The kitchen is equally adept at turning out succulent teriyaki and wonderful squid steak. Be sure to try the salmon skin roll. The place is packed on weekends, so call ahead for reservations. Lunch and dinner.

### SUSHI TAZU
**300 Fillmore Pl., Denver**
**303/320-1672**
**$$**      **CD**

Tazu is a contender for Denver's top sushi bar despite its squeezed-in feel and so-so service. Go for the California rolls and the soft-shell crab, or just stick with the raw materials at hand. The cooked dishes are worth checking out, too. Reservations recommended. Lunch and dinner.

### TOSH'S HACIENDA
**3090 Downing St., Denver**
**303/295-1861**
**$–$$**      **CD**

A colorful, fun eatery that serves fresh Mexican fare in enormous portions, Tosh's is the bright spot in an otherwise drab neighborhood. The chiles rellenos are notable, as are the chips and salsa that come with every meal. Reservations for five or more only. Lunch and dinner. No wheelchair access. See also South Metro.

### TUSCANY AT THE LOEWS-GIORGIO HOTEL
**4150 East Mississippi Ave.**
**Glendale**
**303/782-9300**
**$$$**      **CD**

Luxurious furniture and a refined decor put Tuscany on the list of Denver's most beautiful dining rooms. The dishes are updated Italian with attention to details, such as crusty country breads accompanied by a dense pesto and sparkling water. The Sunday brunch buffet is an overload that ensures diners won't be able to move for the rest of the day. Reservations recommended. Breakfast, lunch, and dinner.

### ZAIDY'S
**121 Adams St., Denver**
**303/333-5336**
**$**      **CD**

A deli with plenty of space for a sit-down meal, Zaidy's leans toward New York but has a distinctive style. Great pastrami sandwiches, potato latkes, and blintzes headline the attractions, and the chopped liver also draws raves. Breakfast, with its lox and bagels and oniony omelettes, has a following, but the Friday night $10 dinner of half a roast chicken with all the trimmings is what really brings 'em in. Reservations for six or more only. Breakfast, lunch, and dinner.

### Z-TECA FRESH MEXICAN GRILL
**550 Grant St., Denver**
**303/765-5878**
**$**      **CD**

Zuma rode in on the wave of fresh variations on a fast-food-Mexican theme, and it's turned out to be one of the keepers. Tortillas wrapped around poblanos with cilantro pesto or grilled zucchini and eggplant are just two of the possibilities from the 14-item burrito menu. No lard or animal fats are used, and the $5-and-under burritos—all containing black or pinto beans, cilantro rice, and cheese or sour cream—are full meals in themselves. You can eat it there or take it with you. Reserva-

# GREATER DENVER

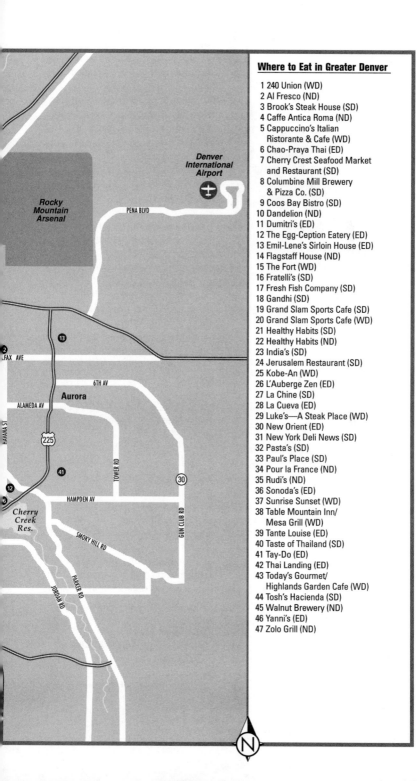

## Where to Eat in Greater Denver

1 240 Union (WD)
2 Al Fresco (ND)
3 Brook's Steak House (SD)
4 Caffe Antica Roma (ND)
5 Cappuccino's Italian Ristorante & Cafe (WD)
6 Chao-Praya Thai (ED)
7 Cherry Crest Seafood Market and Restaurant (SD)
8 Columbine Mill Brewery & Pizza Co. (SD)
9 Coos Bay Bistro (SD)
10 Dandelion (ND)
11 Dumitri's (ED)
12 The Egg-Ception Eatery (ED)
13 Emil-Lene's Sirloin House (ED)
14 Flagstaff House (ND)
15 The Fort (WD)
16 Fratelli's (SD)
17 Fresh Fish Company (SD)
18 Gandhi (SD)
19 Grand Slam Sports Cafe (SD)
20 Grand Slam Sports Cafe (WD)
21 Healthy Habits (SD)
22 Healthy Habits (ND)
23 India's (SD)
24 Jerusalem Restaurant (SD)
25 Kobe-An (WD)
26 L'Auberge Zen (ED)
27 La Chine (SD)
28 La Cueva (ED)
29 Luke's—A Steak Place (WD)
30 New Orient (ED)
31 New York Deli News (SD)
32 Pasta's (SD)
33 Paul's Place (SD)
34 Pour la France (ND)
35 Rudi's (ND)
36 Sonoda's (ED)
37 Sunrise Sunset (WD)
38 Table Mountain Inn/ Mesa Grill (WD)
39 Tante Louise (ED)
40 Taste of Thailand (SD)
41 Tay-Do (ED)
42 Thai Landing (ED)
43 Today's Gourmet/ Highlands Garden Cafe (WD)
44 Tosh's Hacienda (SD)
45 Walnut Brewery (ND)
46 Yanni's (ED)
47 Zolo Grill (ND)

*Z-Teca Fresh Mexican Grill*

tions not accepted. Lunch and dinner. (There are five other Z-Teca locations in Denver.)

## EAST DENVER

### CHAO-PRAYA THAI
**5411 Quebec St., Commerce City**
**303/287-2210**
**$$**  ED

The first Thai restaurant in the United States, Chao-Praya is still run by the family that started it. In the nearly 40 years it's been in operation, the welcoming attitude has never changed, nor has the menu. The kitchen continues to produce exemplary tom ka gai, chicken soup with coconut and lemongrass, and tod-mun, spicy fish patties with hot cucumber salad, and there's not a dud among the house specials. Reservations accepted. Lunch and dinner.

### DUMITRI'S
**1911 South Havana St., Aurora**
**303/752-0553**
**$**  ED

Cheap, filling breakfasts—get in first thing for early-bird specials—and a variety of Greek, Mexican, and American favorites are available at Dumitri's. It opens at 5:30 a.m., and hot-from-the-oven muffins are always waiting. Reservations accepted for six or more only. Breakfast and lunch.

### THE EGG-CEPTION EATERY
**2790 South Havana St., Aurora**
**303/755-9839**
**$**  ED

The decor is semi-country and the juice is fresh-squeezed at this cheery breakfast spot. Oversized omelettes come with fried potatoes and fruit, but save room for the delectable muffins with such fillings as raspberry cream cheese and mandarin orange. Show up early on weekends, since the Egg-Ception fills quickly. Reservations accepted on weekdays only. Breakfast and lunch.

### EMIL-LENE'S SIRLOIN HOUSE
**16000 Smith Rd., Aurora**
**303/366-6674**
**$$**  ED

Simple, honest fare and top-grade steaks rope diners into Emil-Lene's, where a tree grows in the middle of the Western-themed dining room and entrees come with an iceberg-lettuce salad and a side of spaghetti. There's always a fish or chicken special for those who don't want red meat, and the staff is nice to children. Reservations recommended. Lunch and dinner.

### L'AUBERGE ZEN
**9955 East Hampden Ave., Denver**
**303/751-3571**
**$$**  ED

Half-French and half-Japanese—the

chef trained at Japan's haute-cuisine cooking school—L'Auberge Zen does better with its stellar sushi and temptingly light tempura than with the sauce reductions. A pretty dining area (there's also a sushi bar; call for the bargain happy hour times) and graceful service complete a pleasant meal. Reservations recommended. Lunch and dinner; closed Mondays.

### LA CUEVA
**9742 East Colfax Ave., Aurora**
**303/367-1422**
**$**  ED

Green chile that will clear your sinuses and just-fried chips with a potent salsa are but two of the specialties at the decades-old La Cueva, where the Mexican home cooking is made to order and the staff is as upbeat as the decor. Chile addicts can walk away with a pint of La Cueva's powerful version for a few bucks. Reservations accepted for eight or more only. Lunch and dinner; closed Sundays.

### NEW ORIENT
**10253 East Iliff Ave., Aurora**
**303/751-1288**
**$–$$**  ED

The traditional Vietnamese dishes at the uncluttered New Orient are fine, but the daily specials are spectacular turns that marry Asian and Western techniques. For instance, one entree might bring grouper-filled potstickers, another a reduction of fruit with a stir-fry. The interesting and addictive fried chicken comes coated in a sesame-honey crust. Reservations recommended. Lunch and dinner; closed Mondays.

### SONODA'S
**3108 South Parker Rd., Aurora**
**303/337-3800**
**$$**  ED

The sushi is straightforward but well-proportioned and its freshness is unsurpassed at Sonoda's. During peak dining times it's impossible to find a stool at the sushi bar, but rest assured that the service at the tables will be just as fast. The tempura and beef dishes aren't bad, either. Reservations accepted. Lunch and dinner. See also Downtown.

### TANTE LOUISE
**4900 East Colfax Ave., Denver**
**303/355-4488**
**$$$**  ED

Generally considered to be *the* romantic restaurant in Denver, Tante Louise has the class, the elegant decor, the sumptuous victuals, and the extensive wine list to make for an intensely special dining experience. The contemporary cuisine carries French and Italian undertones, and the sommelier, one of the most knowledgeable in the area, is always able to find the ideal match. Reservations recommended. Dinner only; closed Sundays.

### TAY-DO
**2350 S. Chambers Rd.**
**Aurora**
**303/337-0115**
**$–$$**  ED

If you have to stay on the beaten path to find good food, then Tay-Do is not for you. But if you're willing to look deep into a plaza to find some of the most delicious Vietnamese food in Denver, go to the corner of Iliff and Chambers. There you'll be delighted by an elegant but casual decor, a small but sophisticated menu, and the most charming hostess imaginable. The soft-shell crabs—coated with a crumbly batter—are incredible, and the deep-fried crispy squid is

> ## TRIVIA
>
> Henry Kissinger doesn't know it, but he helped Corky Douglass name his restaurant, Tante Louise. Douglass took the place over in 1973, and on the day he was trying to decide what to call it, he happened to glance at a newspaper. Kissinger was on the front page, having been photographed coming out of a restaurant called Chez Tante Louise during the Paris Peace Talks at the end of the Vietnam War.

exquisite. Reservations recommended. Lunch and dinner.

### THAI LANDING
11101 East Colfax Ave., Aurora
303/367-1504
$     ED

The all-you-can-eat weekday lunch buffet for under $5 makes Thai Landing a hot commodity with the surrounding businesses. The rest of the menu, heavy on curries, is a bargain as well. Be sure to mention if spicy isn't your thing, because they don't skimp on the chiles. Reservations are accepted. Lunch and dinner.

### YANNI'S
2223 South Monaco Pkwy.
Denver
303/692-0404
$     ED

At Yanni's the owner jumps from table to table in true Greek fashion offering shots of ouzo and inquiring about customers' meals. More often than not the customers' answers are enthusiastic, because Yanni's knows its Greek.

Marinated octopus and squid, yogurt, tangy dolmades, and flaming kasseri cheese are appetizer highlights, and the parmesan-topped moussaka is one of their signature entrees. A one-of-a-kind baklava ice cream is made on the premises. Reservations recommended. Yanni's serves dinner only. Wheelchair access in the smoking section only.

## SOUTH DENVER

### BROOK'S STEAK HOUSE
6538 S. Yosemite Circle
Greenwood Village
303/770-1177
$$$     SD

One of the few locally owned steakhouses in Denver, Brook's offers rugged decor, large portions, and large prices—just like the big chains. But there's a slightly more personal edge to the service, and the beef, side dishes, and appetizers are tops (especially the oysters Rockefeller). There's a cigar room downstairs and a bar on the main floor, but this place also distinguishes itself from the chains by being fairly kid-friendly. Reservations recommended. Dinner only.

### CHERRY CREST SEAFOOD MARKET AND RESTAURANT
5909 South University Blvd.
Littleton
303/798-2600
$$     SD

Since the seafood is for sale next door to the restaurant, chances are you'll get fresh product at the dowdy Cherry Crest. The kitchen has an easy touch with sauces—nothing arrives drowning—and knows how to cook fish to perfection. Because of the attached retail business, it's not unlikely that you'll encounter several specimens unavailable to other restaurants. Reservations accepted during weekdays only. Lunch and dinner; closed Sundays. No wheelchair access to restrooms.

**COLUMBINE MILL BREWERY & PIZZA CO.**
**5798 South Rapp St., Littleton**
**303/347-1488**
**$–$$**                                            SD
An enormous old grain mill now houses a rustic brewpub that makes equally good microbrews and pizza. The rest of the Italian dishes are just okay, but the thick-crusted pies go better with the beer, anyway. End it all with a traditional but well-executed tiramisu. Reservations accepted for eight or more only. Lunch and dinner. No wheelchair access.

**COOS BAY BISTRO**
**2076 South University Blvd. Denver**
**303/744-3591**
**$$**                                              SD
Just around the corner from the University of Denver, Coos Bay brings together the Pacific Northwest and Italy with ease. The regular menu is small, but it's supplemented by a daily list of specials, including a mess of tapas and several wine-by-the-glass deals, scribbled on the 8-foot blackboards that hang above the vine-accented dining areas. The pizzas are a major attraction, but so is the Multnomah Falls spinach salad with a warm dressing made with pancetta and caramelized onions. Reservations recommended. Lunch and dinner.

**FRATELLI'S**
**1200 East Hampden Ave. Englewood**
**303/761-4771**
**$–$$**                                            SD
Fratelli's is an Italian restaurant that makes good chewy-gooey pizzas, but its breakfasts are worth getting out of bed for. They include a large selection of heart-healthy possibilities, but true breakfast lovers will want to taste one of their superb skillets, with such combinations as the Pennsylvania Dutch rumbled eggs with pork scrapple or the hash of top-round beef and potatoes. Their own blend of coffee beans and a serene decor easy on early eyes make Fratelli's a welcome sight in the morning. Reservations not accepted. Breakfast, lunch, and dinner.

**FRESH FISH COMPANY**
**7600 East Hampden Ave. Denver**
**303/740-9556**
**$$**                                              SD
Consistency is not the Fresh Fish Company's best quality, but the freshness of the fish is never in question, and when the dishes are good, they are very, very good. Uncomplicated preparations are your best bet, and the well-priced, seafood-oriented Sunday brunch is always packed. Reservations accepted for five or more only. Lunch and dinner.

**GANDHI**
**5071 South Syracuse St., Denver**
**303/694-7388**
**$–$$**                                            SD
For a mere $7, diners can treat themselves to Gandhi's lunch buffet of 20 Indian dishes. Dinner brings another, more expensive buffet (there's also a regular menu available), but it's not nearly the great deal that lunch is. From

spinach-fritter appetizers and yogurt-coated salads to a rice-pudding dessert, the inherently healthy Indian food at Gandhi is well-prepared and expertly seasoned. Reservations recommended. Lunch and dinner.

### GRAND SLAM SPORTS CAFE
**9660 East Arapahoe Rd.**
**Englewood**
**303/799-1300**
**$**      **SD**
Grand Slam is a sports bar, to be sure, but it's also a fantastic place to take the family. Tasty, inexpensive burgers, ribs, and other hearty meals are sure to please the adults, while the kids menu offers a drink and dessert with a filling entree for just a couple of bucks. The walls full of televisions and a noisy, fun-filled atmosphere ensure that the young'uns will have a good time. The all-you-can-eat Sunday brunch is another bonus because it stuffs most people for $6.95 and kids under 12 eat for free. Reservations accepted. Lunch and dinner. See also West Denver.

### HEALTHY HABITS
**7418 South University Blvd.**
**Littleton**
**303/740-7044**
**$**      **SD**
Healthy Habits is one of Denver's favorite grazing sites, where one low price gains access to an all-you-can-eat feast from a variety of stations. There's a pizza-and-pasta bar, a soup set-up, a 60-item salad bar, a bakery section and, of course, dessert. As with any buffet, the quality wavers, but you can't beat the bargain. Reservations not accepted. Lunch and dinner. See also Downtown and North Metro.

### INDIA'S
**3333 South Tamarac Dr., Denver**
**303/755-4284**
**$$**      **SD**
Tucked into a shopping plaza, India's doesn't necessarily look like a site for some of Denver's best Indian cuisine, but it is. Watch your chicken come out of the tandoori, juicy and tender inside, crisp out, and be sure to order several things from the appetizer list. Reservations recommended. Lunch and dinner.

### JERUSALEM RESTAURANT
**1890 East Evans Ave., Denver**
**303/777-8828**
**$**      **SD**
The service is appallingly aloof and difficult, but the Middle Eastern fare—considered to be the best in town by most critics—at the itsy-bitsy Jerusalem makes up for the staff's shortcomings. The falafel and the hummus are outstanding, as are the grilled meats. And the restaurant's proximity to the University of Denver, along with its late-night schedule (until 4 a.m. nightly), keeps it constantly full. Reservations recommended. Lunch and dinner.

### LA CHINE
**5071 South Syracuse St., Denver**
**303/220-8885**
**$$–$$$**      **SD**
La Chine is a bit on the expensive side, especially for Chinese food, but judging by the brisk business this exquisitely decorated restaurant does, many Denverites don't care. Some of the reason is the beautiful atmosphere, but most of the credit must go to the savvy cooking. Artfully presented gourmet preparations and extra touches not

normally found in casual Chinese fare—dim sum buns as side dishes, for example—make La Chine a special experience. Reservations recommended. Lunch and dinner.

**NEW YORK DELI NEWS**
7105 East Hampden Ave., Denver
303/759-4741
$ SD
One of the closest imitations of New York deli dining that Denver has to offer, New York Deli News stocks its display cases with fresh, dense pumpernickel, top-drawer pastrami and corned beef, and the blintzes, latkes, chopped liver, and knishes your bubbe used to make. Reservations not accepted. Breakfast, lunch, and dinner.

**PASTA'S**
9126 West Bowles Ave., Littleton
303/933-2829
$$ SD
This family-run, red-white-and-green establishment panders to the American ideal of Italian—lasagne, manicotti, and spaghetti with meatballs—but does it exceptionally well. And it rounds out the expansive menu with some not-so-standard options such as artichokes and chicken in a sun-dried tomato sauce over penne pasta. The amazing garlic knots, a basket of which is relentlessly replenished, will leave you begging for the recipe. Reservations recommended. Lunch and dinner.

**PAUL'S PLACE**
6818 South Yosemite St.
Greenwood Village
303/771-8855
$ SD
Paul's Place is about gourmet fast food, much healthier and better-tasting than anything you'll get at a major chain. Parents weary of the empty calories their children are subjected to elsewhere will be relieved by the low-fat hot dogs, lean burgers, and cholesterol-free mayonnaise sold at Paul's, and they can even rest assured that the onion

Denver Chophouse, p. 67

rings and French fries are dipped in good-for-you-oil. Don't get too carried away by the health of it, though, because Paul's also whips up incredible milkshakes. Reservations not accepted. Lunch and dinner. See also Central Denver.

### TASTE OF THAILAND
504 East Hampden Ave., Denver
303/762-9112
$–$$                                    SD

Owned by a cooking instructor and former native of Northern Thailand, Taste of Thailand relies on what's fresh that day to complement the basics of this eatery's intense curries and spicy stir-fries. Reservations are accepted. Taste of Thailand serves lunch and dinner; the restaurant is closed Sundays. No wheelchair access to restrooms.

### TOSH'S HACIENDA
5071 South Syracuse Pkwy., Denver
303/770-8980
$–$$                                    SD

Tosh's is a colorful, fun eatery that serves fresh Mexican fare in enormous portions. The chiles rellenos are notable, as are the chips and salsa that come with every meal. The typical beans-and-rice affairs are well spiced and taste just-made. Reservations for five or more only. Lunch and dinner. See also Downtown.

## WEST DENVER

### CAPPUCCINO'S ITALIAN RISTORANTE & CAFE
2740 South Wadsworth Blvd.
Denver
303/986-5353
$$                                      WD

Cappuccino's pasta dishes are sound standards, but the stuffed pizza is spectacular: two layers of crust barely hold in a whipped combination of ricotta and romano cheeses. The rich result is heightened by the accompanying red sauce as thick as gravy. Or go for the spinach version overflowing with fresh spinach leaves and provolone. Reservations accepted. Lunch and dinner.

### THE FORT
U.S. 285 at Hwy. 8, Morrison
303/697-4771

*The Fort*

## Food and Fun at The Fort

*The Fort restaurant in Morrison, 18 miles from Denver, initially was intended to serve as a home for owner Sam Arnold, who built the replica of Bent's Fort—the refurbished original is in La Junta, Colorado—for $250,000 in the mid-1950s. The building comprises 80,000 adobe bricks that have to be replaced periodically because of harsh weather conditions, and while it was still being assembled, Arnold decided it would make a good restaurant. It's unique: above the massive structure, attached to the red rocks that jut out around the Fort, is a 43-foot, two-ton steel snake named Lulu, sculpted to resemble a petroglyph from a canyon in Utah. In addition, the lobby to the dining rooms is an open courtyard containing a Plains Indian tipi and an ever-roaring campfire, and strewn throughout the many rooms and outside on the vast patio is an extensive collection of Western and Southwestern memorabilia, including cannons, a 27-star flag, and a pillory. Arnold, who has written several cookbooks on early Western food, is well-known around Denver for his fun-loving antics. He frequently surprises guests who order champagne by popping the cork with a tomahawk, and birthday celebrants are crowned with buffalo horns and ceremoniously presented with a three-foot item that looks like a walking stick. Few guess that the stick is actually a petrified buffalo penis.*

**$$$**      **WD**

Renowned Western historian Sam Arnold turned his replica of Bent's Fort into a restaurant, and what a place it is. One of the most magnificent views of Denver beyond the mountains can be seen from its floor-to-ceiling windows or, in warm weather, the outdoor patio. Arnold's love of food, particularly from recipes out of the Old West, manifests itself in the unique menu, which includes such rare treats as roasted buffalo marrow bones, buffalo tongue, Texas wild boar ham steak, and a salad created by Kit Carson's wife. Warm yourself by the tipi erected at the entrance, and don't leave without sampling the Negrita, a sinful chocolate dessert. Reservations recommended. Dinner only.

**GRAND SLAM SPORTS CAFE**
**810 South Wadsworth Blvd.**
**Lakewood**
**303/922-3400**
**$**      **WD**

Grand Slam is a sports bar, to be sure, but it's also a great place to take the family. Tasty, inexpensive burgers, ribs and other hearty meals please the adults, while the kids menu offers a drink and dessert with a filling entree for a couple of bucks. The walls full of televisions and a fun-filled atmosphere ensure that the young'uns will have a good time. The all-you-can-eat Sunday brunch is a bonus—$6.95 for adults, kids under 12 for free. Reservations accepted. Lunch and dinner. See also South Metro.

### KOBE-AN
**85 South Union Blvd., Denver**
**303/989-5907**
**$$**                                    **WD**

A classy Japanese eatery, Kobe-An competently serves sushi at a small bar or in the sizable dining room. The soft-shell crab roll and the miso soup stand out. Reservations are recommended. Lunch and dinner; closed Sundays.

### LUKE'S—A STEAK PLACE
**4990 Kipling St., Wheat Ridge**
**303/422-3300**
**$$**                                    **WD**

For half the price a large steakhouse chain charges, Luke's sets sizzling steaks down and lets the garlic butter sparks fly. The salmon and other catches of the day are exceptional, too, but it's beef that Luke's does best. Sides of salad and potato are included in the deal, and the bar mixes a mean martini. Reservations not accepted. Dinner only.

### SUNRISE SUNSET
**1424 South Wadsworth Blvd.**
**Lakewood**
**303/986-6065**
**$**                                     **WD**

The top-shelf bacon and ham used at Sunrise Sunset are largely responsible for the high number of repeat customers at this breakfast joint. Both meats come mixed into the skillet meals that also involve fried potatoes, basted eggs, country sausage gravy, or 20 other possible ingredients. When strawberries are in season, things don't get much better than the buttermilk pancakes topped with the fresh fruit and whipped cream. Reservations not accepted. Breakfast and lunch.

### TABLE MOUNTAIN INN/MESA GRILL
**1310 Washington St., Golden**
**303/277-9898**
**$$**                                    **WD**

Southwestern fare, fabulous margaritas, and some unique desserts characterize this Santa Fe–style eatery. The decor is fun and casual, and while service can be slow during busy times, everyone's friendly. The bar is popular for happy hour margaritas, and the wine list isn't bad either. Try the spicy chicken tortilla soup. Reservations recommended. Lunch and dinner.

### TODAY'S GOURMET/HIGHLANDS GARDEN CAFE
**3927 West 32nd Ave., Denver**
**303/458-5920**
**$$–$$$**                                **WD**

Today's Gourmet serves some of the best meals to be had in Denver. The kitchen successfully walks the fine line between healthy/low-fat and rich/heavy while cooking up a full range of traditionally prepared French and quirky, contemporary American. The sit-down Sunday brunch is stellar, with expertly assembled omelettes and the most sinful peach crêpes imaginable. Reservations recommended. Lunch and dinner.

### 240 UNION
**240 Union Blvd., Lakewood**
**303/989-3562**

**$$**                                    **WD**

A contender for Denver's top seafood restaurant, 240 Union counts among its assets Dungeness crab cakes sparked by Chinese five-spice powder with ginger aioli and gently breadcrumb-coated calamari accompanied by a mustard vinegar sauce. The seafood selection changes according to what's fresh, but count on several fish-and-pasta combinations, and don't be afraid to try the non-seafood options—the braised lamb is a stunner. Reservations recom-mended. Lunch and dinner.

## NORTH DENVER

### AL FRESCO
2690 Baseline Rd., Boulder
303/543-9090
**$$–$$$**                             **ND**

Upscale Italian food in an upscale setting is the most accurate way to describe Al Fresco. Try the lightly fried calamari and the creamy minestrone, it's as rich as rich gets. And someone in your party should order the incredible seafood risotto. The wine list is varied and well priced. Reservations recommended. Lunch and dinner. See also Downtown.

### CAFFE ANTICA ROMA
1308 Pearl St., Boulder
303/442-0378
**$$**                                    **ND**

Painted to look like scenes from an Italian courtyard, Antica Roma makes its own pastas and then sauces them with best-quality cheeses, butter, cream, and vegetables. Fish and veal preparations are tenderly poached in herb-touched wines, and the wood-fired oven turns out crisp-edged pizzas onto which are placed prosciutto, artichokes, arugula, and grilled shrimp. Match these marvels with one of the fine Italian wines and you'll forget you're in Colorado. Reservations accepted for six or more only. Lunch and dinner.

### DANDELION
1011 Walnut St.
Boulder
303/443-6700
**$$–$$$**                             **ND**

Another of renowned chef Kevin Taylor's ventures, Dandelion is a stylish spot that serves the most up-to-date in New American cooking. The kitchen is not afraid to take risks, which result in some novel creations, and the waitstaff silently gives impeccable service. One of Dandelion's most popular items is a potato pancake with three types of caviar, and the roast venison and pasta dishes are sure to please. Reservations recommended. Lunch and dinner.

### FLAGSTAFF HOUSE
Flagstaff Mountain Rd., Boulder
303/442-4640
**$$$**                                  **ND**

An internationally recognized wine list and breathtaking view of Denver from its lofty mountain perch have earned Flagstaff a much-deserved reputation as a special-occasion destination. The bill is bound to be big, but you get what you pay for. The menu spans the globe, and the entire experience, from the expensive china to the masterful service to the delicate cookies that arrive with the check, makes diners feel pampered to the fullest. Reservations recommended. Dinner only.

### HEALTHY HABITS
4800 Baseline Rd., Boulder
303/494-9177

**$**                            **ND**
Healthy Habits is one of the area's favorite grazing sites, where one low price gains access to an all-you-can-eat feast from a variety of stations. There's a pizza-and-pasta bar, a soup set-up, a sixty-item salad bar, a bakery section and, of course, dessert. As with any buffet, the quality wavers, but you can't beat the bargain. Reservations not accepted. Lunch and dinner. See also Central Denver and South Denver zones.

### POUR LA FRANCE!
**1001 Pearl St., Boulder**
**303/449-3929**
**$$**                     **ND**
A local chain that originated in Aspen, the casual Pour La France! focuses on light French but steals a few tricks from elsewhere along the Mediterranean. The French-style pizzas are nicely done, and the tomato-Brie pie is divine, as are the desserts from Denver's estimable Blue Point Bakery. Reservations accepted. Breakfast, lunch and dinner. See also Central Denver.

### RUDI'S
**4720 Table Mesa Dr., Boulder**
**303/494-5858**
**$$–$$$**                  **ND**
Vegetarian dishes share the menu with other internationally inspired dishes at the laidback Rudi's. The Indian curries, Greek pastries and Japanese pan-fried noodles are meatless, but the chicken is free-range and the beef prime. Rudi's makes its own rustic breads daily along with a host of soups—the snappy gazpacho is a winner. Reservations recommended. Lunch and dinner; closed Mondays.

### WALNUT BREWERY
**1123 Walnut St., Boulder**
**303/447-1345**
**$-$$**                     **ND**
The Walnut is a brewpub with the usual trendy munchies and well-made microbrews, but it stands out in expensive Boulder by virtue of its cheap eats. An order of wings and one of the hearty soups could constitute a meal, and even with a beer would still come in at under $10. Reservations not accepted. Lunch and dinner.

### ZOLO GRILL
**2525 Arapahoe Rd., Boulder**
**303/449-0444**
**$$**                     **ND**
Chef/owner Dave Query has taken the Southwest to heart by embracing all the elements that make this cuisine great: Mexican, Hispanic, Native American, Tex-Mex and Southern influences are apparent in the well-rounded roster of dishes. Mashed-to-order guacamole fights for attention against duck tacos and a catfish po-boy, at least until dessert time, when it's a daunting task to choose between the grilled banana cream pie spiked with rum or the satin crunch cake with a hazelnut crust. Tables in the understated dining room come only to those willing to wait. Reservations are not accepted. Lunch and dinner.

# 5

# SIGHTS AND ATTRACTIONS

The best place to start looking at Denver's sights is where the city began—at the junction of the Cherry Creek and South Platte River, today's Confluence Park. It is possible to trace the way the city grew by viewing the buildings and landmarks that spread out in different directions from the Confluence through the consecutive periods in Denver's history.

Historic Larimer Square, a stone's throw to the south, and the Auraria campus, just a short jog across Speer Boulevard, showcase well-preserved buildings from the early settlements that became Denver. Also of interest in lower downtown are the old Tivoli Brewery, Union Station, the Oxford Hotel, and the Ice House. For the more adventurous, wander east to LoDo's warehouse section and see some of the now-shabby "palaces" of Denver's former red light district.

Traveling south on 17th Street (and some of the parallel streets), you can see some interesting old Denver buildings mixed in with the modern skyscrapers and office towers. The Daniels and Fisher Tower, the Equitable Building, and the Boston Block are some of the best known. At the end of 17th in upper downtown, there are more Denver landmarks and institutions clustered together—the Civic Center, the Denver Art Museum, Denver Public Library, Trinity Church, and the Brown Palace—to name a few. You might want to start touring this part of town at the Byers-Evans House and view their superb video materials on Denver's history. The nearby Colorado Historical Society has excellent exhibits detailing life in Denver and Colorado from the earliest times through the present.

Metropolitan Denver covers a lot of territory, so there are many more sights to keep you well occupied and intrigued once you leave the Central Denver area. Tea-tasting, bird-watching, and communing with nature are only some of your options once you leave Denver proper.

# DOWNTOWN DENVER

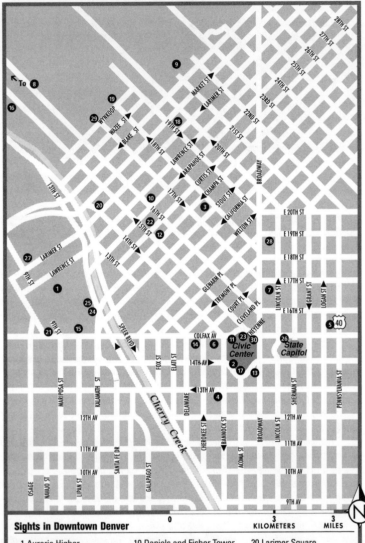

### Sights in Downtown Denver

1 Auraria Higher Education Center
2 Bronco Buster Statue
3 Buerger Brothers Building
4 Byers-Evans House
5 Cathedral of the Immaculate Conception
6 City and County Building
7 "Colorado Wildflowers" sculpture
8 Confluence Park
9 Coors Field
10 Daniels and Fisher Tower
11 Denver Civic Center
12 Denver Gas & Electric Building
13 Denver Public Library
14 Denver U.S. Mint
15 Emmanuel-Sherith Isreal Chapel
16 Forney Transportation Museum
17 Greek Theater
18 House of Mirrors
19 Ice House Ltd.
20 Larimer Square
21 Ninth Street Historic Park
22 Old Prospector Statue
23 Pioneer Monument
24 St. Cajetan's Church
25 St. Elizabeth's Church
26 State Capitol
27 Tivoli brewery
28 Trinity United Methodist Church
29 Union Station
30 Voorhies Memorial Gateway

# DOWNTOWN DENVER

## AURARIA HIGHER EDUCATION CENTER
**Speer Blvd. at Colfax, Denver**
**303/556-3276                        DD**
Metropolitan State College (Metro), Community College of Denver, and the University of Colorado at Denver (UCD) make up the Auraria Higher Education Center. The complex of colleges is located at the site of Auraria, the first of three towns later to merge into Denver. The first settlers of Auraria named their town after a gold-producing region of Georgia that, ironically, yielded as little gold as its hopeful namesake.

## BRONCO BUSTER STATUE
**Civic Center Plaza, Denver      DD**
Alexander Proctor, considered the best animal sculptor of his time, ran into trouble with the human model for this statue. Although the model, named "Slim," performed well on the bucking horse, it turned out he was wanted for horse-stealing. Luckily, the police let Slim continue his modeling duties before hauling him off to jail. The Bronco Buster was dedicated in 1920.

*Bronco Buster Statue*

## BUERGER BROTHERS BUILDING
**1732–40 Champa St, Denver.      DD**
With its Egyptian and Mayan detailing, the Buerger Brothers Building stands as an exotic example of the art deco influence on Denver. Denver architect Montana Fallis designed the building, noted for its glazed terra cotta facade and floral ornamentation, in 1929. Fallis' firm also designed, in 1912, the terra cotta–clad Oxford Hotel addition.

## BYERS-EVANS HOUSE
**1310 Bannock St., Denver**
**303/620-4933                        DD**
Around the corner from the Denver Art Museum stands one of Denver's newly restored treasures, the Byers-Evans home. Thanks to the efforts of the Colorado Historical Society, the home has been open to the public for several years.

The house reflects the character and spirit of two well-known and loved pioneer families—that of William N. Byers, editor of the *Rocky Mountain News*, and of William Grey Evans, son of the first territorial governor, John Evans. Members of the Evans family lived at 1310 Bannock until 1981.

The Byers family called the home "Victoria." The exterior exhibits the exuberant and eclectic mix of architectural styles popular in 1880s Denver. The home's interior is a treasure trove of Victorian antiques, original fixtures, and art. Anne Evans' Southwestern-style apartments, complete with Santa Fe–style fireplaces, have also been restored. The Denver Art Museum next door houses her collection of Southwestern art.

Entrance to the house is through the Denver History Museum in the old carriage house facing 13th Street. The museum offers volunteer-run tours. Visitors can spend hours viewing the fascinating interactive video materials on Denver's history. Tours: Tues–Sun 11–3, starting every half-hour or on the hour depending on the availability of volunteers. Call first if you're on a tight schedule.

### CATHEDRAL OF THE IMMACULATE CONCEPTION
**1530 Logan St., Denver**
**303/831-7010**     **DD**

Completed in 1912, the cathedral is built of Carrara marble and features Bavarian glass windows. It is the "mother church" of the Roman Catholic Church in Colorado and the Bishop presides here. Pope John Paul II stayed at the rectory on the north side of the church in 1993 when he came to Colorado for the World Youth Day celebration. Group tours can be scheduled by calling the office.

### CITY AND COUNTY BUILDING
**1435 Bannock St., Denver**
**303/640-2613**     **DD**

The City and County Building was dedicated in 1932 after years of controversy. Problems ranged from court battles about whether non-Coloradan building materials could be used, to *Rocky Mountain News* and *Denver Post* attacks on the architects' plans, to Mayor Benjamin Stapleton's extravagant vision. The modified Roman-style building was actually completed—to the acclaim of architects across the country during the tenure of Stapleton's successor, Mayor George D. Begole.

The building's grand exterior is made of Colorado Cotopaxi granite and Georgia marble. Colorado travertine, Colorado yule, and pink Tennessee marble, as well as marble from Italy, are some of the fine stones used for the interior.

Mayor Robert Speer's widow, Kate, donated the Speer Memorial Tower Clock and Chimes to the City and County Building. The clock still chimes every quarter-hour in memory of the visionary mayor responsible for so much of Denver's beauty. Tours available: Call at least three weeks in advance.

### COLORADO WILDFLOWERS
**UMB Bank Plaza Building**
**1670 Broadway, Denver**
**303/839-1300**     **DD**

One of Denver's newest institutions has provided the city with one of its newest sights. UMB Bank Colorado commissioned world-renowned glass sculptor Dale Chihuly to create the vividly colored hand-blown glass pieces for the bank lobby. The abstract representations of Colorado wildflowers are mounted on the wall of the lobby facing 17th Street and are highly visible through the bank's sweep of floor-to-ceiling windows. Well-placed lighting illuminates the glass and creates shadows of intertwining light and color—a welcome vision to the drivers beginning their evening commute out of downtown.

### CONFLUENCE PARK
**15th and Platte Sts., Denver**   **DD**

When news broke of gold at Pikes Peak, gold-seekers from every part of the country flocked to Colorado. In 1858, a band of Cherokee Indians, along with some farmers from Georgia, arrived at the spot where Cherry Creek meets the South Platte and started to pan for gold. The site was disappointing, and many of the men left for other gold fields. Those who remained set up a hodgepodge of flimsy shelters that marked the beginning of Denver.

Today, kayakers tumble down the rapids at Confluence Park and bicyclists follow the path that winds along the river. With its great view of the new Elitch Amusement Park across the river, the park is also a favorite spot for picnickers.

**COORS FIELD**
**21st and Blake Sts., Denver**
**303/312-2109            DD**
Dinosaurs roamed here, the Plains Indians camped, and now major league baseball lives in the Platte Valley. Coors Field, the home of the Colorado Rockies team, opened as part of the Platte Development Project in 1995. It is already a well-loved landmark in this long-neglected part of lower downtown.

Named after the Coors Brewing Co. (initial investors in the effort to bring a major league team to the region), Coors Field is one of the few recently constructed baseball-only stadiums in the U.S. The structure harmonizes well with its historic neighborhood. A long-established local company that provided the original brick for much of LoDo also manufactured the red brick for the stadium. The stadium's exterior features architectural motifs from the area's historic buildings, and newer interpretations such as the terra cotta columbines by local artist Barry Rose.

The inside of the stadium feels like an old-time ball field—but with every modern convenience. Each of the specially contoured seats is designed to afford the best view of the field. There are a museum, a brewpub, a restaurant, shops, and a playground and picnic area for kids. With a view of the Rocky Mountains in the distance and games that feature lots of out-of-the-park home runs (is it the altitude?), the stadium offers an experience that many call a baseball-lover's dream come true. Tours: Mon–Fri at 10, 12, & 2. Admission: $5 for ages 12–55, $3 for everyone else.

**DANIELS AND FISHER TOWER**
**1601 Arapahoe St., Denver      DD**
After visiting Venice, Denver busi-

---

## Sixty-Five Million Years Later—the Ocean Comes to Colorado

*Scheduled to open in Denver's Central Platte Valley in summer 1999, Ocean Journey will bring oceans, reefs, tropical rain forests, and a multitude of exotic fish to our land-locked state. Ocean Journey will open at 710 Water Street off I-25 at the 23rd Street exit. Call 303/853-5138 or 800/670-6862 for more information. The Web site is www.oceanjourney.org.*

> **TIP**
>
> Starting at Downtown Denver's Civic Center, you can visit many of Denver's most interesting and historic sights on foot. All within walking distance are the Brown Palace Hotel, the Museum of Western Art, the Denver Public Library, the Denver Art Museum, and the U.S. Mint, as well as many of the historic Capitol Hill homes listed under Central Denver.
>
> For a guided tour of the Civic Center, the Golden Triangle, or Lower Downtown, contact the Denver Foundation for Architecture at 303/779-9193. Experienced volunteers, including Denver area experts, historians, and authors, conduct spring through fall walking tours of many of Denver's most interesting and historic areas. Tours last from one and a half to two hours and cost $3 for DFA members and $5 for non-members. To learn more about the foundation and its offerings, look it up on the Web at www.aiacolorado.org.

nessman William C. Daniels decided to replicate the design of the Campanile in St. Mark's Square for his planned department store. When completed in 1911, the two wings of the store stretched out from the tower from Lawrence to Arapahoe Streets. Today, the tower is all that remains of this once-popular center of Denver shopping. For many Denverites, the D & F Tower symbolizes the need to preserve structures from Denver's past.

### DENVER CIVIC CENTER
**Colfax and Broadway, Denver**
**303/830-1048**      **DD**
Mayor Robert Speer's dream of turning Denver into the "Paris of America" centered on the creation of a gracious plaza surrounded by government and civic buildings that included the already-completed capitol. It took three Speer administrations and the evolution of many plans before the present Civic Center was developed. The State Capitol presides over the area that includes the City and County Building, the Colorado State Museum, Denver Public Library, Denver Art Museum, Greek Theater, Voorhies Memorial Gateway, and notable statues and monuments.

### DENVER GAS & ELECTRIC BUILDING
**15th and Champa Sts., Denver**    **DD**
Driving down 15th Street towards lower downtown at night, the geometrically lit Denver Gas & Electric Building is a striking sight. Constructed in 1910 by Frank Edbrooke & Co., the structure epitomized Denver's newly proclaimed image as the "City of Lights." D G & E also hoped to divert public scrutiny of their monopoly with the dramatic display. (The D G & E president had been jailed in 1906 by Denver Judge Ben Lindsay for election fraud.)

### DENVER PUBLIC LIBRARY
**10 W. 14th Ave. Pkwy., Denver**
**303/640-6200**      **DD**
The Denver Public Library was built in 1956 by Denver architect Burnham Hoyt. The new addition opened in 1995. Designed by world-famous architect Michael Graves and Den-

*Denver Public Library*

ver's Klipp Colussy Jenks DuBois, the addition wraps around the historic building in a jumble of shapes and colors—some have likened it to a box of crayons. The stonework for the new structure is embedded with 150 million-year-old fossils from German limestone quarries.

Curly maple is used in the library addition's dramatic interior. The main entrance leads into three-story Schlessman Hall where information and reference desks surround an atrium. The refurbished Burnham Hoyt section, on the ground floor, houses the new Children's Library and Pavilion and the Marietta Baron Teen Space. Both offer enticing displays, reading areas, and equipment.

The fifth level is—in a word—heavenly. The Western History and Genealogy Department has a comprehensive collection of books, journals, newspapers, maps, manuscripts, photographs, and primary materials recording the Western experience and history. The Gates Western History Reading Room is a beautiful space banked with windows and lovely views. There is a conservation room dedicated to environmental history, a map room, a photodigitization center for accessing historic photos by computer, a manuscript room, and a gallery featuring the work of Western artists such as Albert Bierstadt. One-hour tours: Mon–Fri 11:45 & 2:15, Sat 11, Sun 2, and other times by arrangement. Times may change; it's a good idea to call 640-6206 for reservations.

### DENVER U.S. MINT
**320 W. Colfax Ave., Denver**
**303/844-3582**      **DD**

In 1860 Clark, Gruber & Co. minted their first coins, their name on one side and "Pikes Peak Gold" on the other. Being pure gold, the coins were softer than standard U.S. issue. Even after alloy was added, the coins were 1 percent higher in gold than standard coins. The U.S. government purchased Gruber & Co. in 1863 and used the 16th Street and Market location as an assay office until moving to the present Tuscan-Palazzo–style building in 1904. Tours: Mon–Fri 8–2:45, every 20 minutes. Closed last week in June through July 4. Be prepared for long lines.

### EMMANUEL-SHERITH ISRAEL CHAPEL
**1201 10th St., Auraria Campus, Denver**

*Jennie Rogers*

**303/556-8337**     **DD**
Early Episcopalians built the Emmanuel Church in 1876 on the site of Denver's first Sunday School. Although it later became a synagogue, the structure is Denver's earliest existing church and the oldest example of a Romanesque Revival church. Emmanuel-Sherith is now the Emmanuel Gallery, a collaborative effort of the Auraria Higher Education colleges.

**FORNEY TRANSPORTATION MUSEUM**
**1416 Platte St., Denver**
**303/433-3643**     **DD**
Until 1945 most Denverites took trolleys to get around the city. The Denver Tramway Company power plant provided the steam power to fuel electricity for the trolley system. The mammoth building was constructed in 1901. Local architects and historians still admire the beauty and function of this paragon of industrial architecture.

In 1968 the building was purchased to house the Forney Transportation Museum, a collection of "one of a kind" vehicles. Kids love climbing around on the assorted trains, trolleys, and fire engines parked in the side yard. Ignoring the dim interior, car-lovers drool over such gems as the 1923 Hispano Suiza and Amelia Earhart's "Gold Bug" Kissel. Open daily, call for hours. Admission: $4 adults, $2 ages 12-18, $1 ages 5-11; special group, school, and senior rates.

**GREEK THEATER**
**Civic Center Plaza, Denver**   **DD**
On the south side of the plaza, the Greek Theater was completed in 1919. Allen True painted the murals of the trapper and the prospector on either side of the stage. Surrounded by the Colonnade of Civic Benefactors and facing paths and flower gardens, the theater was originally used for Municipal Band concerts. It still serves as a venue for performances, rallies, and speeches. President Clinton addressed Denverites here during a 1992 campaign stop.

**HOUSE OF MIRRORS**
**1942 Market St., Denver**   **DD**
First known as McGaa, then Holliday, and finally Market, the street running parallel to Larimer was the center of Denver's red light district in the 1880s. By far the fanciest and most renowned house of ill repute was Jennie Rogers' House of Mirrors at 1942 Market Street. Allegedly, the 6-foot-tall Jennie Rogers used blackmail to bully a customer into building the house for her. Designed by architect William Quayle, the building's facade sported phallic-like stone carvings and a sculpture of Jennie herself. Inside, there were banks of mirrors in the entry, crystal chandeliers, orien-

## Wow! Jack Kerouac in Denver

In Jack Kerouac's classic novel about the fifties Beat Generation, On the Road, hero Sal Paradise follows his idol, Dean Moriarty, to Denver. The story is based on Kerouac's real-life friendship with Denverite Neal Cassidy. Here is how Sal describes arriving in Denver: "Said to myself, Wow! What'll Denver be like! I got on that hot road, and off I went in a brand-new car driven by a Denver businessman of about thirty-five. He went seventy. I tingled all over; I counted minutes and subtracted miles. Just ahead, over the rolling wheatfields all golden beneath the distant snows of Estes, I'd be seeing old Denver at last. I pictured myself in a Denver bar that night, with all the gang, and in their eyes I would be strange and ragged and like the Prophet who has walked across the land to bring the dark Word, and the only word I had was, 'Wow!' The man and I had a long, warm conversation about our respective schemes in life, and before I knew it we were going over the wholesale fruitmarkets outside Denver; there were smokestacks, smoke, railyards, red-brick buildings, and the distant downtown graystone buildings, and here I was in Denver. He let me off at Larimer Street. I stumbled along with the most wicked grin of joy in the world, among the old bums and beat cowboys of Larimer Street."

tal rugs, a ballroom, a grand piano, and a wine cellar. The House of Mirrors was so popular that Jennie bought the house next door and decorated it to resemble a harem. After Jennie's death, the equally renowned madame Mattie Silks bought the House of Mirrors. "M. Silks" was printed in tile at the entryway.

Today the house has been renovated as the Mattie Silks restaurant. Owners of the adjoining Lodo Bar and Grill restored some of the original features and guessed at the rest. Across the street at 2009 Market stands another of Jennie Rogers' former bordellos. Still sporting some of its Victorian detail, this house's original glory is a bit easier to imagine.

**ICE HOUSE LTD.**
**1801 Wynkoop, Denver**
**303/298-9191**                             **DD**
The present Ice House structure was built in 1903 as a cold storage plant. Bands of multicolored brick and intricate brick patterns bring interest to the windowless sections of the walls. Owned first by Littleton Creamery and

# Top Ten Buildings in Denver
## by Tom Morris, Denver architect and community activist

Denver native Tom Morris designed the Limon Town Hall, City Park Bandstand, and many other structures. His father, architect Robert Max Morris, was a member of the Denver Atelier, a group of architects and artists who met in the 1930s.

1. **United Bank Walk, Sherman to Broadway.** "The best space in Denver.... Approach from 18th and Sherman and walk through the courtyard. Proceed through the huge, dark tower lobby, then on to the Lincoln east lobby. Cross the bridge that hovers above the traffic below. Go through the Lincoln west lobby where I. M. Pei's tower stands and proceed to the atrium."

2. **West Wall at Gates Rubber Co., 900 S. Broadway.** "This shows that architecture can be a lot less pretentious than it usually is. Fans and ducts, wires, pipes, lights, and all the mean things of industry trip the light fantastic here."

3. **The Boston Block, 17th and Champa Sts.** The Boston firm of Andrews, Jacques, and Rantoul built the Boston Block in 1889 and the Equitable Building at 17th and Stoutin in 1890. Morris likes the stolid buildings here because "a building should sit on the ground."

4. **Boat House at Washington Park, Downing and Louisiana.** "Picturesque."

5. **Central Bank, 1515 Arapahoe St.** "Bill Muchow, one of Denver's great architects, used classic Miesian rigidity to achieve wonderful spaces in this building."

6. **City and County Building, Civic Center.** "Most of Denver's architects worked on this building to survive the Great Depression."

7. **Confluence Park, 15th and Platte Sts.** "I don't ever remember seeing this great place until Joe Shoemaker started saving the Platte."

8. **Anyone's Backyard.** "The best thing about Denver is summer. The heat of the day is sucked away almost the instant the sun sets.... We each create our own space in anyone's backyard to celebrate Denver."

9. **Coors Field, 21st and Blake Sts.** "Major league."

10. **Under the viaducts.** "Talk about three-dimensional space!"

then by Beatrice Creamery, it is said that the plant stored furs and possibly corpses along with the more expected butter, cheese, cream, and ice. The ground floor is now occupied by restaurants. Developers plan to turn the top part of the building into condominium apartments.

## LARIMER SQUARE
**1400 Block of Larimer St., Denver** DD

In 1965 Denver preservationist Dana Crawford spearheaded the effort to restore the buildings of Larimer Street between 14th and 15th Streets. Thanks to creative public financing sources, the street's red brick buildings, constructed during Denver's 1880s boom, are home to shops, restaurants, and galleries. The restoration signaled the beginning of a renaissance in lower downtown and galvanized a citywide preservation movement as well.

The Clayton Building, on the southwest corner of Larimer and 15th Streets, was built between 1880 and 1882 on the site of Denver's first structure, the cabin of claim-jumping Denver City founder General William Larimer. Today a Williams-Sonoma store occupies the ground floor. Denver's first pharmacy opened in 1859 where the Sussex Block buildings (1880) now stand at 1428–34 Larimer Street. The Gallup-Stansbury Building (1873), at 1449–51 Larimer Street, used to house one of the rowdiest establishments of the 1860s, Stansbury's Tambien Saloon.

## NINTH STREET HISTORIC PARK
**Auraria Campus, Denver** DD

The one block of Victorian homes on 9th Street is the oldest restored residential block in Denver. The 14 homes were built in the late 1800s and early 1900s for tradespeople and business owners. Restored by Historic Denver in 1976, they now serve as college administrative offices.

## OLD PROSPECTOR STATUE
**Brooks Towers, Denver**
**1020 15th St.** DD

The Old Prospector that stands guard outside the Brooks Towers condominiums used to hover over the city from the top of the enormous old Mining Exchange Building (circa 1891). When the Mining Exchange was razed in the mid-Sixties, the statue was salvaged.

## PIONEER MONUMENT
**Civic Center Plaza, Denver** DD

Unveiled in 1911, the Pioneer Monument sparked one of the first Civic Center controversies. The monument was executed by French sculptor and "City Beautiful" proponent Frederick MacMonnies to commemorate the end of the Smoky Hill Trail. In keeping with his concept of the West, MacMonnies modeled a miner, a trapper, and a pioneer mother at the base of the statue, and a nearly nude Indian at the top. The glorification of the Indian enraged Denverites, and a likeness of Kit Carson replaced it as the crowning figure.

## ST. CAJETAN'S CHURCH
**9th and Lawrence Sts.**
**Auraria Campus, Denver** DD

In 1926 the Roman Catholic Church commissioned Denver architect Robert Willison to build a church at this site. The first church in Denver for Spanish-speaking peoples, Willison modeled St. Cajetan's after churches in Mexico and New Mexico. When plans for developing the

*Trinity United Methodist Church*

Auraria campus called for razing St. Cajetan's, neighborhood and preservation groups banded together to save it. The Mission Revival building was designated a Denver Landmark in 1970.

### ST. ELIZABETH'S CHURCH
**1060 11th St., Denver**
**Auraria Campus          DD**
Of the three Roman Catholic Churches that graced Denver, which were within blocks of each other, two remain: St. Elizabeth's and St. Cajetan's. St. Elizabeth's, built for the German community, is the older of the two. Struggling German immigrants arriving in Denver received welcome aid from the Franciscans at St. Elizabeth's.

### STATE CAPITOL
**200 E. Colfax Ave., Denver**
**303/866-2604          DD**
Begun in 1886 and completed by Denver architect Frank Edbrooke in 1904, the State Capitol was built on land donated by Henry C. Brown. A farmer/developer, Brown also donated the nearby Brown Palace site. A dome of 200 ounces of gold leaf tops the Federal Revival–style building. A statue of "the most beautiful woman in Colorado" would have graced the dome if legislators had been able to agree on a model.

The interior is designed largely after the nation's Capitol in Washington, D.C. It has the same Greek Cross floor plan with entrances at every side, the same number of rooms, and a rotunda that is the same distance to the floor below. The rotunda features the murals of noted Colorado artist Allen True. Rose onyx from Beulah, Colorado—a material found in no other building in the world—lines the walls. The view from the capitol dome looks out over the Civic Center and is well worth the climb. Tours: Mon–Fri 9:30–2:45, offered every 45 minutes at the north (off Colfax Avenue) entrance.

### TIVOLI BREWERY
**1324 10th St., Denver          DD**
John Good, a master brewer from Alsace-Lorraine, started the Rocky Mountain Brewing Co. in 1860. He later changed the name to Tivoli after the famous gardens in Copenhagen. The existing Tivoli Brewery was constructed in 1890–91 when Philip Zang was the owner. German-born architect F. C. Eberly designed the main building of the complex. The adjoining opera house, where German operettas were performed, was designed by Harold H. Baerresen in 1882. Today the Tivoli Brewery houses class-

# The Sacred 36

Most of Denver's "high society" of the late 1800s built mansions on the hill near the capitol, today's Capitol Hill district. Mrs. Crawford Hill, whose mansion still stands at 150 10th Ave., was the undisputed social queen of her day. Hill established the Denver Social Register and the exclusive Sacred 36 bridge club whose members were the supposed cream of Denver society. Try as she might, Molly Brown could never gain acceptance by the Sacred 36.

It is puzzling why Mrs. Hill deemed the former Hannibal, Missouri, "river girl's" manners so uncouth, in light of her own behavior. A portrait of Mrs. Hill's husband hung on one wall of her front parlor and a larger portrait of her lover on the other. Every spring Mrs. Hill would herald the start of the Denver social season by unveiling a nude marble statue in her garden.

After Molly Brown emerged as one of the survivors—and heroines—of the Titanic, the Sacred 36 finally had to back down. They hosted a luncheon in Molly's honor at the Denver Country Club.

In 1969 Denver stood up for Molly Brown again. The "House of Lions" was slated for demolition by the Skyline Urban Renewal Project. The Tabor Building, the Mining Exchange Building, the Windsor Hotel, and many other significant old buildings had already been razed to make way for urban expansion. Historic Denver, Inc., was formed to oppose the destruction of yet another historic Denver structure. Since saving Molly's house, Historic Denver has gone on to preserve much of Denver's architectural heritage.

Molly Brown's Capitol Hill Walking Tour *(available at the Molly Brown House, $8.98)* provides a self-guided tour of the area's late 1800s and early 1900s homes built by some of Denver's most prominent architects—William Lang, Frank Edbrooke, Fisher and Fisher, J. J. B. Benedict. A range of architectural styles, from Craftsman to Romanesque, Spanish Colonial to Art Moderne, are represented. Some of the more famous Capitol Hill structures—including the Cheesman-Evans-Boettcher Mansion and the Grant-Humphries Mansion—are within walking distance of Molly's home.

rooms and shops for the Auraria campus.

## TRINITY UNITED METHODIST CHURCH
**1810 Broadway, Denver**
**303/839-1493** DD
The architect of Trinity, Robert Roeschlaub, designed some of Denver's finest structures, and this is perhaps the finest of them all. Built in 1888, the church was constructed of a volcanic granite from Castle Rock, Colorado. Red, blue, and silvery mica speckle the light beige stone. The beautiful spire is a welcome sight from many vantage points downtown, including the nearby Brown Palace Hotel. Light diffused through the Tiffany stained-glass windows warms the beautiful sanctuary. Hours of worship: Sun 8:15 & 11. Tours: Sun 12:15.

## UNION STATION
**17th and Wynkoop Sts., Denver** DD
Only the two wings on either side of Union Station remain from the original 1881 structure. It was constructed of pink lava stone, with limestone from Morrison, Colorado, trimming the doors and windows. In 1914 the middle part of the station was reconstructed in a similar Romanesque style. Mayor Robert Speer erected a 65-foot-high steel arch in front of the building in 1906. On one side the lighted arch read "Welcome" and on the other, "Mizpah," which is actually a Hebrew greeting. But visitors somehow got the idea that "Mizpah" was an Indian word for "Howdy." The arch came down in 1931, but some of the signage in LoDo has the street name on one side and "Welcome-Mizpah" on the other.

## VOORHIES MEMORIAL GATEWAY

**Civic Center Plaza, Denver** DD
Denver architects Fisher and Fisher designed the Voorhies Memorial Gateway in 1921. Balancing the Greek Theater and Colonnade to the south, the many-columned, open structure was designed to resemble the Water Gateway at the 1893 Chicago Exposition. Denver banker and mining mogul John H. P. Voorhies and his wife donated the memorial in response to Mayor Robert Speer's famous exhortation to Denverites to "give while you live." The Voorhies lived across the street from where the memorial was built.

# CENTRAL DENVER

## MOLLY BROWN HOUSE (HOUSE OF LIONS)
**1340 Pennsylvania St., Denver**
**303/832-4092** CD
It is ironic that the home of socially unacceptable Molly Brown (and, incidentally, that of her millionaire husband, J. J. Brown, owner of the legendary Little Johnny Mine in Leadville) was the structure that sparked the birth of Historic Denver, Inc. The fantastic-looking Queen Anne home, designed by William Lang in 1889, is guarded by two stone lions at the entry. The restored interior is filled with Victorian antiques and unusual features like the polar bear rug in the front parlor. Tours: Mon–Sat 10–3:30, Sun 12–3:30, beginning every half-hour.

## CHEESMAN-EVANS-BOETTCHER MANSION (GOVERNOR'S MANSION)
**400 E. 8th Ave., Denver** CD
When the Denver Landmark Commission formed in 1967, their first designated landmark was the

# CENTRAL DENVER

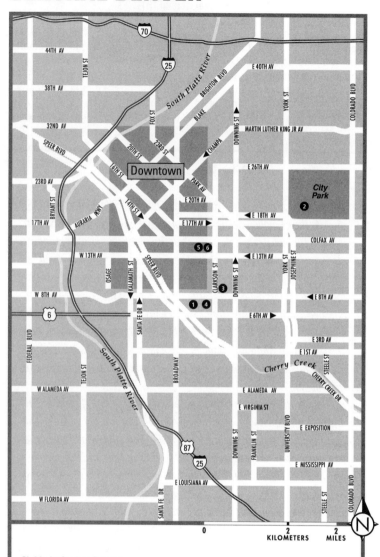

### Sights in Central Denver

1 Cheesman-Evans-Boettcher Mansion
2 City Park
3 Corona-Dora Moore School
4 Grant-Humphries Mansion
5 Molly Brown House
6 St. John's Episcopal Cathedral

Cheesman-Evans-Boettcher mansion. The Colonial Revival home was completed in 1908 for the family of water and real estate tycoon Walter Scott Cheesman, who had died a year earlier. John Evans, Jr., Denver businessman and the grandson of one of Colorado's territorial governors, and Cheesman's daughter, Gladys, married in the house and lived there until 1911.

Claude Boettcher, heir to the family's businesses, including Great Western Sugar Co., Ideal Cement, and Boettcher Investment Co., bought the house in 1926. In 1960 the Boettcher Foundation deeded the mansion to the state of Colorado for the governor's mansion.

## City Park Pavilion

*Designed by architects Humphrey and Fisher and dedicated in 1896, the City Park Pavilion became a vibrant center of activity in Victorian Denver. The two-story Italianate structure housed a kitchen and two steel-barred jail cells in the basement for rowdy park revelers. White-jacketed waiters served elegantly dressed ladies and gentlemen in the ground-floor refreshment parlor and restaurant. Skaters climbed to the second story to warm up and enjoy the mountain views, from Longs to Pikes Peaks, from the building's twin towers. The Municipal Band and famous musicians of the day such as John Philip Sousa played concerts at the open-air Bandstand opposite the Pavilion.*

*Over the years, the Pavilion fell into disuse and disrepair. The original red brick was stuccoed over and the interior gutted. The building housed a museum for a while and then stood empty, a sad and crumbling relic, sealed off and forgotten. In 1990 the Department of Parks and Recreation revived interest in the building with plans to renovate the structure as their central office. Community groups opposed the plan, insisting that the Pavilion be renovated for public use. Today, thanks to bond money and the creative collaboration among architects, developers, city planners, the Department of Parks and Recreation, and community members, the Pavilion and the Bandstand are restored. Weddings, reunions, parties, and jazz concerts take place at the historic site that has received a new lease on life.*

Many Denverites opposed the donation, feeling that the Boettcher family already exerted too much influence on the city and that the governor shouldn't live in such splendor. But the donation was accepted and Colorado governors have lived in the mansion since 1960. Many public and private events take place in the ground-floor Palm Room. Tours: May–Aug 1–3. Just show up at the front door!

## CITY PARK, THE PAVILION, AND FERRILL LAKE AT CITY PARK
**17th Ave. and Colorado Blvd., Denver**
**303/322-3031**      **CD**

This area in the center of City Park is always tranquil. The recently restored Pavilion has a snack bar, and there are picnic tables overlooking the lake to the east and the rose garden to the west. At the boathouse to the south of the Pavilion, you can rent paddleboats for $5 and go out on the water for an hour. There is also a playground set back from the eastern shore that overlooks the lake and the Pavilion.

The Children's Statue, commissioned by former Mayor Robert Speer after a sculpture he admired in Dusseldorf, Germany, is at the south end of the lake and is a favorite spot for picnicking or just watching the ducks paddle by. Paddleboat hours: Memorial Day–Labor Day, Mon–Sun 11–7.

## CORONA-DORA MOORE SCHOOL
**846 Corona St., Denver**      **CD**

Both fanciful and grand, with its billowing rooves, arched portals, and carved facade, the Corona-Dora Moore School was designed in 1889 by Robert Roeschlaub in the Romanesque Revival style. Famous alumni of the school include Douglas Fairbanks, Mamie Doud Eisenhower, Paul Whiteman, and Judy Collins. It is still one of Denver's most vibrant public schools, with an active PTA and superb teachers and administration.

## GRANT-HUMPHRIES MANSION
**770 Pennsylvania St., Denver**
**303/894-2505**      **CD**

Built in 1902 for smelting magnate James B. Grant, Colorado's first Democratic governor, this gracious Colonial-style mansion was an oddity among the castles most wealthy Denverites were building at the time. Standing on a sweeping expanse of lawn overlooking the mountains, the house has a semicircular portico entryway that is supported by Corinthian columns. There are terra cotta flourishes around the windows and archways. Inside the 30-room mansion, Grant installed a billiard room, a bowling alley, and a ballroom that was used for his inaugural ball.

In 1917 Albert E. Humphreys, Jr., an iron and oil magnate and well-known philanthropist, bought the house. Humphrey added a ten-car garage, gas pump, and car wash for his Rolls Royce fleet. In 1976 the house was bequeathed to the state for use as offices. The grounds became a city park.

Although there are no official tours, the Grant-Humphries Mansion is often rented for receptions, meetings, and events. Spaces range from the intimate to the palatial. The sight of a bride coming down the grand staircase has delighted many guests over the years.

## ST. JOHN'S EPISCOPAL CATHEDRAL

# Top Ten Buildings in Denver
## by Barbara Norgren, historic preservationist

Member of the Denver Landmark Preservation Commission, Barbara S. Norgren coauthored *Denver: The City Beautiful* with Thomas J. Noel and runs a historic preservation consulting company.

1. **Trinity Methodist Church, 18th and Broadway (Downtown).** "Denver architect Robert Roeschlaub's work. The stone spire, completely supported from the inside, and the layout of the sanctuary are unusual features."
2. **University Building, 16th and Champa (Downtown).** "When you look up under the eaves, you can see different colors and a great deal of artistry under the curved cornices."
3. **Mountain States Telephone Building, 14th and Curtis (Downtown).** "The building itself was rare in Denver, as it emulated New York skyscraper styles of the time (1929). In the lobby are Denver artist Allen True's exceptional murals, 'History of Communication.'"
4. **Gas and Electric Building, 15th and Champa Sts. (Downtown).** "Absolutely beautiful when all lit up, the building is unusual for its all–terra cotta facade."
5. **Neef House, 2143 Grove St. (NW).** "Built in 1886 for brewer Frederick Neef, this house displays every Victorian ornamentation possible."
6. **St. Elizabeth Chapel, at Provenant Gardens at St. Elizabeth's, 2835 W. 32nd Ave. (NW).** "What a gem. It makes me think of Sir Christopher Wren's churches."
7. **Baerresen House, 1718 Gaylord St. (Central Denver).** "Barbara loves the refined and delicate look of this Dutch Colonial Revival home, built in 1903 by architect Harold W. Baerresen. Of special note is the gambrel roof, echoed by the gambrel roof of the central dormer."
8. **University of Denver Classroom Building (Annex 1), 1445 Cleveland Pl. (Downtown).** "There are few examples of International-style buildings in Denver. I wish this one would get cleaned up and loved."
9. **Buerger Brothers Building, 1732 Champa St. (Downtown).** "There are few art deco buildings in Denver. I love the colors in the designs of the facade."
10. **Elitch Theater (Old Elitch Gardens) (NW).** "This was the longest-lived venue for performing stock companies in the U.S. . . . many Broadway and Hollywood stars got their start [here]."

**1313 Clarkson St., Denver**
**303/831-7115** CD

The cathedral and its adjoining structures cover the entire block between 13th and 14th Avenues and between Clarkson and Washington Streets. The stained-glass windows in the main sanctuary are some of the finest in Denver. Internationally renowned German sculptors Joseph Mayer and Peter Rendl carved the altar and the 17 free-standing figures above it.

St. Martin's Chapel is a little jewel in the center of the enclave. John E. Thompson, one of Colorado's most eminent painters, painted the chapel murals.

## EAST DENVER

**FOUR MILE HISTORIC PARK**
**715 S. Forest St., Denver**
**303/399-1859** ED

Just 4 miles from downtown is the site of Denver's oldest standing structure—a log cabin built on Arapaho and Cheyenne Indian land in 1859. The next year a widow with two children converted the building into a stagestop for travelers on the Cherokee Trail. Another pioneer family acquired the site in 1864, adding 500 acres of ranch land to the area now occupied by office buildings, shops, and restaurants.

The park's devoted volunteer staff offer an authentic and unblinking look into the lives of early Denver pioneers. You can stroll through the living-history farmstead with its chickens and horses and tour the home, filled with period household items and furniture. There are stagecoach tours (weather permitting) on weekends, and a variety of events sponsored—such as the Rocky Mountain Arts Festival and the Organic Farmers Market—throughout the year. There are also week-long summer camps for kids. Tours: Apr–Sept, Wed–Sun 10–4; call for winter hours. Admission: $3.50 adults, $2 seniors (65+) and students (6–15), free for children 5 and under. Stagecoach rides for $1 per person: Weekends 11–2, weather permitting.

**PLAINS CONSERVATION CENTER**
**21901 E. Hampden Ave., Aurora**
**303/693-3621** ED

Visitors to the 1,900-acre Plains Conservation Center experience the prairie environment that metropolitan Denver has displaced. Areas of western wheatgrass, needlegrass, and blue grama substitute for well-groomed blue grass lawns; squirrels and pets give way to red-tailed hawks, golden eagles, prairie dogs, coyote, badgers, American pronghorns, burrowing owls, and the lark bunting, Colorado's state bird.

A sod homestead depicts the lives of the early settlers in eastern Colorado. There is a shelter area for picnics, and the John Race Memorial Amphitheater affords sweeping views of the Front Range from Pikes Peak to Rocky Mountain National Park. This striking, windswept world is preserved entirely through private contributions. Memberships in the non-profit Friends of the PCC come in different categories, and offer special privileges.

At present, the Plains Conservation Center is open only for scheduled group tours. June through September, however, monthly moon walks are offered 7:30 p.m. to 9:30 p.m. that include a campfire and marshmallow roast at $4 per person. Wagon rides are also offered. Call for times.

## RICHTOFFEN CASTLE
(Montclair)
**7020 E. 12th Ave., Denver**    **ED**

Baron Walter von Richtoffen was a Prussian nobleman and the uncle of the famous "Red Baron." He burst upon Denver sometime in the 1870s and, energized by the youth and vigor of the city, proceeded to hatch scheme after scheme that never quite materialized.

The baron's castle, a limestone fortress complete with crenelated parapet, was built east of the city and "out on the plains" between 1883 and 1887. The site was part of an envisioned suburb of Denver, but for quite a while the castle, sporting a moat, greenhouse, underground passageway, and *Molkerei* (milk house), was the only structure around.

The baron lost his fortune in the silver crash, but his fantastic castle still stands, surrounded by the beautiful Montclair neighborhood he did not live to see. This is a great area for a bike ride.

# WEST DENVER

## BUFFALO BILL MEMORIAL MUSEUM AND GRAVE
**987 1/2 Lookout Mountain Rd.
Golden
303/526-0747**    **WD**

When Wyoming native William F. Cody, otherwise known as Buffalo Bill, died in Denver, city officials quickly whisked him up to Lookout Mountain for burial. Wyoming citizens were not happy to be deprived of their favorite son and potential tourist attraction and demanded the body be turned over to them for burial. Denverites responded by pouring tons of concrete over the grave, ensuring that Buffalo Bill would never move from the spot. A winding scenic road takes you to the site, overlooking Denver and Golden. The grave itself, surrounded by a black wrought-iron fence, is pretty dreary—a sad tribute to the irreverent and hard-drinking showman.

The adjoining museum contains photographs, posters, costumes, saddles, and guns from Cody's Wild West Show. There are also exhibits on the Pony Express and life on the frontier, and a collection of the dime novels (often portraying Buffalo Bill as the hero) so popular in the late 1800s. Hours: May–Oct, Mon–Sun 9–5; Nov–Apr, Tues–Sun 9–4. Admission: $2 adults, $1 children, $1.50 seniors.

## MOTHER CABRINI SHRINE
**20189 Cabrini Blvd.
Golden
303/526-0758**    **WD**

Fifty years ago, Mother Frances Xavier Cabrini became the first American citizen canonized as a saint by the Roman Catholic Church. The first pilgrimage in her honor took place in 1947 when 10,000 people climbed what was then a cattle track to the Mother Cabrini Shrine in Golden. In 1950 Pope Pius XII named Saint Cabrini the patron saint of emigrants.

Having founded her own order in Italy, Sister Cabrini arrived in New York City at Pope Leo XIII's urging in 1889. She traveled the United States, setting up schools, orphanages, and hospitals. In the early 1900s, Sister Cabrini sent missionaries to the Denver area to set up an orphanage. In 1912 she traveled by horse-and-buggy with members of her order to dedicate the present site as the orphanage's summer camp. It was here that she tapped a rock with her

## Sightseeing Excursion: Cherokee Ranch and Castle

*About 30 minutes from Denver, Cherokee Ranch and Castle is well worth a visit. It is one of Colorado's most spectacular residences, built in the style of a 1450s Scottish castle.*

*Situated on four thousand acres of open land with sweeping views of the Front Range, Cherokee Castle was designed by Denver architect Burnham Hoyt between 1924 and 1926. The castle's 26 rooms occupy 10,000 square feet and are filled with priceless antiques, paintings, and architectural features collected from around the world.*

*In 1954, Mrs. Tweet Kimball purchased the castle and surrounding property and also brought the first herd of Santa Gertrudis cattle to Colorado to start what is still a working ranch. To protect the land and its abundant wildlife, Kimball—who still lives at the castle—created the Cherokee Ranch and Castle Foundation.*

*The foundation provides group tours and rents the castle for special events. Board meeting space is also available. The sight is open to the public by reservation only. Contact the foundation at P.O. Box 472, Sedalia, CO 80135, 303/688-5555.*

---

cane and produced a spring of clear water for the camp. She laid her cane down on the spot where the summer camp was built.

The nickels, dimes, and pennies donated by pilgrims largely paid for the 22-foot-high, 25-ton statue of Mother Cabrini that stands on the hill overlooking Denver and Genessee. More than 350 steps lead to the top—and a truly spectacular view of the surrounding area.

Today, Sister Ignatius Miceli, who arrived at the Mother Cabrini convent in 1954 when the area was still a rural summer camp, is the shrine's chief historian. She urges visitors to climb the steps to the statue and shrine, stroll through the convent and the lovely perennial gardens, and absorb the beauty of this unique place.

### COORS BREWERY COMPANY TOURS
**13th and Ford Sts., Golden**
**303/277-BEER**  WD

Adolph Coors, Sr., was born in Barmen, Prussia, in 1847. He overcame poverty, the oppressive reign of Prussia's King William I, the rigors of immigration to America (he was a stow-away on a U.S.-bound ship),

# GREATER DENVER

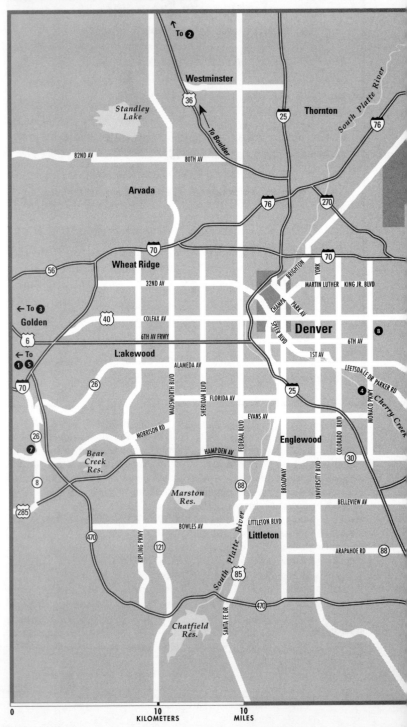

## Sights in Greater Denver

1. Buffalo Bill Memorial Museum and Grave (WD)
2. Celestial Seasonings Tour of Tea (ND)
3. Coors Brewery Company Tours (WD)
4. Four Mile Historic Park (ED)
5. Mother Cabrini Shrine (WD)
6. Plains Conservation Center (ED)
7. Red Rocks Amphitheater (WD)
8. Richtoffen Castle (ED)

and the challenges of a new country to fulfill his dream of establishing a brewery. Inspired by the springs of the Clear Creek valley near Golden, Coors founded a business that not only survived the Depression and Prohibition, but prospered and expanded.

Plan to spend 1 1/2 hours on the Coors Brewery tour, which includes a guided walk through the brewing and packaging plant, complimentary beer sampling in the hospitality lounge, and shopping in the Coors & Co. Gift Shop. Free. Tours: Mon–Sat 10–4. (Children 18 and under must be accompanied by an adult.)

### RED ROCKS AMPHITHEATER
**North of Morrison on Hogback Rd. (between U.S. 40 and U.S. 285)**
**303/692-8801 or 303/640-7300  WD**
It was the dream of George Cranmer, Denver's Manager of Parks during Mayor Ben Stapleton's administration, to build an outdoor theater between the towering 400-foot-high sandstone rocks at Red Rocks Park. With the nearly-donated design work of architect Burnham Hoyt, a labor force of WPA workers, and much political maneuvering, the 9,000-seat theater was developed during the Depression and completed in 1938. Wolfgang Wagner, son of composer Richard Wagner, came from Germany to supervise, without pay, the acoustical fine-tuning of the space.

Today, there are still few greater pleasures in the Denver area than sitting out under the stars or in the clear bright Colorado sunshine to enjoy a concert at Red Rocks. The view of Denver's skyline across the expanse of plains is spectacular. Sometimes you can just make out the white canopy of DIA floating in the distance.

## NORTH DENVER

### CELESTIAL SEASONINGS TOUR OF TEA
**4600 Sleepytime Dr.**
**Boulder**
**303/530-5300                        ND**
Ever wonder how they get all those tea leaves into those tiny little bags? The Celestial Seasonings Co. will reveal this mystery to you and much more. The entertaining tour takes you through the factory, the research and development center, and the art department. Of course, there is tea-tasting at the end.

Celestial Seasonings founder Mo Siegel started collecting wild herbs and making them into teas in 1969 when he was 19 years old. Today his Boulder-based company is the largest herbal tea manufacturer in the country. Siegel is known for his laid-back, socially conscious management style, and the company has maintained the feel of its cottage industry roots through the years.

At the gift shop, you can sample any tea you like. The outdoor herb garden, laid out in the traditional English style with paths, trellises, and bowers, is a lovely place to sit and chat.

To reach Celestial Seasonings from Denver, take I-25 north to U.S. 36 west. As you near Boulder, exit onto Highway 157 heading north. Continue as 157 turns into Highway 119 heading northeast. Turn right on Jay Road and proceed to Spine Road. Turn left, then left again on Sleepytime Drive. Tours: Mon–Sat every hour 10–3.

# 6

# KIDS' STUFF

When you ask them what they want to do, most kids say they just want to play. Metro Denver has some great parks where kids of all ages can climb, run, roll, and make things. There are also museums, theaters, rec centers, entertainment events, and places to see animals that kids—and adults—enjoy.

## ANIMALS AND THE GREAT OUTDOORS

**ALAMO-PLACITA PARK**
3rd Ave. and Emerson St.
Denver                    CD
Although it is close to Speer Boulevard, Alamo-Placita is a small, peaceful little park. There are several basketball courts and a nice playground. Smaller kids love to run around the flower beds. From spring through fall the city plantings produce spectacular blooms and color.

**BARR LAKE**
13401 Picadilly Rd.
(off I-76), Brighton
303/659-6005              ND
More than 350 bird species flock to the Barr Lake prairie reserve, bird sanctuary, and wildlife refuge at various times throughout the year. You won't need to walk the entire 9-mile trail that circles the lake to see—and hear—some wonderful birds. Start at the Nature Center and walk to the gazebo boardwalk at the lake's south end. From the gazebo, you can sit behind an observation blind and view bald eagles that inhabit a cottonwood across the way. Snowy egrets, cormorants, black-crowned night herons, and great blue herons also nest in the southwest part of the lake. Sitting behind any of the other four observation blinds, you might also see red foxes, badgers, coyotes, deer, and some of the other wildlife that inhabit the area. Hours: Wed–Sun 9–4. Admission: $4/vehicle or a Parks Pass.

*Red Fox at Barr Lake State Park*

**BELLEVIEW PARK**
**W. Belleview Ave. and Huron**
**Englewood**
**303/761-1140             SD**
Big Dry Creek flows through the grassy expanse of Belleview Park. Besides wading in the stream, kids love the space playground that features a former U.S. military plane. Kids can climb in the cockpit and onto the wings. At the park's west end, there is a petting zoo and a miniature train that chugs over a trestle and through a tunnel. Miniature train hours: Tues–Sun 10–5. Admission: 40¢.

**BUTTERFLY PAVILION AND**
**INSECT CENTER**
**6252 W. 104th Ave., Westminster**
**303/469-5441             ND**
Wear brightly colored clothing and move slowly, and a butterfly with wings shining like blue neon lights might just land on your shoulder. Wear perfume, and the possibilities are endless. The 17,000-square-foot Butterfly Pavilion includes a glassed-in rain forest conservatory where butterflies of every imaginable color and shape flutter among rubber trees, bougainvillea, and hibiscus. There is also an insect center with honeybee hives, microscopes, and chrysalis-viewing areas. Hours: Tues–Sun 9–5. Admission: $6.50 adults, $4.50 seniors, $3.50 children ages 4–12.

**CITY PARK**
**Colorado Blvd. and 17th Ave.**
**Pkwy.**
**Denver             CD**
City Park is a great place for kids. Besides being bordered by the Denver Zoo and the Denver Museum of Natural History, there are two playgrounds within the park itself, at the east and west ends. Picnic tables are all over—by the playgrounds, under trees, and at the lily pond in the park's southeast corner.

At Big Lake, between the museum and the Pavilion, you can rent paddleboats, fish off the shore, or just watch the ducks go by (but please don't feed them, begs the Parks and Rec Dept.!). The smaller Duck Lake, to the north, is another favorite spot for duck-watching. There are beautifully maintained tennis courts at

## Top Ten Best Things to Do in Denver
by Jacob Petersen Paul, age 5

1. Climb on rocks
2. Run on grass
3. Follow streams
4. Make things out of pine cones
5. Roll down hills
6. Watch clouds
7. Count ducks and talk to ducks
8. Build a fort with sticks
9. Sing
10. March around in a circle

the park's northwest corner. Denver Parks and Rec offers a summer tennis program for a minimal cost.

For many small children, the park's pièce de résistance is a tree-shaded "canyon" area off a path leading south from the museum. The old City Ditch (Smith's Ditch) that provided water for all Denver in the late 1880s and early 1900s used to wind its way through the boulders here. You and the kids can take a small safari and trace the dry bed of the ditch from the canyon area southwest to where it connects with the small lake just south of Big Lake.

### DENVER BOTANIC GARDENS
**1005 York St., Denver**
**303/331-4000**     **CD**
Talk about a place to run around in! Even during winter months, kids can gallop through the spacious outdoor gardens, over bridges, up hills, and around the beds while you drink in the beauty of the place. The indoor conservatory features a variety of tropical and semi-tropical plants. The gardens sponsor Saturday morning arts and crafts classes for kids.

Hours: Winter daily 9–5; summer Wed–Fri 9–8, Sat–Tues 9–5. Admission: $3 adults, $1.50 students and seniors over 65, $1 children 6–16.

### DENVER ZOO
**City Park**
**2300 Steele St., Denver**
**303/331-4111**     **CD**
You can be 99.9 percent certain your kids will be happy to visit the Denver Zoo. Besides the Children's Zoo, with animals to feed and pet and a covered wagon they can climb on, there are more than 2,500 other animals exhibited in natural settings spread over the zoo's 35 acres. Exhibits include a large primate area, a "cat" house, indoor and outdoor aviaries, enclosures for elephants, giraffes, zebras, black rhinoceros, and more. Chimps swing from tree to tree on Monkey Island, and seals and penguins glide through outdoor streams. You can watch enormous polar bears swimming and playing from above-and-below viewing sites at the Northern Shores exhibit. Clouded leopards, howler monkeys, vampire bats, poison dart frogs, and snakes

*Denver Zoo*

such as the green tree python live in the indoor rain forest at Tropical Discovery. The newest exhibit, Primate Panorama, is a 5-acre facility devoted to the habitat of more than 25 species of primates. Daily feeding times are 2:30 p.m. for sea lions, 10:15 a.m. and 4 p.m. for penguins, and 3:30 p.m. for the big cats. Special events include the "Wild Lights" Christmas display from late November through December and the Summer Safari program for kids. Hours: Mon–Sun 10–5 (admission gate closes at 4). Open year-round, holidays included. Admission: $6 ages 13–61, $3 seniors 62 and over, $3 children 4–12, children 3 and under free.

### OBSERVATORY PARK
**Evans and Fillmore Sts.**
**Denver**     **SD**
Surrounded by a pleasant neighborhood and beautiful homes, Observatory Park is intersected by a street. The area to the south has a great shaded playground, nice bathrooms, and lots of grass. It's easy to keep little kids in sight in this small, contained space. The area to the north houses the University of Denver's dome observatory, open for star-watching on clear nights, and there are also several basketball courts.

### WASHINGTON PARK
**Downing St. and Louisiana Ave.**
**Denver**     **CD**
Another old and spacious Denver park, Washington Park has many features that appeal to kids. A wonderful playground with wooden slides and climbing structures stands near the boathouse—a spot where in-line skaters perform their most daring feats. The two lakes provide duck-watching and boat-floating while more structured play goes on at the south-end tennis courts. There are wide grassy expanses for playing tag, and there is always some kind of fascinating activity to watch while resting up.

## MUSEUMS AND LIBRARIES

### CHILDREN'S MUSEUM
**2121 Children's Museum Dr.**
**Denver**
**303/433-7433**     **CD**
At the Children's Museum, kids can schuss down a plastic bristle-coated ski hill or learn to navigate through the world in a wheelchair. The Science Lab has computers and carpentry tools along with materials for making electricity or testing water pressure. For an intimate look into the natural world, kids can climb into a see-through working beehive. Hands-on exhibits change regularly and there is a children's theater with varying show-times as well. The Children's Museum is in a very pleasant

## Top Ten Places to Take Kids in Denver
by Steve Lass and Diana Poole

Steve and Diana are well qualified to comment on what kids like to do in Denver. Thanks to the couple's 4-year-old triplets, Zack, Sarah, and Sam, this family has sampled every possible way to expend energy within a five-state area.

1. Denver Zoo
2. Denver Museum of Natural History
3. Littleton Historical Museum
4. Butterfly Pavilion
5. Denver Puppet Theater
6. Elitch Gardens
7. Colorado Rockies games at Coors Field
8. Children's Museum
9. Denver Victorian Playhouse
10. Belleview Park

location on the Platte River across from Elitch Gardens. There is a playground outside and picnic tables. Hours: Tues–Sun 10–5 and until 8 the first Friday of the month. Admission: $5 ages 3–5, $2 ages 1–2.

**DENVER ART MUSEUM**
**100 West 14th Ave. Pkwy., Denver**
**303/640-7577**        **DD**
Saturdays are a great day for families at the Denver Art Museum. The first and third Saturday of every month, families meet at the Kids Corner in the main floor lobby for Family Workshops (best for families with kids ages 5–9). Each workshop centers on creative projects relating to particular art exhibits. Every second, fourth, and fifth Saturday, Family Backpacks are available, full of hands-on games and activities to use while touring the galleries. A new museum feature, Art Stops, features custom-designed kits of creative materials on each floor. Interpreters use the kits to help visitors explore the creative process of different mediums on display (beadwork, sculpture, painting, basketry). Call for a schedule of the popular summer art classes. Hours: Family Workshops 11, 12:30, & 2. Museum admission: Free on Saturdays. Family Workshops and Backpacks are free, also.

**DENVER FIREFIGHTERS MUSEUM**
**Fire House No. 1**
**1326 Tremont Pl., Denver**
**303/892-1436**        **DD**
Do you know why Dalmatians are associated with firehouses? The dogs ran alongside the horses that pulled the old fire carriages and sped up their pace. At the scene of the fire, the Dalmatians stood guard over the horses while the firemen battled the flames. To learn more, dash on over

*Children's Pavilion, Denver Public Library*

to the 1909 Fire House No. 1, now the Denver Firefighters Museum, and see Denver's original hand-drawn, horse-drawn, and gasoline-powered firefighting equipment. Tours are for adults and kids alike, but kids get to don boots, jackets, helmets, and oxygen masks, climb in the engines, sound the alarm, put their feet to the stationary pedal, and take off to save the day. Hours: Mon–Fri 10–2. Admission: $2 adults, $1 children.

**DENVER MUSEUM OF NATURAL HISTORY**
**City Park**
**2001 Colorado Blvd., Denver**
**303/322-7009,**
**303/370-6300 for IMAX**     **CD**
The expansive glass-enclosed entrance to the Denver Museum of Natural History sets the stage for the delight and wonderment that kids experience as they explore the museum. The Prehistoric Journey exhibit features full-size dinosaurs and walk-through dioramas of fossils and skeletons. On the second floor, kids can access various hands-on displays about the five senses at the Hall of Life with "credit cards" issued at the exhibit's entry. Life-like dioramas representing different animals in their native environments cover several floors. There are also exhibits of butterflies and insects. The IMAX theater shows films of adventure and the natural world on their huge $4^{1}/_{2}$-story screen. (These can be scary for little kids—check first.) Hours: Daily 9–5. Museum admission: $6 adults, $4 seniors 65 and older, $4 children 3–12. IMAX admission: $5 adults, $4 children and seniors. Planetarium admission: $3.50 adults, $2.50 children and seniors or free with museum admission.

**DENVER PUBLIC LIBRARY**
**Children's Library**
**10 W. 14th Ave. Pkwy., Denver**
**303/640-6384**     **DD**
One of the country's first children's libraries was established in Denver, in

1894. Today, the Denver Public Library continues the tradition with a Children's Library that is not only well stocked for preschoolers to teenagers but is extremely beautiful as well. A stuffed Pooh Bear looks out a window near computers featuring everything from Dr. Seuss books to *The Way Things Work* and access to the Internet. There are cushions and reading nooks everywhere. Special events like magic shows, puppet shows, and story hours take place in The Children's Pavilion, a tower-shaped space surrounded by huge windows overlooking the Civic Center. Hours: Mon–Wed 10–9, Thur–Sat 10–5:30, Sun 1–5.

### LITTLETON HISTORICAL MUSEUM
**6028 S. Gallup St., Littleton**
**303/795-3950                           SD**
Your kids can't imagine a world without Big Macs and electric blankets? Take them to the Littleton Historical Museum, where the family cooks meals in kettles on the hearth and sleeps on straw mattresses in the upstairs loft. The museum is the site of two living history farms, from the 1860s and the 1890s, respectively.

*Annie Zook and her puppets*

Staff and volunteers in authentic costumes invite visitors to join them in a typical day of pioneer life. You can wander through historic farm buildings that include barns, sheds, a blacksmith shop, an ice house, and a schoolhouse. There are chickens, goats, sheep, pigs, Holstein oxen, and Belgian draft horses in the busy farmyard. Be sure to ask lots of questions—the "homesteaders" won't know about french fries, but they will show you how to churn butter and pitch hay! Hours: Tues–Fri 10–5, Sat 10–5, Sun 1–5. Free.

## PUPPETS AND THEATER

### DENVER PUPPET THEATER
**5136 W. 38th Ave. at Irving, Denver**
**303/987-3612 or 303/757-8702    SD**
Puppeteer Annie Zook makes the puppets and writes the stories, based on folk tales and fairy tales, for her one-woman show. The theater stays open a half hour before and a half hour after the performances to give kids a chance to handle the puppets themselves. Kids from 3 to 13 years of age enjoy these engaging puppet shows. Ask about the birthday party packages and the summer puppet camp. Hours: Thur & Fri 10 & 1, Sat 11 & 1, Sun 1. Admission: $3/person over 1 year old.

### DENVER VICTORIAN PLAYHOUSE
**4201 Hooker St., Denver**
**303/433-4343                           WD**
Kids don't just watch Cinderella get pushed around by the wicked stepsisters at the Denver Victorian Playhouse. They go up on stage and help her sweep the cinders into the fireplace so she can get to the ball on time. The playhouse stages dramas, musicals, comedies, and mysteries

## Theater and the Elitch Gardens

*John and Mary Elitch purchased a 17-acre apple orchard at 38th and Tennyson in northwest Denver in 1890. They purchased the land to serve as a home and a garden to support their downtown restaurant, but their dream was to build a theater for first-class productions. John died a year after the purchase, and Mary, who came to be known as the "Lady of the Gardens," developed the site, fulfilling her husband's and her own dream.*

*The picturesque Elitch Theater, with its festive cupola and gingerbread trim, eventually housed the longest-running stock show company in the country. Not only vaudeville and light opera, but dramas—some criticized for the shocking inclusion of "damn" in their dialogue—were featured. Cecile B. DeMille, Douglas Fairbanks, and Grace Kelly began their acting careers at Elitch. Sarah Bernhardt, Frederic March, and Patricia Neal also performed here.*

*Mary helped promote her theater by developing the surrounding gardens and adding a zoo, a miniature railroad, and a steam-powered carousel. Over time, the rides became more popular than the theater. Mary Long, who had married her assistant Thomas Long in 1900, was forced to sell the gardens in 1916 to pay her debts. She had not only established one of Denver's best-loved institutions, but also supported a tradition of classical music and light opera in Denver at a time when the city's tastes were flagging.*

*In the early 1920s, the Trocadero Ballroom was built. Until it closed in 1975, the Trocadero was the epitome of romance in Denver. The most famous bands of the times played here as Denverites swirled across the 15,000-square-foot dance floor imagining they were Ginger Rogers and Fred Astaire. The scent of flowers and the moonlight streaming in the open pavilion made this a place that was magical and, as it turns out, irreplaceable.*

for children, as well as different productions for adults. Individual works may appeal to toddlers, teens, adults, and senior citizens. Call to make reservations. Admission varies with performances.

## THEME PARKS

### ELITCH GARDENS AMUSEMENT PARK
**I-25 and Speer Blvd., Denver**
**303/595-4FUN or 800/ELITCHS**    **CD**

After 104 years of operation in northwest Denver, Elitch Gardens moved to the Central Platte River Valley in downtown Denver in 1995. The 67-acre park features rides like Twister II, a wooden roller coaster, Disaster Canyon, a river rapids ride, and the giant rotating swing, Avalanche. There are also lots of rides for littler kids, like the carousel and bumper cars. The 300-foot-high Total Tower offers 360-degree views of downtown Denver and the Rocky Mountains. The park is very expensive and the flower gardens have yet to take off, but hopefully the new Elitch will restore the charm and ambiance of the old park in time. Open May 26 to November 2. Hours: Sun–Thur 10–10, Fri & Sat 10–11. Admission: $23.95 adults, $12.95 children 3–7, $15.95 seniors 55–69, seniors 70 and older free.

### LAKESIDE AMUSEMENT PARK
**4601 Sheridan Blvd.**
**(I-70 and Sheridan), Denver**
**303/477-1621**    **WD**

With all the hoopla over the new Elitch's, you might think there was no alternative. Lakeside is a very pleasant park that sits next to Lake Rhoda. Its nationally renowned roller coaster can be seen from I-70 traveling west

*Lakeside Amusement Park*

to the mountains. Established in 1912, Lakeside offers a variety of rides to terrify and/or delight the visitor. Kiddie Playland features its own miniature roller coaster and a pond with remote-controlled boats. Admission: Gate, $1.50 per person over 2 years old. Unlimited rides, Mon–Fri $9.75 and Sat–Sun $11.25. Hours: Open weekends in May; open 7 days/week June–Labor Day; main park open Mon–Fri 6 p.m.–11 p.m., Sat and Sun noon–11 p.m.; Kiddie Playland open Mon–Fri 1 p.m.–10 p.m. and Sat and Sun noon–11 p.m.

## STORES FOR KIDS

### THE BOOKIES
**4315 E. Mississippi Ave., Denver**
**303/759-1117**    **ED**

"Sometimes a person needs a story more than food to keep alive." That's the motto at The Bookies. The adapted quote from author Barry Lopez embodies the vision that has kept

## Top Ten Things for Older Kids To Do in Denver
by Alyssa Tweed, age 9

Alyssa Tweed is president of her fifth grade class at Stedman Elementary School in northeast Denver. Alyssa and her classmates suggest a few more fun things to do in Denver from the older kid's point of view.

1. Elitch Gardens Amusement Park
2. Skate City Aurora, I-225 and 6th Ave., Aurora, 303/344-3321. There are two other indoor roller-skating rinks in Metro Denver: Skate City Littleton and Skate City Meadowood. Hours: Sat 10–10. Admission: $3 until noon (adults free); $3.25 noon–6; $3.75 6–10. Skate rental included.
3. Evergreen Lake Ice Skating, Evergreen Recreation Center, Highway 74, Evergreen, 303/674-2677. Admission: $1.75 adults, $1.25 youths 5–18, 50¢ kids under 5. Skate rental available.
4. Swimming—try your neighborhood recreation center. There are nice pools at the Washington Park Recreation Center, the East Denver YMCA, and the Golden Recreation Center, to name a few.
5. Sports events. The Rockies, Broncos, Nuggets, and now the Zephyrs all provide great sports entertainment.
6. Sports leagues. Join a soccer, basketball, or baseball league.
7. Visit a pet store, such as one of the 14 Pet City shops in Metro Denver.
8. Go to a park. City Park by the Denver Zoo and the Denver Museum of Natural History is one of the best.
9. Children's Museum. The News Room, where you try out being a part of the newscast team, is my favorite.
10. Go to the movies!

the store a vibrant Denver institution for over 20 years. The Bookies has 48,000 children's titles, a large selection of teacher resource books, and some adult fiction. A newsletter publishes Bookies' schedule of events, such as teacher workshops and programs by visiting children's authors. Hours: Mon–Sat 10–6, Sun 12–5.

**FAO SCHWARTZ**
3000 E. 1st Ave., #136, Denver
303/333-5100                    CD
Things are never dull at this Cherry Creek Mall toy store, where stuffed giraffes and monkeys hang from a ceiling-high tree and electric trains toot along tracks winding through beeping and gyrating displays. Wear earplugs while your kids luxuriate in this "toy heaven." Hours: Mon–Fri 10–9, Sat 10–7, Sun 11–6.

**KAZOO & COMPANY**
2930 E. 2nd Ave., Denver
303/322-0973                    CD
Ever since Beth Griffiths opened her Cherry Creek store in 1981, both kids and adults have loved the place. Kazoo & Company features well-made, durable "toys that play with the imagination," and that means no Nintendos live here. Instead, there are kits for making your own books or jewelry, telescopes, building blocks, stuffed animals, and innovative games. Kids can register for the Birthday Club and get a coupon toward the toy of their dreams. Hours: Mon–Fri 10–6, Sat 10–5:30, Sun 12–5:30.

**TARGET STORES**
4301 E. Virginia Ave., Denver
303/399-0890                    CD
For one-stop shopping and good deals on everything from diapers to snacks, clothes, games, and toys, Target is a good bet. There are 12 stores throughout the metro area. Hours: Daily 8 a.m.–10 p.m.

**THE WIZARD'S CHEST**
230 Fillmore St., Denver
303/321-4304                    CD
Located in its own magic castle in Cherry Creek, The Wizard's Chest is filled with games and gadgets that young to old to very old kids enjoy. The young staff loves showing you how everything works. There is one whole floor of costumes. Hours: Mon–Fri 10–8, Sat 10–5:30, Sun 12–5:30.

## RESTAURANTS KIDS LOVE

**GRISANTI'S CASUAL ITALIAN RESTAURANT**
4100 E. Mexico Ave., Denver
303/782-5170                    ED
Kids get balloons and talk to the chefs while kneading their own pizza dough at this family restaurant. Entrees include spaghetti, pizzas, calzones, and seafood. There are locations in Aurora, Arvada, and Englewood. Hours: Mon–Fri 11–10, Sat & Sun 11–11.

**LIKS ICE CREAM AND FROZEN YOGURT**
2039 E. 13th Ave. at Vine St.
Denver
303/321-1492                    CD
Liks offers super-premium ice cream and frozen yogurt in every imaginable flavor. Unless there's a snowstorm, the outdoor patio is packed with lip-smacking clientele most weekends throughout the year. Hours: Winter daily 6 a.m.–10 p.m., summer daily 6 a.m.–11 p.m..

**OLD SPAGHETTI FACTORY**
1215 18th St., Denver
303/295-1864                    DD
Housed in a historic cable car building in downtown Denver, the Old Spaghetti Factory offers pasta dishes at very reasonable prices. Hours: Mon–Thur 11:30–2 for lunch, 5–10 for dinner; Fri & Sat 5–11; Sun 4–10.

# 7

# MUSEUMS AND GALLERIES

An appreciation for beauty has characterized many Denverites since the city began. The empty, sun-filled plains with the gorgeous mountains behind attracted settlers who brought imagination, vigor, and wonder to their harsh and seemingly limitless environment.

Present-day Denver museums and galleries reflect this same dynamic spirit and inventiveness. You will find every type of art from the decorative to the provocative and even outrageous in this welcoming, laid-back city. Do not necessarily expect traditional, western themes. The plains seem to inspire all sorts of unpredictable and wonderful creations.

## ART MUSEUMS

### DENVER ART MUSEUM
**100 West 14th Ave. Pkwy., Denver**
**303/640-4433**     **DD**
Another century-old Denver institution, the Denver Art Museum (DAM) has occupied the striking I. M. Pei–designed building off the Civic Center since 1971. The museum's six floors feature collections of native and Asian arts, architecture, modern and contemporary paintings and sculpture, and pre-Columbian and Spanish Colonial arts. The "Art of the Americas collection" is especially renowned.

DAM has a fresh and exciting look since reopening in fall 1997. A new entrance on Acoma Street provides easy access to the spacious and well-priced parking lots across the street. The ground-level restaurant, Palettes, offers inventive cuisine in a glassed-in space overlooking the Acoma Plaza and di Suvero's striking red sculpture, *Lao Tzu*. Outside the new Adventures and Arts education center off the 14th Street entrance, Montana artist Deborah Butterfield's life-size bronze horses graze in the Kemper Courtyard. On the museum's sixth floor, the Euopean and American galleries now

*Denver Art Museum*

display artwork by theme instead of chronologically.

DAM sponsors annual shows and competitions featuring regional artists and hosts an outstanding array of touring exhibitions. A Toulouse Lautrec exhibit will take place from April 10 to July 4, 1999. Special educational features of DAM include "Art Stops," custom-designed kits with touchable materials available at each floor and holiday "Adventure Backpacks," a series of hands-on games and activities offered throughout the museum. "Choice Tour" is a free 45-minute introduction to the DAM collections offered daily at 1:30 p.m. Hours: Tues–Sat 10–5, until 9 on Wed, Sun 12–5, closed Mon and major holidays. Admission: $4.50 adults, $2.50 seniors and students, children 5 and under free. Free admission every Sat.

## MIZEL MUSEUM OF JUDAICA
560 S. Monaco Pkwy., Denver
303/333-4156　　　　　　ED

The Mizel Museum of Judaica celebrates Jewish heritage through paintings, photographs, sculpture, glass, quilting, and many other mediums. Traveling exhibitions as well as the work of regional artists are featured. Exhibits such as "Mediums of Remembrance," featuring works inspired by the Holocaust, "Intimate Portraits: Colorado Jewish Women, 1860-1960," and "Cultural Threads: Ceremonial Textiles Around the World," not only reflect the Jewish experience but also testify to all peoples who have survived oppression. "Bridges of Understanding" is a Mizel Museum program that celebrates the similarities and differences among all the ethnic/religious groups living in Colorado. Hours: Mon–Fri 10–4, Sun 12–4. Free admission.

*Frida Kahlo,* Self-Portrait with Monkey

## MUSEO DE LAS AMERICAS
**861 Santa Fe Dr., Denver**
**303/571-4401**     **CD**

During his internship at the Denver Art Museum, José Aguayo saw the need for an artistic and cultural forum for Denver's Hispanic community. Under Aguayo's leadership, the Museo de las Americas opened in 1991. Many different people from Denver's artistic, historic-preservation, and business communities came together to support the effort. The Museo is located in the heart of a Latino neighborhood that is sprouting new businesses, shops, and cultural offerings.

"Pinturerías: The Art of the Art of the Bullfight," "Eppie Archuleta: Master Weaver of the San Luis Valley," and "Nuestros Artistas," featuring 19 of Colorado's best-known Latino artists are but a few of the exhibits that have attracted thousands of visitors to the intimate and appealing gallery space. Traveling exhibits change every few months, and the Museo's own permanent collection of paintings, ex-votos, and retablos is expanding. The Museo de las Americas is fast becoming one of Denver's most vibrant cultural institutions. Hours: Tue–Sat 10–5. Admission: $3 adults, $2 seniors, and $1 students, children under 10 and members are free.

## ROCKY MOUNTAIN QUILT MUSEUM
**1111 Washington Ave., Golden**
**303/277-0377**     **WD**

The pattern "Hands All Around" is the symbol for the Rocky Mountain Quilt Museum, where more than 120 quilts are on display. Golden resident, quilter, and quilt collector Eugenia Mitchell donated the bulk of the permanent collection. The museum is run largely by volunteers who try to convey the spirit of the old-fashioned quilting bee, where together much can be accomplished and much shared. In addition to presenting six quilt exhibits each year, the museum has a reference library and offers classes for beginning to advanced quilters. Hours: Tues–Sat 10–4. Admission: Members, free; non-members, $2. *(Note: Not shown on maps in this chapter.)*

# SCIENCE AND HISTORY MUSEUMS

## BLACK AMERICAN WEST MUSEUM AND HERITAGE CENTER
**3091 California St., Denver**
**303/292-2566**     **CD**

Did you know that one out of three cowboys was black, or that one of the first discoveries of gold was by a black miner in Idaho Springs? The Black American West Museum is a treasure trove of photographs, mem-

*Navarre Building*

## The Lady Doctor

The beautiful Victorian structure that houses the Black American West Museum was the home and office of Dr. Justina Ford, the first African American woman doctor in the state of Colorado. Dr. Ford arrived in Denver in 1902 with a degree from Hering Medical College in Chicago. Because of her race and gender, she was denied access to area hospitals. Despite the discrimination she suffered, Ford established a practice in gynecology, obstetrics, and pediatrics out of her home. The museum displays the office with the original furnishings and medical equipment that Ford used. "The Lady Doctor," as she was lovingly called, delivered more than 7,000 babies from her home office.

---

orabilia, books, attire, and artifacts documenting the experience and contributions of African Americans who settled the West. It is one of the few places in town where both children and adults will find equal enjoyment, browsing and marveling at the colorful and well-displayed exhibits.

Check out the display of jazz in Denver from the 1890s on with photos of Duke Ellington, Count Basie, and Jimmy Lunsford at the Rossonian Hotel and Lounge. And don't miss the saddle that belonged to O. J. Jackson, founder of the all-black settlement of Dearfield, Colorado. The museum's originator and director, Paul Stewart, relates stories and details about his collections that will enhance your visit. Hours: Mon–Fri 10–5, Sat & Sun 12–5. Admission: $3 adults, $2 seniors, $1 youth 13–17, 50¢ children, tots under 3 are free.

**COLORADO HISTORY MUSEUM**
1399 Broadway, Denver
303/866-3681       **DD**
For 115 years, the Colorado History Museum has provided collections and exhibits documenting life in Colorado and the West, both past and present. A trip to the modern museum building, just across from the Denver Public Library, affords the visitor glimpses into the lives of the Native Americans who first lived

*Paul Stewart*
*Black American West Museum*

in Colorado, miners who came in search of gold, and legendary figures such as Silver King H. A. W. Tabor and his wife, Baby Doe. The new "*La Gente:* Hispanos in Colorado" exhibit explores Hispano history and culture in Colorado. "Buffalo Soldiers West" tells the story of the black soldiers who came to settle in the West after the Civil War. Displays include the work of famous Western photographers such as William Henry Jackson, dioramas, apparel, mining equipment, and even an old sod house. Permanent exhibits include the "Cheyenne Dog Soldiers," a unique look at this division of the Cheyenne Nation, and "Colorado's Window to the Past," an exhibit that allows visitors to peer through a glass wall into a storage room housing the museum's wide variety of collections. Hours: Mon–Sat 10–4:30, Sun 12–4:30.

Tyrannosaurus rex *in the Natural History Musuem*

## DENVER MUSEUM OF NATURAL HISTORY
City Park, 2001 Colorado Blvd.
Denver
303/322-7009
303/370-6300 for IMAX         CD

How would you like to meet Tyrannosaurus Rex, watch mice playing basketball, and view the stars all in one stop? The Denver Museum of Natural History, with its planetarium, IMAX theater, and permanent and traveling exhibits, appeals to all ages. There are wildlife dioramas, gem and mineral exhibits, and butterfly collections. The "Hall of Life" exhibit offers a hands-on journey through the body and the five senses. Special exhibits such as "Prehistoric Journey" have received rave reviews nationwide. IMAX theater presents a slate of films on its giant 4$^1$/$_2$- by 6$^1$/$_2$-story screen that immerse the viewer in a wide range of outdoor adventures. Gates Planetarium can take you to the stars through its powerful Minolta Series IV Star Projector, which creates images of over 8,500 stars and star clusters. The Coors Mineral Hall looks at geologic history and includes the Sweet Home Rhodochrosite Pocket—a reconstructed wall of rhodochrosite crystals originally found in Alma, Colorado. Museum hours: Daily 9–5. Museum admission: $6 adults, $4 children 3–12, $2 seniors 65 and older. IMAX admission: $5 adults, $4 children and seniors. Planetarium admission: $3.50 adults, $2.50 children and seniors or free with museum admission.

## WINGS OVER THE ROCKIES AVIATION AND SPACE MUSEUM
7750 E. Irvington Pl., Denver
303/360-5360         ED

Housed in Hangar 1 of the now-closed Lowery Air Force Base, Wings

Over the Rockies fills the cavernous 5-acre space with a collection of 21 airplanes restored by pilots and mechanics who served in World War II. On view are everything from a B-1A Stealth bomber to an H-21C "Flying Banana" helicopter, a one-man glider, and a space station module. Check the museum for the Open Cockpit Days when kids—and their adults—can climb in the planes and pretend to fly their own missions. Enthusiastic volunteers, mostly former pilots and mechanics, are on hand to help. To reach the museum, enter the former base through the 1st Avenue gate, then travel east on Irvington Place to Hangar 1. Hours: Mon–Sat 10–4, Sun 12–4. Admission: $4 adults, $2 children 6–17 and seniors 60 and over, children 5 and under free.

## ART GALLERIES

**CAMERA OBSCURA GALLERY**
**1309 Bannock St., Denver**
**303/623-4059** DD

Camera Obscura's director, Hal Gould, has exhibited photographs on this same corner, across from the Denver Art Museum, since 1963. Gould pioneered acceptance of photography as an art form from the time the Denver Art Museum would not allow a photograph on their walls. Ask to see Gould's remarkable collection of photographs by artists Paul Strand, Edward Weston, and William H. Jackson. The changing exhibits of vintage and contemporary photographs are always superb. Hours: Tues–Sat 10–6, Wed until 8, Sun 1–5.

**DAVID COOK/FINE AMERICAN ART**
**1637 Wazee St., Denver**
**303/623-8181** DD

Located next door to the Oxford Hotel in LoDo, David Cook's gallery specializes in historic Native American art, Colorado paintings, and Arts & Crafts furniture. Plains beadwork, Navajo textiles, Pueblo pottery, baskets, jewelry, and New Mexican art are displayed. The gallery buys and sells collections and offers appraisals,

---

## Galleries Galore

*Denver has so many fine galleries, it is hard to mention them all. Some of the more traditional galleries in Denver, featuring works by nationally and internationally recognized artists, are the Knox Galleries, the Carson Gallery, Gallery One, Mudhead Gallery, and Saks Galleries. Galleries specializing in alternative and contemporary works include the pioneering Pirate Contemporary Art Oasis along with the newer Zip, Edge, and Hyphen-8. The Bug sponsors video works and performance art.*

# Top Public Art Works in Denver
by Denver documentary filmmaker Mary Jones,
member of the 1996 Alliance For Contemporary Art (AFCA),
and her fellow board members

1. **Davies Chuck Wagon Diner** and **Horse Sculpture**, 9495 W. Colfax Ave., Lakewood. This 48-ton prefabricated diner was shipped intact to Denver from a New Jersey manufacturer in 1957. Individual jukeboxes grace every table and a 10-foot cowboy points to the plaster horse sitting over the entry of the silver structure.
2. **Herbert Bayer sculpture**, I-25 & S. Broadway. The bright yellow sculpture by the Austrian-born Bauhaus master can be seen from I-25. Part of the Denver Art Museum's collection, it stands at the south end of the light rail line, in front of the Buckhorn Exchange Restaurant.
3. **Tony Ortega**, *Juntos/Together*, 1991; 10th and Osceola. Hand-set porcelain tile mural.
4. **Art at Coors Field**. Art installations at Coors Field. Perhaps the most visible is *Evolution of the Ball* by Lonnie Hanzon. The free-standing ceramic tile archway is on the west side of the stadium.
5. **Red Grooms sculpture**, Denver Art Museum (DAM). The portrayal of American Indians attacking a covered wagon did not sit well with residents of the Lawrence Street Apartments when the commissioned piece landed in their courtyard. Native American groups didn't care much for the sculpture, either. After it was scuttled unceremoniously from one location to another, DAM finally took the sculpture under its wing.
6. **Kenneth Snelson**, *Soft Landing*, 1982; 1225 17th St. (17th St. Plaza Bldg.)
7. **Harry Bertoia**, *Sounding Sculpture*, 1976; 17th and Curtis (Ideal Plaza)
8. ***The World is a Stage***, 721 Santa Fe Dr., on the south wall of the Denver Civic Theater. This colorful mural was created by Denver artists and school children in memory of Enrique Montoya.
9. **Martha Keating** and **Bob Luna**, *Neighborhood Epic*, 1994; 20th St. Viaduct (Highlands neighborhood west of I-25). The porcelain tile mosaic with hand-fired ceramic tiles is mounted on the viaduct walls across the street from Our Lady of Guadalupe Church. The ten mosaics depict different stages in Denver history, starting with dinosaurs, and include the different ethnic groups who contributed to Denver's growth as a city.
10. **Mark di Suvero**, *Lao Tzu*, Acoma Plaza between the Denver Art Museum and the public library. This 18-ton painted steel sculpture, a new installation, is part of the DAM's permanent collection.

restorations, and consulting. Hours: Mon–Sat 10:30–6, Sun 12–5 (call to confirm Sunday hours).

### ELIZABETH SCHLOSSER FINE ART
311 Detroit St., Denver
303/321-4786　　　　　　　　CD
At the intimate and accessible Schlosser gallery, you will find museum quality nineteenth- and twentieth-century art. Paintings, watercolors, pastels, and prints by artists including Charles Partridge Adams, Birger Sandzen, and Frank Mischau are displayed. There is also a fine selection of estate jewelry and antiques. Hours: Tues–Sat 12–5.

### MOSADI'S COLLECTIONS
624 E. 17th Ave., Denver
303/863-0700　　　　　　　　CD
As you enter the gallery owned by the very warm and vibrant Ernest Bonner, prepare yourself for a world unto itself. Jazz music drifts through the beautifully restored four-story home that houses an outstanding collection of artworks by Haitian, Caribbean, African, and African American artists. Mosadi's has artwork from 43 nationally and internationally recognized artists, but the gallery represents 150 in all.

### 1/1 GALLERY
1058 Delware St., Denver
303/893-2360　　　　　　　　DD
1/1 is a gallery as unique and intriguing as its name. Among the eclectic collection of artworks showcased are Merv Lapin's Chinese peasant paintings; ink wash pieces by An Yun Peng, curator of the Jilin Public Art Museum; fiber and bead jewelry by Sharon Wenzel; and the lively, often whimsical paintings, prints, and watercolors of Denver artist Patty Cramer. Call for hours.

### OLD MAP GALLERY
1746 Blake St., Denver
303/296-7725
www.oldmapgallery.com
This gallery in lower downtown takes visitors back to times long forgotten and almost unrecognizable. The map connoiseur and history buff alike will find endless treasures—from maps of the California gold rush, Africa in the mid-1800s, William Tecumseh Sherman's Civil War marches, and eighteenth-century Cyprus to maritime atlases. Shoppers can browse through the gallery's catalog on-line.

### PISMO CONTEMPORARY ART GLASS
235 Fillmore St., Denver
303/333-2879　　　　　　　　CD
PISMO's features glass wall sculptures, vases, and jewelry by local and international artists including Dale Chihuly. There is an extremely wide price range at this glittering and glowing gallery. PISMO Art Furniture, a few blocks away, offers furniture either painted or carved from natural woods by local artists. Handmade one-of-a-kind accessories are also displayed. Hours for both galleries: Mon–Sat 10–6, Sun 11–5.

### ROBISCHON GALLERY
1740 Wazee St., Denver
303/298-7788　　　　　　　　DD
Expect the unexpected at the Robischon Gallery, but rest assured that you will see high-quality, provocative artwork. For 20 years, this gallery has shown the work of contemporary artists—focusing on the Rocky Mountain region, but also including established and emerging artists from across the country. The adventurous collector will find timeless and enduring art

at Robischon's. Hours: Tues–Fri 10–6, Sat 11–5.

**RULE MODERN & CONTEMPORARY**
111 Broadway, Denver
303/777-9473                                    CD
Robin Rule likes the strong, graphic statements that underlie her design background. The Rule gallery specializes in modern and contemporary painting, sculpture, and photography, with an emphasis on abstraction. Dale Chisman, Lawrence Argent, and Jeff Starr are only a few of the regional artists featured at this up-and-coming art venue.

**SANDY CARSON GALLERY**
1734 Wazee St., Denver
303/297-8585                                    DD
Providing consulting services for businesses, corporations, designers, and private collectors, the 20-year-old Sandy Carson Gallery has a vast selection of quality artwork by regional and national artists. Contemporary canvases, works on paper, ceramics, glass, and furniture are available.

**SAVAGEAU GALLERY**
2230 E. Colfax Ave., Denver
303/355-6101                                    CD
A maverick artistic beacon at his York and E. Colfax location, Steve Savageau specializes in nineteenth- and early twentieth-century art, with an emphasis on the work (especially vintage work) of Coloradan artists. The representative of many prominent Coloradan family estates, the Savageau Gallery also offers fine framing services.

---

## More Public Art

New works signal efforts to make Denver a "City of Sculpture." Three of most exciting are:

- Jonathan Borofsky's Sculpture Park at the Denver Performing Arts Complex. The Denver Art, Culture, and Film Foundation commissioned the artist to create 60-foot-tall whimsical dancing figures. The sculptures should be installed by the year 2000.
- Donald Lipski's The Yearling, 14th Avenue Parkway outside the children's wing of the Denver Public Library. A 20-foot-tall red chair with a life-sized palomino perched on top.
- Fernando Botero's Man and Woman. On loan from the Marlboro Gallery in New York, the two sculptures reside in Denver temporarily. The Kemper Family Foundation is offering $100,000 in matching funds in hopes of keeping the world-class sculptures in town.

# 8
# PARKS AND GARDENS

*Due largely to the vision of several early mayors, Denver is filled with green parks, tree-lined parkways, and towering statues and monuments. Mayor Joseph Bates first insisted the city needed parks in an 1872 inaugural address. In 1874, William Byers, editor of the* Rocky Mountain News, *wrote that Denver would not be a perfect city until "a public park is provided like Central Park on Manhattan Island." Then came Robert Speer, the man most credited for starting Denver's park and parkway system. Before he was elected mayor, Speer attended the 1893 Chicago Exposition. He returned with dreams of turning the hastily designed Denver into a "City Beautiful" modeled after ideas presented at the exposition.*

*Speer had his work cut out for him. He had to convince the majority of citizens, politicians, and business people that creating aesthetically pleasing open space was as important as building a warehouse or commercial building. The idea of a city purchasing open space just to keep it open seemed ludicrous to many.*

*Nonetheless, as soon as Denver elected Speer mayor in 1904, he put his plans in motion. The mayor developed previous plans to connect each of the city's parks by long, green parkways, as well as encouraged Denver's elite to donate money for civic sculpture—the renowned "Give While You Live" campaign. While not all of his dreams were realized, strong elements of his grand plan still dominate the city's landscape today.*

*Cheesman Park*

## DENVER AREA PARKS

### CHEESMAN PARK
**8th Ave. and High, Denver    CD**
Cheesman Park was established in 1892 on an 80.7-acre rectangle that was formerly Denver's first cemetery. Vincent Scully, a prominent Yale University art historian, has described Cheesman as one of the country's finest urban spaces. Denverites, who pack the park year-round, agree. The Greek-style Cheesman Memorial Pavilion, donated in memory of Walter Cheesman by his wife and daughter, presides over the park to the east. Architects designed the marble monument with Tuscan columns and pillars, pavilions at either end, and a Doric frieze. The Parthenonlike structure is a popular meeting and sunset-viewing spot. Frisbee and volleyball games pack the park, located west of the Denver Botanic Gardens, in warm weather.

### CITY PARK
**17th Ave. Parkway and Colorado Blvd., Denver    CD**
Mayor Richard Sopris, sometimes referred to as the father of City Park, started in 1881 to transform the northeast Denver park from a sagebrush tract into a picturesque garden. Today, City Park is an oasis of rose gardens, huge trees, lakes, and classical architecture. Dog walkers and exercisers circle the "Big Lake" path and race through the park on quiet streets blocked off from traffic year-round. Local musicians drum in the historic bandstand on the lake's

---

**TIP**

The Colorado Symphony Orchestra performs summer concerts in Washington, City, and Sloan's Lake Parks. Call the symphony or check the local newspapers for dates.

west shore. A resurgence of activity around the Pavilion has occurred since the city completed restorations on the nineteenth-century structure in 1995. A horseshoe pit lies next to the park tennis courts in the northwest corner. During the summer months, a concessionaire rents colorful paddleboats on Big Lake. The busy east end of City Park holds the popular Denver Museum of Natural History and the Denver Zoo. Heavy traffic and parking lot space make the area less appealing, but the museum's west entrance affords spectacular sunsets and city views.

## CRANMER PARK
**3rd and Clermont, Denver          ED**
During George E. Cranmer's tenure as Manager of Parks and Improvements, he developed Mountain View Park—literally in his own front yard. The 23-acre site, which was later renamed Cranmer Park, includes a sundial and flagstone mountain-viewing deck. Peakfinders lining the mosaic mountain panorama point to sites including Red Rocks Park, Longs Peak, and the Central City Opera House. The 7-foot equatorial sundial, completed in 1941 by engineer S. A. Ionides, was destroyed by vandals in 1965. Local school children raised money for the reproduction that stands on the Cranmer Park Terrace today.

## GENESEE PARK
**I-70 and Genesee Exit, Denver WD**
A small herd of bison was transported from Wyoming's Yellowstone Park to Genesee Park outside of Denver in 1914. At the time, fewer than 600 bison existed in the United States. The move was intended to protect the endangered species by dispersing the populations. People can view the rare Genesee herd roaming its 1,000-acre home anytime of the year. During the winter, the city feeds the bison on the north side of I-70 every

City Park Pavilion

> ### Wynken, Blynken and Nod
>
> Mayor Robert Speer commissioned the Wynken, Blynken and Nod sculpture that is now located on the east side of Washington Park. Colorado sculptor Mabel Landrum Torrey created the sculpture in honor of the Eugene Field poem "The Dutch Lullaby." Field was well loved in Denver. In addition to writing beloved children's poems, Field was also known as a practical joker. One of his better-known jokes stemmed from a delayed Oscar Wilde trip to Denver. When Field heard that the famous playwright's train was late, he dressed up a Denver Tribune editor as a Wilde look-alike and paraded him around town. Other jokes centered around the opera. Field was not a fan of H. A. W. Tabor or of opera stars such as Sarah Bernhardt who performed at the Tabor Opera House. He used to tie strings to curtain-call bouquets so they could be pulled back from the performers.

morning. The 30-count herd roams back and forth between the south, middle, and north pastures in the summer. Take I-70 west to the Genesee Exit to reach the viewing area on the south side of I-70. The city keeps another herd of 30 bison in Daniels Park, on Castle Pines Parkway.

**SLOAN'S LAKE PARK**
**17th Ave. and Sheridan, Denver**
**WD**
Although a sprawling view of the downtown Denver skyline opens from Sloan's Lake Park, the city's humming center seems a million miles away. The park, located 5 miles west of downtown, is a peaceful haven for the surrounding community. A running trail circles the large lake, and soccer fields, picnic tables, and playgrounds fill the grassy open space. The park serves as a good entry point for people exploring historic northwest Denver. A silver torpedo on the southwest shore of Sloan's Lake commemorates WWII submarine veterans. Getting there: Take Colfax west to Sheridan, then right on Sheridan two blocks to 17th Avenue. Right on 17th into park.

**WASHINGTON PARK**
**Louisiana Ave. and**
**Downing St., Denver         CD**
South Denver's Washington Park is the city's answer to San Francisco's Golden Gate Park. It's where many locals go to run, bike, rollerblade, play tennis, and picnic. The 160-acre park was designed in 1899 on land that was originally pure prairie. Mayor Robert Speer's administration brought in sand from Cherry Creek and water from the City Ditch to turn the Washington Park lake area into Denver's first beach in 1912. The historic Bathhouse and Boathouse, both recently renovated, stand guard

Wynken, Blynken and Nod, Washington Park

around Smith Lake as a reminder of these earlier times. Most of the park's streets are closed to vehicle traffic, so there is plenty of room for pedestrian traffic.

## Gardens

**DENVER BOTANIC GARDENS**
1005 York St., Denver
303/331-4000                    CD

The Denver Botanic Gardens treats visitors to a myriad of authentic international garden displays. A tea house built in Japan completes the Japanese Garden of Pine Wind. The humid tropical conservatory has the brilliant color and heady smell of a Hawaiian rain forest. The Plains Garden is a reminder of what pre-developed Denver vegetation looked like. The Romantic Gardens, the newest addition to the grounds, takes visitors to a tranquil world of aromatic cottage gardens and gently spilling waterfalls. The Gardens holds summer jazz, world music, and dance concerts in its outdoor amphitheater.

---

## Monumental Civic Pride

*Some of Denver's finest monuments were commissioned for placement in City Park. The Sullivan Gateway, located at the Colfax and Esplanade entrance, is one of the more spectacular. Leo Lentelli sculpted two 40-foot-high pylons to represent the major factors in Colorado's economic development: mining and agriculture. Joseph Addison Thatcher donated $100,000 in 1918 to build Thatcher Memorial at the southern 17th and Esplanade park entrance. The fountain features a figure of liberty surrounded by three L's—learning, loyalty, and love. Ed Rose's 1976 Martin Luther King, Jr. statue stands west of the Pavilion. Although awaited with great anticipation, community members greeted the statue's unveiling with criticism, claiming it portrayed the great civil rights leader more as a caricature than an important man.*

Plan to arrive at least an hour before the shows to find hillside seating with a good view. Hours: Daily 9–5, except May–Sept, when the gardens are open until 8 Tues–Sat. Admission: Oct–Apr $3 adults, $1.50 seniors and children 6-16; May–Sept $4 adults, $2 seniors and children; children under 5 always free.

**HUDSON GARDENS**
**2888 W. Maplewood Ave., Littleton**
**303/797-8565** SD
Until June 1996, the Denver Botanic Gardens had little, if any, competition. In comes the grand 30-acre Hudson Gardens. Under the guidance of renowned master horticulturist Andrew Pierce, the Gardens made the Littleton desert bloom with 16 distinct regional gardens. The displays, such as the Fragrance, Rose, Butterfly Bank, Conifer Grove, and Wetland Gardens, feature plants that grow naturally in Colorado. More than 7,500 flowers fill the Oval Garden alone. The Gardens also hope to fill an education niche by offering water-use and gardening education programs. Hours: Wed–Sun 10–dusk. Admission: May–Sept $4 adults, $3 seniors over 60, $2 children 6–16; Oct–Apr $3 adults, $2 seniors, $1.50 children.

*State Parks and Recreation Areas*

When Denverites feel like going to the beach, they head to one of the local state parks. Cherry Creek, Chatfield, Barr Lake, and Aurora State Parks are recreational oases. Any of the state parks can be an easy family day trip. There is a $5 per vehicle fee to enter the parks.

**AURORA RESERVOIR**

## Top Ten Park Views
### by Rod Lister, Denver Parks and Recreation

1. City Park, view from the west steps of the Denver Museum of Natural History
2. Daniels Park, view from the picnic shelter
3. Inspiration Point Park
4. Cheesman Park, view from the Pavilion
5. Genesee Park, view from the Genesee Mountain Summit
6. Ruby Hill Park, view from the summit
7. Cranmer Park, view from the mountain-viewing terrace
8. Red Rocks Park, view from the top of the amphitheater
9. Sloan's Lake Park, view from the west side of lake
10. Buffalo Bill's Grave on Lookout Mountain

## The City Ditch

*The city of Denver bought the City Ditch, a 27-mile irrigation canal, in 1875 to bring water into the thirsty city. Water in the gravity-flow ditch, the precursor to modern Denver's water system, flowed from Chatfield Dam north to City Park's "Big Lake." The City Ditch, or Smith Ditch as it was also called, after its early designer John W. Smith, filled both Washington Park lakes, irrigated homes around the Denver Country Club, and eventually ended in City Park. Residents watered yards, flower beds, gardens, and trees by tapping into the main ditch. More than 1,000 miles of smaller canals were diverted from the City Ditch by the 1930s. Without this early irrigation system, arid Denver would never have become the green city it is today. The ditch allowed landscape architects to transplant eastern pine, junipers, Carolina poplars, and red oaks throughout the city. All of the small tributary ditches were filled in by 1935 after children playing in the water came down with typhoid fever. Today, only the Washington Park section, a peaceful stream running through the park, runs above ground. The City Ditch is the oldest part of the Denver Parks system and was designated a Denver Landmark in 1977.*

**5800 S. Powhaton Rd., Aurora**
**303/690-1286 or 303/766-0020**
**(wind information)**     **ED**
The local sailing community welcomed peaceful Aurora Reservoir with open arms. Sailors love the reservoir's consistent winds and the noticeable absence of loud motorboats. The park allows only electric motors on the water. Scuba divers can explore the Cessna aircraft sunken in 20 feet of water off the northeast shore. An 8.5-mile paved bike path circling the reservoir is a good place to view summer storms passing in from the Front Range. The reservoir also offers picnic areas, concession stands, and boat rentals and lessons. Park hours: Dawn to dusk.

**CHATFIELD STATE PARK**
**11500 N. Roxborough Park Rd.**
**Littleton**
**303/791-7275**     **SD**
The U.S. Army Corps of Engineers began construction of the Chatfield Dam in 1967 after a South Platte River flood caused considerable damage and concern in the surrounding residential area. The result is a 5,600-acre recreation area in the southwest corner of Metro Denver. The reservoir is divided into separate boating, sailing, swimming, fishing, and water skiing areas. Bird

## The Park People

*The Park People is an all-volunteer organization that carries on the vital tradition of developing, enhancing, and maintaining Denver's parks. Since 1966, the Park People has endowed Denver with trees and restored Civic Center monuments, park pavilions, fountains, playgrounds, historic sites, and countless other treasures. The headquarters for the Park People is in the Eugene Field house in Washington Park. To become a member or for more information, call 303/722-6262. Or write the Park People at 715 S. Franklin St., Denver, CO 80209.*

watchers forge through the prairie grasses looking for great blue herons, one of the 180 bird species sighted at Chatfield. Bikers, hikers, and horseback riders can explore the park on miles of paved and dirt trails. Boat and horse rentals are available. Hours: 5 am–10 pm.

**CHERRY CREEK STATE PARK**
**4201 S. Parker Rd., Aurora**
**303/690-1166**  **ED**
It's possible to get lost among the miles of trails winding through dry river beds and the open plains in Cherry Creek State Park. Pick up a free map at the entrance booth and explore the area by foot, bike, or on horseback. The reservoir will delight water-sports fanatics. Boaters should drive defensively as you will share the waterways with other motorboats, sailboats, and jet skiers. The park also has a rifle range, model airplane runways, horse stables, and boat rentals and lessons. Park hours: Summer 6 am–10 pm, winter 7–7.

# 9
# SHOPPING

Until the 1950s, tiny downtown Denver was the center of all shopping, and all services as well. As residents and newcomers started to fill up the empty plains around them in wider and wider circles, new shopping areas followed. Now, like the city itself, shopping is spread all over the metropolitan area.

## SHOPPING AREAS

### ANTIQUE ALLEY
Several blocks of South Broadway are lined with shops and cooperatives specializing in antiques of various styles and periods. There are also a few fine antique stores on North Broadway.

### CHERRY CREEK
The Cherry Creek Shopping Center houses the huge and glittering Cherry Creek Mall, home to world-class shopping with such well-known department stores as Saks Fifth Avenue and Neiman Marcus, as well as 130 specialty shops and restaurants. The adjacent Cherry Creek North Shopping District offers a more relaxed environment along three tree-lined avenues and plazas. Shoppers can stroll to specialty shops, restaurants, boutiques, and galleries.

### DOWNTOWN AND LOWER DOWNTOWN
Shops line the 16th Street Mall that runs through the center of downtown. A dazzling and welcome newcomer to 16th Street shopping is Denver Pavilions, a huge outdoor center on the mall between Tremont and Welton Streets. NikeTown, Virgin Records, Hard Rock Café, Barnes and Noble, and Wolfgang Puck Café are only some of the stores and restaurants bringing new life to this part of town. The United Artists theater is the first new downtown movie theater

since old-timers like the RKO Orpheum and the Denham gave up the ghost in the early sixties. Shoppers can take the mall shuttle bus and easily access shops in LoDo and upper downtown. LoDo shopping is centered in historic Larimer Square, Writer's Square across the street, and the neighboring Tabor Center. It's pretty and interesting to stroll through the area, even if you don't find anything to buy. Sakura Square, three blocks away, features imported goods from Japan.

## HIGHLANDS

Across the Speer Street Viaduct from downtown lies the Highlands neighborhood and the Highlands shopping district. Founded by General Larimer in 1858, Highland (originally without the "s") was one of the three towns that merged to become the city of Denver in 1860. Because of its higher elevation, Highland became one of Denver's first suburbs. Here, home owners could breathe fresher air and escape other evils of the city below. Alcohol was prohibited in early Highlands, and the area had the most churches in town.

## OLD SOUTH GAYLORD

Old South Gaylord Street is a block-long shopping district marking the point where the streetcar line from downtown Denver once ended in the "country." Recently restored, the street is one of Denver's oldest shopping areas.

## SOUTH FEDERAL BOULEVARD

This street is home to many Asian restaurants, shops, and businesses.

## WEST 32ND STREET

Neglected for many years, several newly renovated blocks along West 32nd Street now form a pleasant shopping district, with specialty stores, restaurants, and a coffee shop. Spiritual, neighborly, eclectic—there is a unique ambiance to this area.

## SPECIALTY STORES AND MARKETS

### *Antiques*

**ANTIQUE EXCHANGE CO-OP**
**1500 S. Broadway (Antique Alley)**
**Denver**
**303/777-7871** CD
The 15 Antique Exchange shops specialize in every genre, from European to cowboy to western. The atmosphere is friendly and relaxed.

**ANTIQUE GUILD**
**1298 S. Broadway (Antique Alley)**

*Larimer Square*

Denver
303/722-1816    CD
Louis XV dressing tables, American Empire sofas, Bavarian blanket trunks, antique guns, and hand-painted folk art figurines are scattered throughout the barnlike Antique Guild space. Dealers here are knowledgeable and eager to talk about their treasures without pressuring you to buy.

**ANTIQUE MALL OF LAKEWOOD**
9635 W. Colfax Ave., Lakewood
303/238-6940    WD
The Antique Mall of Lakewood features eighteenth-, nineteenth-, and twentieth-century antiques on its three floors of showroom space. The mall's café serves lunch daily.

*Far East Center, South Federal Boulevard*

**CLUTTERED CLOSET**
2600 E. 12th Ave., Denver
303/331-9305    CD
Customers love this neighborhood hangout where you can buy everything from a 99-cent button to a priceless antique.

**ERON JOHNSON ANTIQUES, LTD.**
451 N. Broadway
(Antique Alley)
Denver
303/777-8700    CD
Eron Johnson moved its 18,000-square-foot showroom from downtown to this location in January 1996. The new space, formerly an auto showroom, has been renovated with antique architectural pieces. The store specializes in eighteenth- and nineteenth-century furniture, accessories, paintings, silver, and architectural and garden ornaments. Restoration and appraisals are offered.

**METROPOLITAN ANTIQUE GALLERY**
1147 N. Broadway (Antique Alley)
Denver
303/623-3333    CD
Transforming an ugly purple building bordering downtown into a classy gallery was the Metropolitan's first gift to Denver. The next was bringing a fresh perspective to Denver's antiques scene. With close ties to estate houses in New York, owner Craig Nassi specializes in rare, museum-quality pieces. Whether it's a Gothic altarpiece from France or a Louis XVI window casing, you'll always find something spectacular at this store.

**ROSVALL AUCTION ANTIQUES GALLERY**
1238 S. Broadway (Antique Alley)
Denver
303/722-4028    CD
Rosvall auctions everything you can imagine—from household items and

> ## Downtown Denver, Way Back When
>
> Jane O'Donnell, born in Denver in 1912, remembers the early downtown area:
>
> *As a child, it was a long-anticipated excursion on the streetcar for a day of shopping and a trip to the top of the Daniels and Fisher Tower (which now can barely be found amidst the tall buildings) to look out over the entire city. Possibly, if we had been good all week, we were taken to Baur's famous restaurant to indulge in chicken à la king in a patty shell and chocolate ice cream. . . . There was a lovely small-town feeling about Denver until World War II engulfed the city and the rest of the world.*

antique and modern furniture to cars. So it pays to attend the weekly noon viewings at the store. Sometimes there are estate sales. Public auctions Wednesday at 6:30.

### SANDPIPER ANTIQUES
**1524 S. Broadway (Antiques Alley), Denver**
303/777-4384    CD
You never know what you might find at Sandpiper Antiques—a Queen Anne game table, a Wells Fargo trunk, an early Victorian secretaire. The store also has unusual and charming folk art sculptures.

## *Apparel*

### AMERICAN VOGUE
**10 South Broadway, Denver**
303/733-4140    CD
Some of the classiest vintage clothing can be found at American Vogue and its sister store six blocks away, American Aces. The collection runs the gamut from comfortable Katharine Hepburn to classic Audrey Hepburn, and you'll find hats, jewelry, shoes, and a wide variety of accessories.

### APPLAUSE
**2827 E. Third Ave. (Cherry Creek) Denver**
303/321-7580    CD
Grandmothers and grandmother wannabees hover longingly about the racks of exquisitely designed infants' and children's clothing at Applause. There are gauzy ballet dresses, cuddly sleepers, flowered slouch hats, shoes, barrettes—you name it. Applause offers a great selection of unique, high-end women's clothing as well. There are two Applause stores in Boulder

### BARBARA & COMPANY
**7777 E. Hampden Blvd., Denver**
303/751-2618    SD
A favorite with the style-conscious woman, Barbara & Co. carries sophisticated contemporary clothing. Lines include Zelda, Tahari, Kenar, and Ghost. There is a large selection of belts, hats, scarves, and accessories. Salespeople devote

undivided attention to the customer. Appointments are welcome.

## BOLDERSPACE PERSONAL ENVIRONMENTS
**1512 Larimer St., Denver**
**303/623-7600**      **DD**

If you are looking for something sophisticated, unique, and comfortable to wear, try the Denver branch of Bolderspace. This Boulder-based store features an eclectic selection of women's clothing, including its own Shali label. Manufactured in Boulder, Shali dresses, jackets, and shawls are elegant creations of hand-woven silk. Prices are in the mid- to upper range.

## BROOKS LTD.
**2426 E. Third Ave. (Cherry Creek) Denver**
**303/377-2606**      **CD**

For more than 20 years, owner Brooks has designed women's fashions at this Cherry Creek North location. Her small boutique attracts women of all ages, income levels, and professions who share a desire for something unique in their wardrobes. Day-into-evening ensembles, formal attire, and weekend wear are all offered. All styles, designs, and fabrics are interchangeable. Brooks especially likes working individually with clients to create designs tailored to their needs.

## CHERRY CREEK TAILORING
**227 Clayton St. (Cherry Creek) Denver**
**303/321-6278**      **CD**

Do you have a favorite garment that just doesn't fit? No matter the type of hem, seam, or fabric, miracle workers Hamdi and Kiraz Sahin will come to your rescue. A poster of the owners' native Turkey presides over this tiny basement shop.

## CHILDREN'S EXCHANGE
**560 S. Holly, Denver**
**303/321-3897**      **CD**

A decades-old establishment, the Children's Exchange is a consignment store offering every type of clothing (except socks) for boys and girls to age 14. The store also sells infant accessories and some better-brand toys. Its motto is "second hand but not second best."

## CIRCA 19 HUNDRED
**1415 Larimer St., Denver**
**303/534-4940**      **DD**

Clothes and accessories that evoke a bygone era, primarily the twenties, thirties, and forties, are Circa 19 Hundred's trademark. There are sweaters, jewelry, and hats in the $40 range, sophisticated suits from $300 to $400, and everything from filmy drop-waist dresses to T-shirts, pants, and embroidered blouses in between. Also at 2849 Third Ave., Denver, 303/316-8340.

## GRASSFIELD'S
**2850 E. Second Ave. (Cherry Creek), Denver**
**303/388-5727**      **CD**

Max Grassfield has owned and operated his full-line men's clothing store since 1960. The store carries elegant suits and business attire, sportswear, shoes, belts, and neckwear. Max and his staff offer warm personal service and expertise. Many women frequent the store to buy clothing for their fashion-shy men. Now women can browse for their own fashion statements. Erica McNeish offers her expertise in the

## Top Ten Bargains in Denver

by Marilyn Mitchell, owner of As You Wish, a business specializing in "personal services that make life easier."

1. **Capitol Hill Books**—300 Grant St., 303/837-0700. This pulse-of-the-city bookstore features new and used books at exceptional prices.
2. **CARL**—303/758-1551, www.carl.org (Web), or csn.carl.org (Telnet). The CARL system offers online library access and has spread to various libraries across the country and around the world.
3. **Country Club Flowers**—3434 E. Colfax Ave., 303/399-3838. Here you'll find nicely priced cut flowers and artful arrangements.
4. **E. Central**—303/830-0123. E. Central offers the best Internet access in Denver. One of the company's many features is an online cultural events calendar for the Denver metro area.
5. **El Taco de Mexico**—714 Santa Fe Dr., 303/623-3926, and 2463 Sheridan Blvd., Edgewater, 303/237-7174. Here you'll enjoy authentic Mexican counter food: hand-dipped rellenos, thin and flaky tortillas, steamy frijoles, menudo, and chorizo. Don't miss the relleno burrito.
6. **Goin Tree Service**—303/366-8021. Offering meticulous and reasonably priced tree pruning, Goin Tree operates with integrity and environmental awareness.
7. **Lana's Resale Boutique**—2434 E. Sixth Ave., 303/322-0555, and 2371 E. Evans, 303/765-4776. Lana Mercer offers an eclectic mix of quality used clothing (emphasizing natural fibers) at excellent prices.
8. **Massage Therapy Institute of Colorado**—1441 York St., Suite 301, 303/329-0512. You can receive a full-body massage for $20 in the Student Clinic. All massages are fully supervised.
9. **Summer in the Park**—303/640-1038. Enjoy free concerts, craft shows, musicals, and plays throughout the summer in Denver's parks.
10. **Lumber Baron Inn**—2555 W. 37th Ave., 303/477-8205. The inn is not only a treasured landmark and bed and breakfast but it is also available for business meetings, weddings, and parties.

new Grassfield's for Women area, where Barry Bricken, Iris Singer, and Samuelson Sportswear are featured.

### IRIS FIELDS
**1099 S. Gaylord St., Denver**
**303/777-0516** CD
Iris Fields features out-of-the-ordinary, contemporary women's fashions in a relaxed and friendly environment. Styles range from dressy to sporty.

### LAWRENCE COVELL
**225 Steele St. (Cherry Creek)**
**Denver**
**303/320-1023** CD
Lawrence and Cathy Covell go all the way to New York and Milan for the designer clothing they carry in their Cherry Creek store. The shop features sophisticated men's and women's clothing, sportswear, and accessories, with a special emphasis on Italian collections. The Covells offer many exclusive lines and outstanding service.

### MOTIONS, INC.
**2060 S. University Blvd., Denver**
**303/777-7274** CD
In business since 1954, Motions is Denver's premier dance clothier—the oldest such store in Colorado. The emphasis here is on proper fit and flattering color and design. Motions offers a large selection of dance, fitness, skate, gymnastics, and active wear.

### RICH RAGS
**600 Downing St., Denver**
**303/861-2130** CD
There are enough sequins, flounces, and plunging necklines at Rich Rags to satisfy any party goer. You can rent or purchase from the outstanding selection of consignment prom dresses and women's formalwear. The store has a large selection of women's daywear as well. Styles tend toward the sophisticated.

### SHOE BIZ
**2636 E. Third Ave. (Cherry Creek)**
**Denver**
**303/333-7000** CD
They come in cowhide, stingray, ostrich, and eel, in sizes 3 AAA to 15 EEE. So you should be able to find a pair of boots you like—and that fit—at Shoe Biz. The store has a full-service in-house repair shop. (Three other downtown locations)

### THE SNOB SHOP
**2804 E. Sixth Ave., Denver**
**303/355-6939** CD
Whether you're looking for a wedding dress or a pair of Levi's, the Snob Shop might be just the place you need. Discriminating in its selection of consignment goods, the store features both men's and women's clothing, shoes, jewelry, and accessories. The staff is friendly and helpful.

### TAPESTRY
**286 Fillmore St. (Cherry Creek)**
**Denver**
**303/393-0535** CD
"You don't want the cookie-cutter look that the malls provide? Then come to Tapestry!" says Carolyn Fineran, who started the store 20 years ago in Cherry Creek North. Brocaded vests, unusual belts, and unique fabrics and styles typify the Tapestry look. The store is known for its one-of-a-kind wearable art pieces and individual service.

## *Art Supplies/Framing*

### DENVER ART SUPPLY
**1437 California St., Denver**

> ### Top Ten Ways to Keep Your Skin from Drying Out in Denver
> by Nina Laughlin, owner of the Alchemist
>
> 1. Exfoliate dry skin with an agave cloth, bristle brush, or loofah.
> 2. Use a moisturizing liquid soap to clean skin.
> 3. Rub Dr. Hauschka or blackthorn massage oil onto wet skin.
> 4. Follow with a shea butter lotion.
> 5. Drink lots of water.
> 6. Take flax seed oil internally in capsule form.
> 7. Don't soak in the bath unless you're using an oil-based bath product.
> 8, 9, and 10. Visit a humid place as often as possible.

**303/534-1437**   **DD**

If Denver Art Supply doesn't have it, artists don't use it. Not only is the selection one of the best around, the staff is composed of artists who know their crafts. The stores also offers an excellent array of creative art kits for kids, and the prices are very reasonable.

**FRAME OF MIND, INC.**
**5214 E. Colfax Ave., Denver**
**303/388-1048**   **ED**

Owner Mike Jacobsen in an artist and photographer with an eye for color and design. His skill at displaying art to its best advantage is matched by a wide range of framing selections and good prices.

**H. R. MEININGER CO.**
**499 Broadway, Denver**
**303/698-3838**   **DD**

Another longtime Denver institution, Meininger has one of the city's largest selections of supplies and equipment for fine art, drafting, and engineering. Meininger also offers a fine selection of craft supplies and framing services.

### Arts, Crafts, and Gifts

**ARTISAN CENTER**
**2757 E. Third Ave. (Cherry Creek)**
**Denver**
**303/333-1201**   **CD**

Every inch of the Artisan Center is packed with colorful, often whimsical craft items. Kites, glass pieces, birdhouses, and mobiles hang from the ceiling. There are clocks, weavings, mirrors, and paintings on the walls. With all the jewelry, pottery, sculptures, placemats, and candles, it's a wonder there is room left for customers to browse. This is a great place to find a unique and reasonably priced wedding gift.

**THE BAOBAB TREE**
**1518 Wazee St., Denver**
**303/595-0965**   **DD**

Greeting the shopper at the Baobab

Tree are enough giraffes, parrots, and bamboo chairs to make you feel you're on safari. In fact, the store's owners travel to the southern tip of Africa to find the contemporary arts and crafts they showcase. Prices vary from $1 to $15,000.

### DESERT HEART, INC.
2220 E. Colfax Ave., Denver
303/370-1338     CD

"Whatever feels like it wants to live here" is what you'll find at Desert Heart. The list includes candles, beads, incense, and the Desert Heart line of jewelry. You might even get a tarot reading if you ask.

### GALERIA MEXICANA
3615 W. 32nd Ave. (Highlands)
Denver
303/964-9050     CD

Galleria Mexicana feels like a festive south-of-the-border marketplace. The owners import furniture, pottery, jewelry, clothing, and crafts from the towns and small villages of south-central Mexico. There is a good selection of painted Oaxacan animals and lots of one-of-a-kind folk art. Prices range from 50 cents to $2,000.

### KOBUN-SHA
1255 19th St., Denver
303/295-1845     DD

Kobun-Sha is tucked around the corner from the Pacific Mercantile Market in Sakura Square, Denver's center of Japanese-owned businesses. Hand-painted silk wall hangings, fans, and tea sets are among the items on display. There are reasonably priced kimonos, calligraphy inks and papers, origami materials, screens, rice paper lanterns, and more. Browse through the large selection of hand-painted note cards.

### MANOS FOLK ART
101 Broadway, Denver
303/778-8262     CD

Manos Folk Art features such treasures as West African masks, Indonesian wood sculptures, and placemats and weavings from Peru and Guatemala. Other imports include wood and wrought-iron furniture and ethnic jewelry and clothing. High-quality Mexican folk art and furniture are the store's specialties.

### NATIVE AMERICAN TRADING COMPANY
1301 Bannock St., Denver
303/534-0771     DD

Located across from the Denver Art Museum, the Native American Trading Company is a cross between a museum, a gallery, and a store. The company features a select collection of antique Native American rugs, blankets, artifacts, jewelry, pottery, beadwork, and baskets. Also on display is the work of early southwestern artists like photographer Edward Curtis.

### SQUASH BLOSSOM GALLERY
1428 Larimer Sq., Denver
303/572-7979     DD

This is one of the best places in Denver to find both antique and contemporary jewelry and crafts of the Americas. The gallery features ear-

---

**TRIVIA**

In the early 1950s, Denver architect Temple H. Buell, often called the Father of the Mall, conceived of and built one of the first shopping malls in the country: the Cherry Creek Mall.

rings, bracelets, and necklaces by internationally recognized artists such as Ray Tracey and Jimmy King. There is a selection of jewelry by Colorado Senator Ben Nighthorse Campbell and by well-known Hopi, Zuni, Navajo, and Mexican artists. Plains beadwork and basketry, as well as a fine collection of Zuni fetish carvings, make the gallery a haven for admirers and collectors of Native American art. At the annual February sale, all merchandise is marked down 20 to 50 percent.

## Audio Visual

**LISTENUP AUDIO-VISUAL**
685 S. Pearl St., Denver
303/778-0780　　　　　　　　CD

A decades-old Denver fixture, Listenup is the area's premier specialty audio-visual retailer. The company that installed the sound systems at Mile High Stadium and Fiddler's Green will be happy to install a system in your home as well.

**ROBERT WAXMAN CAMERA & VIDEO**
1545 California St., Denver
303/623-1155　　　　　　　　DD

Robert Waxman Camera opened for business in downtown Denver 36 years ago. Today, Waxman is the largest camera and video dealer in the West. Located in the old Denver Dry Goods building, it is also the largest camera store in the world on one floor. There are eight other stores on the Front Range and a new store on the Internet. Waxman's offers a complete lineup of camera and video equipment and accessories, as well as state-of-the-art film developing and classes.

## Books, Magazines, and Newsstands

**ABRACADABRA ANTIQUARIAN BOOKSHOP AND BOOK SEARCH**
32 S. Broadway, Denver
303/733-5700　　　　　　　　CD

**THE ARK BOOKSTORE**
399 Federal Blvd., Denver
303/922-8405　　　　　　　　WD

**BARNES & NOBLE**
960 S. Colorado Blvd., Denver
303/691-29987　　　　　　　　CD
Eight other locations

**THE BOOKIES**
4315 E. Mississippi Ave., Glendale
303/759-1117　　　　　　　　SD
Specializing in children's books

**CAPITOL HILL BOOKS**
300 E. Colfax Ave., Denver
303/837-0700　　　　　　　　DD
New and used books

**GIBSON'S BOOKSTORE**
1404 Larimer St., Denver
303/620-0034　　　　　　　　DD

**HUE-MAN EXPERIENCE, THE AFRICAN-AMERICAN BOOKSTORE**
911 Park Ave. W., Denver
303/293-2665　　　　　　　　CD

Colin Powell is just one of many famous authors who have signed books at the Hue-Man Experience. For 11 years, this bookstore has provided the Denver community with African and African American books, greeting and note cards, calendars, and fine art prints, plus excellent service and expertise.

**LINDA LEBSACK BOOKS**
1228 E. Colfax Ave., Denver

## The Tattered Cover

*One of the largest bookstores in the United States, the Tattered Cover offers comfy chairs for reading, an attentive and book-loving staff, and a dedication to books and freedom of speech. Frequent book signings feature authors such as Frank McCourt, Kurt Vonnegut, Larry McMurtry, and Margaret Atwood.*

303/832-7190     CD
Specializing in antiquarian books and Colorado history

**MAGAZINE CITY**
200 E. 13th Ave., Denver
303/861-8249     CD
Both new and old magazines and newspapers

**NEWSSTAND CAFE INC.**
630 E. Sixth Ave., Denver
303/777-6060     CD
Magazines, papers, books, and coffee

**TATTERED COVER BOOKSTORE**
2955 E. First Avenue, Denver
303/322-7727     CD

**TATTERED COVER BOOKSTORE LODO**
1628 16th St., Denver
303/436-1070     DD

**WALDENBOOKS**
Aurora Mall, Aurora
303/364-5312     ED
Eight other Denver locations

### Cookware

**COOK'S MART LTD.**
3000 E. Third Ave., Denver
303/388-5933     CD
You'll find every pot, pan, gadget, and doodad you ever dreamed of at this cook's paradise. There are shelves of glassware, pottery, china, and flatware. Prices are moderate to high—you can definitely find a cheaper can opener at Kmart, but it won't be as much fun.

### Flowers and Gardening

**ARAPAHOE ACRES NURSERY AND LANDSCAPING**
9010 S. Santa Fe, Dr., Littleton
303/791-1660     SD
For the widest variety of hardy trees and shrubs, go to Arapahoe Acres. The knowledgeable staff will help you find the best plant for every area of your yard.

**BOUQUETS**
2029 E. 13th Ave., Denver
303/333-5500     CD
The locally grown, fresh-cut flower arrangements from Bouquets have enchanted Denverites since the store's opening in 1985. Backing up local opinion, *Bon Appetit* magazine chose Bouquets as one of the top ten florists in the country. The store also sells stationary, bird-houses, books, vases, and candles. There is a beautiful new Bouquets in LoDo.

**BIRDSALL & CO.**
1540 S. Broadway, Denver

## Top Ten Places to Buy Wine (or Not)

by Dr. Phillip Walravens, Denver pediatrician, chef, and epicure, who acquired his love of wine in his native Europe

**Category 1: Megastores with incredible variety and choices seldom found elsewhere in the world**
1. Argonaut Liquors: 700 E. Colfax Ave., 303/831-7788
2. Applejack Liquor: 3320 Youngfield, Wheatridge, 303/233-3331
3. Broadway Wine & Spirits: 2468 Baseline Rd., Boulder, 303/494-0177

**Category 2: Close runner-up to Category 1**
4. Arrow Liquormart: 4301 E. Virginia Ave., 303/399-2123

**Category 3: Best quality and great expertise; more limited choices. Check case-lot sales**
5. Vineyard Wine Shop, Inc.: 261 Fillmore St., 303/355-8324

**Category 4: Best bargains if you know what you're looking for**
6. Logan Liquors: 100 S. Logan St., 303/744-0731

**Category 5: Surprising and excellent choices at times**
7. Bonnie Brae Liquor & Wine Mart, Ltd.: 785 S. University Blvd., 303/733-7261
8. Mayfair Liquors: 1385 Krameria St., 303/322-0810
9. City Wine: 347 S. Colorado Blvd., 303/393-7576

**Category 6: Price abuse at the only accessible store in the Cherry Creek area**
10. Chateau Liquors: 2627 E. Second Ave., 303/333-5425

---

303/722-2535　　　　　　　　SD
"The right tool for the right person at the right price" is the motto at Birdsall & Co. In addition to a large selection of imported tools, the store offers one-of-a-kind art objects for the garden. Many of the stepping stones, sundials, fountains, twig trellises, and botanical prints are created by local artisans and artists.

**ECHTER'S GREENHOUSES, INC.**
**5150 Garrison St., Arvada**
**303/424-7979**
Echter's offers a wide variety of plants, shrubs, and trees. The cactus

selection and seasonal plant offerings are exceptional. Upscale gift items and patio furniture are also available.

**PAULINO GARDENS**
**6280 Broadway, Denver**
**303/429-8062**      **ND**
Paulino Gardens is a sprawling center with possibly the widest variety of well-priced, healthy plants in metro Denver. The service is friendly and efficient.

## Flea Markets

**ARAPAHOE FLEA MARKET**
**3400 S. Platte River Dr. Englewood**
**303/789-2710**      **SD**

**MILE HIGH FLEA MARKET**
**7007 E. 88th Ave., Henderson**
**303/289-4656**      **ED**

## Food

**ALFALFA'S MARKET**
**900 E. 11th Ave., Denver**
**303/832-7701**      **CD**
This spacious Capitol Hill market offers fresh organic produce, meats, seafood, gourmet delicacies, and a large selection of vitamins and beauty products. The juice bar serves fresh juice and vegetable drinks. Try wheatgrass and garlic if you want a real morning jolt. There are four other metro Denver locations. If you go to the Cherry Creek store, take a deep breath and brace yourself for the horrors of the parking lot.

**ASIAN MARKET**
**333 S. Federal Blvd., Denver**
**303/937-1431**      **CD**
At the lively and fragrant Asian Market, you can find everything from sweet chile sauce to grated cassava, lychee nuts, mangos, and persimmons.

**PACIFIC MERCANTILE MARKET**
**1925 Lawrence St., Denver**
**303/295-0293**      **DD**
Where else in Denver can you find octopus, sake, dried seaweed, kelp, and lotus root all in one place? In addition to food, this Japanese market has a fine selection of cookbooks, utensils, pottery, and every accessory your forays into Japanese cuisine might require.

## Home Furnishings

**FRANKLIN PRICE ORIENTAL RUGS**
**1825 Blake St., Denver**
**303/295-1824**      **DD**
For moderately priced, high-quality oriental rugs, kilims, Navajo rugs, and assorted textiles, both old and new, you can't do better than this LoDo shop. Whether you want to talk about rugs, learn about them, or bargain for them, the charming and knowledgeable Franklin Price will make your experience memorable. Services include washing, repair, restoration, consultation, and appraisals.

**NATURAL IMPACT**
**821 Santa Fe Dr., Denver**
**303/620-9889**      **CD**
Natural Impact features owner Tommy Evans's handcrafted southwestern/Spanish-style furniture. Wooden cabinets, beds, chairs, and tables are hand-finished and highlighted to bring out the grain. Every piece is glued or hand-pegged. The unique designs are reasonably priced, and furniture can be made to order.

**SHAVER-RAMSEY ORIENTAL RUGS AND ARTS**
**2414 E. Third Ave., Denver**

## Japanese in Denver

A bronze bust of Governor Ralph Carr in the plaza of Sakura Square commemorates the Japanese community's gratitude to the Colorado governor for his support during World War II. The late Yutuka Inai, who founded Pacific Mercantile in 1942, wrote in his memoirs that Governor Carr welcomed the Japanese to Colorado during the war in the face of widespread U.S. hostility toward people of Japanese descent.

The name of Inai's market was originally Japanese Mercantile. In early 1945, a member of the Denver City Council expressed concern that references to Japan might bring unwanted controversy to the store. So Inai renamed it Pacific Mercantile. His memoir was printed on July 4, 1989, when he was 94 years old.

---

**303/320-6363**   CD
Shaver-Ramsey has received national recognition for the quality of its oriental rugs, kilims, and textiles. Also featured are artifacts and antiques from around the world—santos from the Philippines, Japanese *tansu*, and an exceptional collection of ethnic jewelry.

### *Jewelry*

**JOHN ATENCIO**
**1440 Larimer St., Denver**
**303/534-4277**   DD
John Atencio offers a unique collection of contemporary, award-winning jewelry featuring colored stones and diamonds. The Expressway and Silhouette collections feature rings with companion earrings, bracelets, and pendants. Elements, featuring pieces in sterling silver with 18-karat gold accents and colored gemstones, is the newest series. There are five more John Atencio stores in Colorado.

**KIM JEWELERS**
**333 S. Federal Blvd., Denver**
**303/935-4466**   CD
The owner of Kim Jewelers, Minh Su, offers a wide selection of high-quality jade jewelry from Hong Kong. There is also a good selection of diamond jewelry from Israel.

### *Music*

**TWIST AND SHOUT**
**300 E. Alameda Ave., Denver**
**303/722-1943**
The name says it all. This place has Grateful Dead rugs hanging from the ceilings, guitars for sale along the walls, and notices of local band concerts everywhere. There is a vast selection of jazz, blues, Latin, country, folk, and bluegrass CDs, tapes, and records. The plastic leopard-skin seats on the listening room stools are an especially nice touch.

**WAX TRAX RECORDS**
**619 E. 13th Ave., Denver**

*Tabor Center*

**303/860-0127**     **DD**
The price is right and the atmosphere funky at Wax Trax, which also has stores at 620, 626, and 638 E. 13th Avenue. You'll find new and used reggae, rap, rock, jazz, and blues. These folks like a challenge—the more obscure your record or CD request the better. If anyone can find Eric Clapton's *John Mayll and the Blues Breakers* it's Wax Trax.

## Souvenirs

**BLACK AMERICAN WEST
MUSEUM AND HERITAGE CENTER**
**3091 California St., Denver**
**303/292-2566**     **CD**

**COLORADO HISTORICAL SOCIETY**
**1300 Broadway, Denver**
**303/866-4993**     **DD**

**COLORADO ROCKIES DUGOUT**
**1730 Sherman St., Denver**
**303/832-8326**     **DD**

**GOLD STAR
DOWNTOWN GIFTS**
**662 16th St., Denver**
**303/534-6772**     **DD**

**MUSEUM OF NATURAL
HISTORY SHOP**
**2001 Colorado Blvd., Denver**
**303/370-6366**     **CD**

## Sporting Goods

**COLLINS' BICYCLES**
**3217 E. Colfax Ave., Denver**
**303/322-1786**     **CD**
For 61 years, Denver youngsters have tried out their first bikes at Collins'—careening out the front door and around the block. The tiny bustling store has rows of bicycles, new and used, stacked to the ceiling. The founder's grandson, owner Tito Collins, offers retail and repair services along with the charm and good will locals have enjoyed for generations.

**GART SPORTSCASTLE**
**1000 Broadway, Denver**
**303/861-1122**     **CD**
Golf carts carry customers up and down the six floors of the Gart Sports-

castle, where every sports need can be filled. The store also features a putting and driving range, a ski machine, and a rooftop tennis court where customers can try before they buy. Gart's annual Sniagrab Sale takes place on Labor Day weekend, when ski equipment and clothing are slashed to significant discounts. The April Garage Sale provides discounts on summer sporting goods.

**GREAT PACIFIC PATAGONIA**
1431 15th St., Denver
303/446-9500    DD

If there is one common denominator to Denverites, it is their love of the outdoors. And Great Pacific Patagonia offers all the trappings every outdoor lover needs or wants. In addition to the complete Patagonia line of outdoor clothing for adults and kids, the store offers clinics on fly fishing and other activities and sponsors slide shows and talks by famous mountain climbers and other sports figures.

**SPORTS PLUS**
1055 S. Gaylord St., Denver
303/777-6613    CD

Tired of buying new parkas every year for those sprouting kids? Or just want a good deal for yourself? Sports Plus sells both new and used quality sporting goods. You'll find sportswear and equipment for bicycling, golf, tennis, skiing, hockey, ice skating, and in-line skating.

## Other Notable Stores

**THE ALCHEMIST**
2737 E. Third Ave., Denver
303/337-7567    CD

Owner Nina Laughlin has used herbal potions and remedies since

*Barney Launcelot Ford*

childhood. Her store depicts an old European pharmacy with all types of head-to-toe grooming products for men and women. Besides a wide assortment of soaps, shower gels, and body lotions, there are aromatherapy products and unusual European perfumes.

**CALICO CORNERS**
6625 Leetsdale Dr., Denver
303/320-5338    ED

Calico Corners carries a large selection of upholstery and drapery-weight decorator fabrics. The store will make draperies and upholstery to customer specifications. There are often great sales here and wonderful bargains on seconds.

**JIM'S SEWING MACHINE AND VACCUUM CLEANER CO.**
3201 N. Speer Blvd., Denver
303/455-5052    WD

## A Black Pioneer

*Barney Launcelot Ford escaped from slavery in the mid-1800s and fled to Chicago, where he worked with the Underground Railroad. It was in Chicago that he chose a new name—after the Launcelot Ford steam locomotive.*

*Ford then moved to Colorado and worked for the rights of black Americans. He promoted Colorado's entry into the Union as a free state with suffrage for all men.*

*He purchased a building for $673 in 1862 and opened a barbershop. When it was destroyed by fire, he built another structure and opened the People's Restaurant on the ground floor, a barbershop and hair salon in the basement, and a saloon on the third floor.*

*Barney Ford was nominated for the territorial legislature, and in 1881 he became a member of the Colorado Association of Pioneers. He and his family are buried at Riverside Cemetery in Denver. Near the corner of 15th and Blake Streets in LoDo, a plaque marks the spot of Ford's original barbershop.*

---

A few blocks from the West 32nd Street shops, Jim's provides repair services and what locals claim are the best deals on used vaccuum cleaners in the city (and maybe the state). Jim's has been in business at this location for 26 years.

## SHOPPING MALLS AND CENTERS

**AURORA MALL**
14200 E. Almeda Ave., Aurora
303/344-4120 ED

**BUCKINGHAM SQUARE SHOPPING CENTER**
1306 S. Havana, Aurora
303/755-3232 ED

**CHERRY CREEK NORTH SHOPPING CENTER**
3003 E. Third Ave., Denver
303/394-2903 CD

**CHERRY CREEK SHOPPING CENTER**
3000 E. First Ave., Denver
303/388-3900 CD

**CINDERMARK ASSOCIATES**
701 W. Hampden Ave., Englewood
303/761-6368 SD

**CROSSROADS MALL**
1600 28th St., Boulder
303/444-0265 ND

**HERITAGE SQUARE**
Hwy. 40 and Hwy. 98, Golden WD

## TIP

After a hard day at the mall, rest your shop-weary bones at the Izba Spa (1441 York St., Suite 101, 303/321-1239). Owner Leo Byssokob will give you a traditional Russian Banya treament that clears the body of toxins and the mind of—everything.

**LAKESIDE MALL**
5801 W. 44th Ave., Denver
303/455-7072  WD

**NORTH VALLEY MALL**
500 E. 84th Ave., Thornton
303/288-6895  ND

**PARK MEADOWS TOWN CENTER**
8401 Park Meadows Dr., Littleton
303/792-2862  SD
www.parkmeadows.com

**SOUTHGLENN MALL**
6911 S. University Blvd., Littleton
303/795-1511  SD

**SOUTHWEST PLAZA**
8501 W. Boles Ave., Littleton
303/973-5300  SD

**THE SHOPS AT TABOR CENTER**
1201 16th St., Denver
303/446-0535  DD

**TAMARAC SQUARE SHOPPING CENTER**
7777 E. Hampden, Denver
303/745-0055  SD

**TIFFANY PLAZA MALL**
7400 E. Hampden, Denver  ED

**UNIVERSITY HILLS MALL**
2700 S. Colorado Blvd., Denver
303/758-2663  CD

**VILLA ITALIA SHOPPING CENTER**
7200 W. Alameda, Lakewood
303/936-0594  WD

**WESTMINSTER MALL SHOPPING CENTER**
Boulder Turnpike at 88th and Sheridan, Westminster
303/428-5634  ND

**WRITER SQUARE**
1512 Larimer St., Denver
303/628-9056  DD

*Factory Outlet Stores*

**CASTLE ROCK FACTORY SHOPS**
5050 Factory Shops Blvd.
Castle Rock
505/688-4494  SD

**CURRENT FACTORY OUTLET**
3550 S. Inca, Englewood
303/762-9803  SD

**ROCKY MOUNTAIN FACTORY STORES**
I-25, exit 257B, Loveland  ND

**SILVERTHORE FACTORY STORES**
145M Stephens Way, Silverthorne
970/468-9440 or 800/969-3767  ND

# 10
# SPORTS AND RECREATION

It's probably due to the weather—Denver enjoys more than 300 days of sunshine a year. Or perhaps it's the city's proximity to the mountains. Whatever the reason, Metro Denver is a mecca for outdoor fanatics. You find them cross-country skiing through the city parks, or commuting on the busy streets on their bikes. The Cherry Creek Trail teems with downtown joggers during the lunch hour, and avid windsurfers speckle the local reservoirs each summer afternoon. Landlocked Denver even supports more than its share of scuba diving and marine shops and no fewer than five professional sports teams. So just name your recreational passion, and you're sure to find it somewhere around Denver. If you prefer to watch, you'll find spectator sports listed at the end of this chapter.

## BICYCLING

Bicycle magazine voted Denver one of the top ten cycling towns in North America in 1996. The features earning the city its sixth place honor include the 12-mile Cherry Creek Trail (often called a "bicycle expressway"), convenient bike racks located throughout the city, and the popular Bike Month, during which bikers gain free admission to local attractions. Contact Colorado State Parks at 303/866-3437 for a complimentary metro area bike map.

### Road Biking
#### CHERRY CREEK TRAIL
The 12-mile paved trail winds from Confluence Park near downtown to Cherry Creek Reservoir east of the city. Bikers travel along the river bed below Speer Boulevard and into the flat eastern plains. The trail is relatively flat until it nears the

state park, where a steep hill gets the heart pounding. Bikers access the Speer Boulevard section from ramps located along the street. The path gets crowded with rollerbladers, bikers, and walkers during warm-weather weekends. Bring water for the trip.

### HIGHLINE CANAL TRAIL
City records indicate that more than 800,000 people use the Highline Canal Trail each year. This easy trail skirts Chatfield State Park along the tree-lined Highline Canal, one of Denver's original waterways, from County Line Road to Roxborough Park Drive. Bikers can access the trail at County Line Road, Santa Fe Drive, Waterton Road, and Roxborough Park Drive. Thorn-proof bicycle tires are strongly recommended.

### PLATTE RIVER AND ARAPAHOE COUNTY GREENWAY
The Platte River Greenway passes through more than a dozen parks as it winds from 38th and Washington Streets south along the South Platte River. The paved trail turns into the Arapahoe County Greenway near Ruby Hill Park, then continues south to the South Platte Park. Families will enjoy this easy trail as the terrain is mild and there are plenty of stopping points. The Greenway connects with the Bear Creek Trail, ending at the Bear Creek Reservoir, near Hampden Avenue. Access the trail from Confluence Park at 15th and Platte Streets, or from Ruby Hill Park near Evans and Broadway.

## *Mountain Biking*

### HAYDEN/GREEN MOUNTAIN PARK TRAILS
Intermediate mountain bike trails wind through the park and climb 1,200 feet to the Green Mountain Summit. Trailheads are located on Rooney Road south of I-70 and on Alameda between Florida and Utah Streets. To reach the park, drive west on 6th Avenue to the Union Exit. From there, head south on Union to Alameda and turn right. You'll see the park on the right side.

### JEFFERSON COUNTY OPEN SPACE TRAILS
Mountain bikers can find challenging trails in any of the Jefferson County Open Space Parks. At **Mount Falcon Park** bikers access beginning loops from the Indian Hills trailhead off Highway 285, or difficult steep climbs from the Highway 8 Morrison trailhead. Trails lead up the foothills on a narrow road through forests and meadows. Mt. Evans appears in the distance from Indian Hills, and the top of Mt. Falcon yields views of Red Rocks Park and the plains. The challenging **Dakota Ridge Trail** in **Matthews/Winters Park** starts at the Hogback Park parking area across the highway from Matthews/Winters Park. The 5-mile trail travels across the ridge, crosses Highway 26, and connects with the Red Rocks Trail south of Red Rocks Park. Dakota Ridge calls for more technical biking, but the trail evens out across the highway.

Contact Jefferson County Open Space at 303/271-5925 for free park maps and more information.

## BOATING

*For a landlocked area, Metro Denver provides an impressive array of boating options on nearby lakes and reservoirs.*

## TIP

Several bike clubs around the metro area organize weekly rides in the city and foothills. Denver Bicycle Touring Club (303/756-7240) is the largest, with 1,500 members. Jefferson County's Team Evergreen and the Rocky Mountain Cycling Club are two additional options.

### AURORA RESERVOIR
**5800 S. Powhaton Rd., Aurora**
**303/690-1286, 303/766-0020**
**(wind line)**     **ED**

The 820-acre Aurora Reservoir prohibits gas motors and jet skis, making it a haven for sailors. The surfer's beach, north of the swim beach, has sandy and grassy areas perfect for launching sailboards. A concrete boat ramp makes it easy to put larger boats in the water. From the reservoir, sailors have a sweeping view of the Front Range and in-coming Colorado storms. Boat and sailboard rentals and lessons are available through the reservoir concessions. Entrance: $3 vehicle pass and $3 city boat permit. Hours: Year-round dawn to dusk.

### CHATFIELD RESERVOIR
**11500 N. Roxborough Park Rd.**
**Littleton**
**303/791-7547 (Chatfield Marina)**
**303/791-6104 (boat rentals)**     **SD**

Designated water skiing, swimming, and wakeless areas on Chatfield Reservoir help control the busy summer boating traffic. Sailors, jet skiers, and motorboaters are all welcome on the 1,450-acre reservoir. The Chatfield Arena, open April through October, provides boating supplies, boat and sailboard rentals

*Platte River Greenway*

and lessons, and fuel docks from the reservoir's South Ramp. Boat ramps are located on the north and south sides of the reservoir. Entrance fees: $5 vehicle pass and $3 city boat permit. Park hours: Year-round 5 a.m.–10 p.m.

**CHERRY CREEK RESERVOIR**
**4201 S. Parker Rd., Aurora**
**303/690-1166** ED
The only Cherry Creek sailboaters who appreciate the motorboaters are those stuck by the north dam wall and in need of rescue. Otherwise sailboats and sailboards must compete with power boats and water skiers on the 880-acre reservoir. Boat rental and lessons are available from the marina on the west side of the reservoir. Entrance fees: $6 vehicle pass and $3 city boat permit. Park hours: Summer 6 a.m.–10 p.m., winter 7–7.

## BOWLING

**HOLIDAY LANES**
**10350 W. Colfax Ave., Lakewood**
**303/238-0407** WD
It's 3 a.m. and you have nothing to do? Never underestimate Denver's all-night possibilities. Holiday Lanes provides 24-hour bowling for avid bowlers and night owls. Wile away sleepless nights, or days, on one of the center's 30 bowling lanes or 12 pool tables. The restaurant and bar close at 2 a.m. Bowling costs $1.75 per game during the day and $2.50 after 6 p.m.

## CAMPING/BACKPACKING

Miles of secluded national forest backpacking trails, some leading to high mountain lakes and others to aspen-filled meadows, are easily accessible within a few hours' drive of Metro Denver. Backpackers should contact the appropriate national forest for maps, backcountry tips, and specific camping regulations before starting off on a trip. The forest service also maintains campgrounds easily reachable by vehicles.

**ARAPAHOE/ROOSEVELT**
**NATIONAL FORESTS**
**101 Chicago Creek, Box 3307**
**Idaho Springs, CO 80452**
**303/567-2901** WD

**PIKE/SAN ISABEL**
**NATIONAL FORESTS**
**19316 Goddard Ranch Court**
**Morrison, CO 80465**
**303/275-5610** WD

**ROCKY MOUNTAIN**
**NATIONAL PARK**
**National Park Service**
**Estes Park, CO 80517**
**970/586-1206** ND

**U.S. FOREST SERVICE**
**Box 25127**
**Lakewood, CO 80225**
**303/275-5350** WD

## DAY HIKES

So many possible day hikes wind throughout the Denver area foothills and state parks that an entire book could be dedicated to them. The following is a list of a few favorites within an hour's drive from Denver.

**GOLDEN GATE**
**CANYON STATE PARK**
**3873 Highway 46, Golden**
**303/592-1502** WD

The 14,000-acre Golden Gate Canyon Park offers hikers more than 35 miles of hiking on 12 park trails. Trails pass over wooden bridges, past mountain streams, and into pine-forested canopies. Each trail is named after an animal native to the region and marked with the animal's footprint. The park uses the same symbols as ski areas to indicate degree of difficulty. Circles are easy, squares are moderate, and diamonds are difficult. Even with a park trail map, the trails can be confusing to follow. Be sure to follow the right footprint at the head of every diverging trail. The moderate **Raccoon Trail** ascends to the Panorama Point, where majestic views of Mt. Evans, Longs Peak, and the Indian Peaks dominate the horizon. Cross-country skiers can access any trail in the snowy winter months. Getting there: Take Highway 6 west to Highway 93 in Golden. Continue north on Highway 93 about a mile to Golden Gate Canyon Road. Turn left and follow the winding road 15 miles to the park entrance.

### JEFFERSON COUNTY OPEN SPACE
**Golden**
**303/271-5925**     **WD**

Jefferson County voters approved a .5 percent sales tax in 1972 to preserve a wide range of open space lands in the county. The result is 11 mountain and urban parks, replete with hiking, mountain biking, and horse trails, streams, wildlife and regional history, all within an hour's drive of Denver. **Mt. Falcon Park** is a favorite. John Brisben Walker, a wealthy Denver businessman, bought the land in the early 1900s. He planned to build a summer home for U.S. presidents next to his own home. Walker's house burned down in 1918, but hikers can see the huge stone wall and fireplace remnants of the former castle residence off the Castle Trail. The Summer White House site can also be accessed from the Castle Trail. Dogs must be on leashes. Getting there: Take the Indian Hills Exit from Highway 285. Follow Parmalee Gulch Road for 2 1/2 miles to Picutis Road. Follow signs to the parking area.

### TOO LONG TRAIL/ BERGEN PEAK PARK
**Bergen Park**     **WD**

The moderate Too Long Trail passes through a meadow burgeoning with wildflowers, majestic ponderosa pines, and tall grasses on its way to the top of Bergen Peak. The trail leaves the meadow and begins

## TRIVIA

Unknowingly, I-70 commuters pass by 120-million-year-old rock formations on either side of the interstate every day. To educate people about the area's ancient history, the U.S. Geological Survey erected the Hogback Park geological walk in 1971. Although the area needs some maintenance work, the brief geological survey is well worth a short stopover. The tour guides visitors through 300 million years of Colorado geologic history that spotlights ancient seas, tidal swamps, mountains, dinosaurs, and volcanic eruptions. Turn south off the Red Rocks Exit, then turn left into the first parking lot.

## Matthews/Winters Park

*The area surrounding Matthews/Winters Park played an important role during the Rocky Mountain gold rush. Mt. Vernon Canyon, one of the early routes to the Central City gold fields, lies within the park boundaries. Dr. Joseph Casto, an Ohio lay preacher-turned-land promoter, founded the town of Mt. Vernon by the canyon in 1859. Dr. Casto hoped to make his fortune from the gold rush by establishing Mt. Vernon as a major supply town along the mining route. In the name of development, Casto advertised free lots in the* Rocky Mountain News *to anyone willing to build on them. Mt. Vernon had 44 registered voters by 1860. Initially, Mt. Vernon residents were Kansas Territory citizens. However, the considerable distance from the territory made governing difficult, and the Jefferson Territory, a local government, formed in 1859. Mt. Vernon's boom was short-lived as Denver soon became Colorado's economic center.*

climbing through a Douglas fir and aspen tree grove. Hikers often spot deer, blue grouse, and porcupine along the trail. Breathtaking views of Mt. Evans, Mt. Bierstadt, and Longs Peak to the west and the Colorado plains to the east open out from the peak summit. The round trip is about 8.6 miles. Getting there: Take I-70 west to Exit 252. Turn left off the highway, and then right onto Highway 74. The trailhead is located from a small parking lot on the right-hand side 1 mile south of Bergen Park.

## FISHING

More than a million people fish in Colorado streams and reservoirs each year. The following section lists fishing options near Metro Denver. Restrictions vary on the different waters. Some stipulate catch-and-release; others, a limit on the number of fish you can catch, so it's important to contact the Colorado Division of Wildlife at 303/297-1192 for specific regulations and a copy of Colorado Fishing Season. Fishing licenses are available at sporting goods stores. Call 303/291-7533 for 24-hour recorded fishing information.

There are two prime stretches of fishing water near Denver on the **South Platte River.** The more popular, and crowded, stretch runs from Cheesman Reservoir to Strontia Springs Reservoir. The fishing community counts this Gold Medal river one of the best rainbow and brown trout fisheries in the nation. Take U.S. 85 to state Highway 67. The second stretch runs from Strontia Springs to the Chatfield Reservoir close to Denver. This area is less crowded and has a high fish concentration. Access this area by foot or bike from the

# Top Ten Places to Bird-watch in Metro Denver

by Jim Wade, Denver lawyer and bird-watcher,
and Hugh Kingery, editor of the *Colorado Reading Bird Atlas*

1. **Barr Lake, northeast of Denver in Barr Lake State Park.** Good for viewing seasonal waterfowl and shore birds; a gathering place of pelicans; bald eagles often nest on the west shore.

2. **Chatfield State Park, southwest of Denver.** Seasonal waterfowl on the reservoir; a large rookery with herons and cormorants; walk the river on the south side to see the cottonwood river bottoms and nesting land birds.

3. **Waterton Canyon, southwest of Denver.** Good for warblers in migrating season together with nesting grosbeaks and buntings; in winter you can see water ouzels here and on the stream flowing into Chatfield Reservoir.

4. **Roxborough State Park, southwest of Denver and south of Waterton Canyon.** A splendid place for birding in the foothills zone; expect to see scrub jays, swifts, towhees, canyon wrens, and the like; also eagles, falcons, and ravens.

5. **Rocky Mountain Arsenal, northeast of Denver.** There is an eagle roost watch from 3:00 to dusk in the winter.

6a. **South Platte Park, Mineral St. and Santa Fe Blvd.** Cottonwood river bottom and ponds. Similar to Chatfield and Waterton Canyon.

6b. **South Platte River, north of I-70,** particularly the stretch from 64th Ave. to 120th Ave. Good for waterfowl, gulls, and shorebirds in season.

7. **Castlewood State Park, Douglas County, south of Denver.** Birds of the foothills, including soaring turkey vultures and white-throated swifts.

8. **Wheatridge Greenbelt at Prospect Park**

9. **Hogback Hawk Watch, Dinosaur Ridge (Exit 259):** Drive south on the ridge from the southeast corner of I-70 and Hwy 28. March 20 through May 10, best in April; see hawks actually migrating.

10. **Genesee Mountain Park, west of Denver.** Ponderosa pine birds such as mountain chickadee, nuthatches, Williamson sapsuckers, bluebirds, juncos, and jays.

*Fishing in the Denver area*

Kassler Water Treatment Plant off South Wadsworth.

The **Big Thompson River** flows east out of Rocky Mountain National Park. The river maintains a natural brown trout population as well as stocked rainbow trout. The Big Thompson season runs from May to September. Fishing with flies is recommended July to September. This is catch-and-release water.

The **Evergreen to Bear Creek Reservoir section of the Bear Creek** has consistent levels of 10- to 12-inch rainbow trout. This medium-sized stream is located off Colorado Highway 74. Reach Highway 74 from I-70.

Many Denver area reservoirs provide excellent fishing opportunities. Premier trophy walleye fishing is at its peak from May to June at **Cherry Creek Reservoir. Aurora Reservoir** offers game fishing of rainbow trout, walleye, wipers, largemouth bass, and yellow perch. At **Chatfield Reservoir** in south Denver, fishing enthusiasts will find large walleye, yellow perch, and rainbow trout. Night fishing in the Plum Creek area yields channel catfish. Both a State Parks Pass, available at the park gates, and a Colorado fishing license are required for all fishing.

There is additional fishing in the city park lakes. Young and old toss their line into lakes at **City, Washington,** and **Sloan's Lake Parks.** A fishing license is required.

## FITNESS CLUBS

### COLORADO ATHLETIC CLUB
**1630 Welton St., Denver**
**303/623-2100**  DD

The International Wellness Center and Athletic Club is a six-story, 75,000-square-foot club. The club's proximity to the convention center and the 16th Street Mall make it convenient to downtown hotels and conventioneers. The center has basketball, squash, and racquetball courts, in addition to fully equipped weight and fitness rooms. The wellness center offers aroma- and massage therapy. International Health and Racquet Sport Association (IHRSA) members can use the club. Fees: $10/day, $30/week, $90/month.

**DOWNTOWN YMCA**
**25 E. 16th Ave., Denver**
**303/861-8300**         **DD**
Visitors can work out at the downtown YMCA for $10, or $5 if you come in with a member. YMCA members from different areas can use the club for $5. This fitness center has it all. Guests have access to the swimming pool, basketball courts, handball courts, aerobic machines, free weights, and Nautilus equipment. Hours: Mon–Thur 5:30 a.m.–10 p.m., Fri. 5:30 a.m.–9 p.m., Sat. 7–6, Sun. 10–5.

**WASHINGTON PARK RECREATION CENTER**
**701 S. Franklin St., Denver**
**303/698-4962**         **CD**
The rec center isn't pretty or sweet-smelling like the posh clubs, but this city-run facility is well worth the price of admission. With an indoor swimming pool, aerobics room, full fitness center, and locker room, the facility meets most needs. Try to avoid the 5 p.m. rush hour. Visitors are welcome at any of the city's recreation centers. Day pass fees: Denver residents $2 adults, $1 children; non-residents $4 adults, $2 children. Annual passes also available. Hours: Mon & Wed 6 a.m.–10 p.m., Tues & Thur 9 a.m.–10 p.m., Fri 6 a.m.–9 p.m., Sat 8 a.m.–3 p.m., closed Sunday.

## GOLF

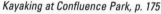

The following public golf courses are available to both residents and non-residents. The Metro Denver area is packed with private clubs, but these aren't as useful to visitors.

**Denver Municipal Golf Courses** allow visitors to play on any of the city's seven courses. Call for the course nearest you. Non-residents may purchase a $10 annual access card to reserve a tee time three days in advance. Call 303/784-4000 to access the city's automated tee

*Kayaking at Confluence Park, p. 175*

Confluence Kayaks

# Top Ten Public Courses for Views and Prices in Metro Denver
by Sharon Sakagawa, hairstylist and avid golfer

Sharon and her husband, Richard, spend every weekend, weather permitting, searching the metro area for the perfect golf course. After years of hard work, here is their list.

1. Mariana Butte in Loveland, 970/663-3483
2. Fox Hollow in Lakewood, 303/986-7888
3. Riverdale Dunes in Brighton, 303/659-4700
4. Raccoon Creek in Littleton, 303/973-9690
5. Willis Case in Denver, 303/458-4877
6. South Suburban in Littleton, 303/770-5500
7. Legacy Ridge in Westminster, 303/438-8997
8. Indian Peaks in Lafayette, 303/666-4706
9. Foothills Golf Course in Lakewood, 303/989-3901
10. The Meadows in Jefferson County, 303/972-8831

time service. Flip through the options for confirmations, cancellations, directions, reservations, green fees, hours, and course descriptions. Fees range from $12.75 to $19.75 for non-residents, depending on number of holes and weekend or weekday play, and from $9.50 to $14.50 for Denver County residents, depending on number of holes and time of play. **City Park**, 2600 York Street; **Evergreen**, 29614 Upper Bear Creek; **J. F. Kennedy**, 10500 E. Hampden Avenue; **Mira Vista** at Lowry, 10110 E. Golfers Way; **Overland**, 1801 S. Huron Street; **Wellshire**, 3333 S. Colorado Boulevard; **Willis Case**, 4999 Vrain Street.

## HORSEBACK RIDING

**BEAR CREEK LAKE PARK**
Old West Stables
**14700 Hwy. 8, Morrison**
**303/697-9666**     **WD**
Old West Stables, located across the street from Bear Creek Park, guides year-round horseback riding tours through the 2,500-acre Bear Creek Lake Park. Guides lead one- and two-hour rides through the 14 miles of designated horse trails. Trails cross the park's cottonwood-lined river and wind across the flat prairie land. Fee: $13/hour. Children must be at least 7 years old.

**CHATFIELD STATE PARK**
**B & B Livery**
**11500 N. Roxborough Park Rd.**
**Littleton**
**303/933-3636**     **SD**
The B & B Livery at Chatfield State Park, 15 miles southwest of Denver, leads guided tours through the park's 24-mile trail system. Trails follow the Chatfield Dam shoreline and wind

through park vegetation and wildlife areas. The stables are open daily May to September, 9 a.m. to 5 p.m.

**CHERRY CREEK STATE PARK**
**4201 S. Parker Rd., Aurora**
**303/690-8235**  CD
Over 12 miles of horseback riding trails wind through the plains and ravines in Cherry Creek State Park. The 4,000-acre park, home to plains wildlife such as deer, coyote, pheasant, and jackrabbit, is a small oasis in the city. The Paint Horse Stables, located near the east gate entrance, offers tours during the summer season.

## HUNTING

Tales of abundant waterfowl, small game and big game animal populations within a few hours' drive from Denver bring hunters flocking to the state for the annual hunting season. The Department of Wildlife has divided the big game season into separate archery, muzzle loading, and rifle seasons. Hunters must apply to the Department of Wildlife for some big game licenses, and others are unlimited in number and may be purchased at any time from the Department of Wildlife or sporting goods stores. The department issues elk, big horn sheep, mountain lion, deer, moose, antelope, and bear permits. The small game season runs September to February, and hunters can purchase these permits at sporting goods stores and Department of Wildlife offices. Common Colorado small game include rabbit, coyote, beaver, and bobcat. The waterfowl and upland bird season, including blue grouse, bobwhite quail, goose, pheasant, and turkey, usually runs September through December. Do not hunt on private lands, and always check with the Department of Wildlife at 303/297-1192 for specific regulations before hunting. Call 303/291-7529 for 24-hour recorded big game information, 303/291-7546 for information on small game, and 303/291-7548 for info on waterfowl.

## IN-LINE SKATING

The flat Metro Denver plains make for good in-line skating. The best routes are away from Denver's busy traffic on one of the city's bike trails. Close to Denver, skaters speed down the **Cherry Creek Trail**, **South Platte Trail** and connecting paths, and the **Washington Park** loop. In the north metro area, the **Wheatridge Greenbelt** bike trail runs along the Clear Creek stream. The **Highline Canal** in south Denver goes from C-470 around the Chatfield Reservoir.

## KAYAKING

*Kayakers practice their rolls in Chatfield, Cherry Creek, Soda Lake, and Aurora Reservoirs.*

---

**TIP**

Confluence Kayaks, located at 1539 Platte Street, one block north of Confluence Park, offers kayak lessons and a fully outfitted kayak store. Call 303/433-3676 for more information.

> **TIP**
>
> In-line skate rentals are available throughout Metro Denver. Skate Tech, 724 S. Pearl, and Sports Plus, 1055 S. Gaylord, are both convenient to Washington Park. Grand West Outfitters at 801 Broadway is reasonably near the Cherry Creek Trail.

**CLEAR CREEK RIVER**
Clear Creek has many possible kayak runs. The owners of Confluence Kayaks in Denver recommend the Lower Clear Creek section for advanced boaters. This section of Class 4 water runs from mile 267 off Highway 6 to Lion's Park in Golden. Watch out for two potentially hazardous diversion dams along the route.

**SOUTH PLATTE RIVER**
There are two kayak runs on the **South Platte River**. The most convenient to Denver is in Confluence Park near the intersection of 15th and Platte Streets. The city built a short boat chute that starts beneath the upper bridge. Kayakers usually use the chute as a training area. There's an easy take-out point at the brick courtyard to the left of the rapid. The second run is a 6-mile stretch below the **Chatfield Dam** in Jefferson County. The intermediate Class 2/3 rapid runs to the **Union Avenue Boat Chutes** take-out point.

## SCUBA DIVING

**AURORA RESERVOIR**
5800 S. Powhaton Rd., Aurora
303/690-1286                    **ED**
The rangers at Aurora Reservoir sunk a Cessna 310 aircraft in 28 feet of water for scuba divers to explore. The reservoir waters provide up to 20 feet of visibility. Access the site from the scuba beach on the northeast corner of the reservoir. Local dive shops hold certification classes at Aurora Reservoir. Park entrance: $5 daily vehicle pass. Park hours: Year-round dawn to dusk.

## SKATING

**EVERGREEN LAKE HOUSE**
303/674-2677 (hotline)          **WD**
The Evergreen Lake House provides the best outdoor skating in the area. All skating depends on ice and weather conditions, so call the hotline before making a trip. Admission: $2 adults, $1.75 youth 12–18, $1.50 children under 12. Rentals: $2/hour. Regular hours: Mon 1–7, Wed 4–7, Fri 4–9, Sat 9–9, Sun 9–7.

**UNIVERSITY OF DENVER
ICE ARENA**
2250 E. Jewell Ave., Denver
303/871-2235                    **CD**
The DU Ice Arena, home to the Division I DU Pioneer hockey team, offers year-round one- and 1 1/2-hour public skating sessions. The arena's hours change weekly, so call the hotline number in advance. Admission: 1 1/2 hour sessions $3 adult, $2.50 children; one-hour sessions $2. Rentals: $1.50.

# DOWNHILL SKIING

Some of the world's best skiing lies within 90 miles of Denver. Acres of natural and man-made snow, varied ski terrain, and high-tech ski technology await skiers in Colorado ski-country. The Colorado ski season opens around Thanksgiving and runs into June, depending on where you choose to plant your poles. The best skiing months vary annually. Some years the best snow hits the mountains before the winter holiday season, other years it's dry until mid-winter. But snowmaking abilities at most of the state's ski areas create snow even when nature provides little or none. Spring skiing is also a great experience as skis glide through soft snow down the mountain. The following lists day skiing within two hours' drive of Denver and accessible off I-70.

## ARAPAHOE BASIN
**P.O. Box 38**
**Keystone, CO 80435**
**970/925-1220**

A-Basin has been a local favorite for decades. It's close to Denver, nestled within the Arapahoe National Forest, and offers some of the state's most challenging skiing off only five lifts and within 490 acres. Experts should try North Glade and Palivacinni, one of the state's steepest faces, off the Palivacinni lift. Long intermediate runs, like West Wall, are accessible from the Lenawee lift. At 13,050 feet, A-Basin is the highest lift-served ski area summit in the country. This fact keeps A-Basin open until June, but it can also make the area bitterly cold. Come prepared. Getting there: Take I-70 west to the Loveland Pass Exit (#216). Travel over the pass and directly into A-Basin. Or drive through the Eisenhower Tunnel to the Dillon Exit (#205). Turn left onto Highway 6 and drive about 12 miles to the area. All parking areas are within a short walking distance to the lifts.

## BRECKENRIDGE SKI RESORT
**P.O. Box 1058**
**Breckenridge, CO 80424**
**970/453-5000**

The Breckenridge ski area spans four connecting peaks in Summit County's scenic Ten-Mile Range, making it one of the largest ski areas in Colorado. With 126 trails, 17 lifts, and acres of bowl skiing, Breckenridge truly has something for everyone. Experts can ski the new chutes on Peak 9, and beginners can explore the more intermediate runs on Peak 8. Breckenridge made itself snowboarder-friendly by building a half-pipe and terrain garden on Peak 8. Breckenridge is a popular, and very busy, resort destination spot. New condos, hotels, shops, and restaurants have crowded the historic mining town since the 1980s. Call 970/453-5000 for general information, 970/453-6118 for ski conditions, or 800/221-1091 for lodging. Getting there: Take I-70 west to Exit 203. Turn left onto Highway 9 and continue about 12 miles to Breckenridge. Close-in parking is expensive. Shuttles bring skiers in from outlying lots.

## COPPER MOUNTAIN RESORT
**P.O. Box 3001**
**Copper Mountain, CO 80443**
**970/968-2882**

Copper Mountain's 1,370-acre trail system is naturally divided into beginning, intermediate, and advanced terrain, making it a good family resort. Beginning skiers can practice new techniques on wide, groomed trails on the mountain's west side. Experts will find steep and challenging mogul runs off the A and B lifts on the east mountain face and any of the four mountain-top bowls. Long cruisers and short bump runs meet intermediate skiers' needs. The Copper Mountain Village offers AAA four-star lodging, restaurants, shops, and indoor tennis. Call 970/968-2882 for general information, 970/968-2100 for a snow report, or 800/458-8386 for lodging. Getting there: Take I-70 west from Denver to the Copper Mountain Exit about 75 miles from Denver. Shuttles drop skiers off at different parts of the ski area.

**ELDORA SKI RESORT**
**P.O. Box 1697**
**Nederland, CO 80466**
**303/440-8700**

Families love Eldora. Kids can sleep in later, and parents don't have to battle I-70 ski traffic. Located 21 miles west of Boulder, Eldora offers the closest downhill skiing to Denver. While the area lacks the diversity of larger ski mountains, beginning to advanced skiers will find fun runs ranging from the challenging Corona Bowl to wide-open, groomed slopes on the front face. The Eldora Nordic Center maintains 30 miles of popular cross-country ski trails. The RTD runs daily bus service from Boulder to the ski area mid-November to April. Getting there: Take I-25 north to the Highway 36 West Exit. Take Highway 36 to Canyon Boulevard (Highway 119). Turn left and continue through Boulder Canyon and Nederland. Eldora is 4 miles west of Nederland.

**KEYSTONE RESORT**
**P.O. Box 38**
**Keystone, CO 80435**
**800/258-9553 (information, ski conditions and lodging)**

Keystone offers skiers endless possibilities. Skiers can ski Keystone, Vail, Arapahoe Basin, and Breckenridge with the same Interchangeable Lift Ticket, and the area lights 35 percent of the mountain until 9 p.m. for night skiers. Additional terrain on North Peak and the Outback gives skiers miles of long groomed and mogul runs. Cross-country skiers can get into the backcountry with the Keystone Nordic Center. Lodging, restaurants, shops, and ice skating are available in abundance in Keystone Village. Getting there: Take I-70 west to the Loveland Pass Exit (#216). Follow the pass 6 miles past Arapahoe Basin to Keystone. Or take I-70 through the Eisenhower Tunnel to Exit 205, then drive 6 miles on Highway 6 to Keystone. Buses shuttle skiers from outlying parking lots.

**LOVELAND SKI AREA**
**P.O. Box 899**
**Georgetown, CO 80444**
**303/569-3203 or 800/225-LOVE**

Loveland is the day skier's paradise. Loveland skiers don't have to worry about crossing the pass or Eisen-

---

**TIP**

If you're coming from the Front Range, never buy a ski lift ticket at the ski area. Denver area merchants sell tickets in advance at a significant discount. Gart Bros., King Soopers, Safeway, and Total Gas stations all offer this skier-friendly service. Multi-day lift tickets are also cheaper.

hower Tunnel. Located only 56 miles from Denver, the biggest concern is choosing where to ski on the 836 acres of terrain. Loveland lift tickets are among Colorado's least expensive, and the ski area offers a "Loveland Pass" with discounted tickets and ski free days. The mountain usually receives the bulk of eastern-moving storm fronts. A chairlift connects Loveland Valley, the beginner area, to Loveland Basin, giving skiers access to a variety of trails. Getting there: Take I-70 west from Denver to Exit 216 and the Loveland parking lots. The parking lots are within walking distance of the lifts.

**VAIL**
**P.O. Box 7**
**Vail, CO 81658**
**970/476-5601 (information)**
**970/476-4888 (snow report)**
**800/525-2257 ext. 213 (reservations)**
The rich and famous fur coat–wearing crowd, as well as the grungy-looking ski bums, take advantage of the 4,000 acres of skiing at Vail. *Ski Magazine* and *Snow Country Magazine* have voted Vail the No. 1 ski resort in the United States for years. Judging from the miles of diverse ski runs and bowl areas, it's easy to see why. The down side is the cost. From parking to lift tickets to food, Vail is one of the country's most expensive ski areas. If you can get beyond the pretense and the glitz, Vail has a lot to offer. The renowned Back Bowls give skiers more than 2,600 acres of nearly treeless skiing. The rest of the mountain is divided fairly equally between beginning, intermediate, and expert runs. Getting there: Take I-70 west about 100 miles to the Vail Exit. Daily jets from most major U.S. cities service the Vail/Eagle County Airport 35 miles west of Vail. Daily shuttles also run between the Vail Airport and Denver International Airport.

**WINTER PARK/MARY JANE**
**P.O. Box 36**
**Winter Park, CO 80482**
**970/726-5514 (information)**
**303/572-SNOW (snow report)**
Many native Denverites started making the two-hour ride to Winter Park and Mary Jane as Pee Wee skiers on the Amtrak Ski Train. Today the area remains a local favorite. Winter Park and Vasquez Ridge provide miles of beginning and intermediate runs while Mary Jane is where the hard-core mogul-seekers go. Skiers rave about the above timberline and gladed tree skiing in the Parsenn Bowl. All areas are connected and reachable by ski lift or ski run. Winter Park has consistently high snowfalls averaging above 30 feet every year. Getting there: Take I-70 west to the Highway 40 Exit. Follow the highway over Berthoud Pass. The first parking lots service Mary Jane. Continue down the highway for Winter Park lots. The Ski Train takes skiers from Denver's Union Station to the base of Winter Park every weekend from December to April. For more information, call 303/296-4754.

## CROSS-COUNTRY SKIING

There are literally hundreds of cross-country skiing options close to Denver, ranging from the Front Range to the Summit County area. Weather permitting, skiers who don't want to battle I-70 on a busy ski weekend head to **Roxborough State Park**, **Golden Gate Canyon State Park**, **Jefferson County's Meyers Ranch**

Park, Chatfield State Park, and Cherry Creek State Park, to name-only a few. There is also great skiing off the summit of Guanella Pass near Georgetown. The Keystone, Breckenridge, Frisco, and Copper Mountain Nordic Centers all mark and maintain Nordic trails for cross-country skiers.

## SLEDDING

Sledders young and old careen down the long hill on the face of Jefferson County's **Meyers Ranch Park** during the Front Range's snowy winter months. Innertubes, toboggans, flyers, and even plastic trash bags reach high speeds maneuvering the crowded course. Most sledders obey the rules of the hill. No. 1: don't start down until the course is clear. The park is located off Highway 285 16 miles west of Denver. The small hill in front of the **Denver Museum of Natural History** in City Park is a fun place for smaller sledders.

## TENNIS

*You can usually find a good pick-up tennis game at the local public tennis courses in Metro Denver. The city has recently resurfaced courts at Denver's **City** and **Washington Parks**. City Park, Washington Park, and **Congress Park** all have well-maintained, lighted courts.*

**CENTENNIAL TENNIS CENTER (INDOOR FACILITY)**
5800 S. Federal Blvd., Littleton
303/794-6933  SD
South Suburban Parks and Recreation runs this year-round indoor facility. The center has six courts, a ball machine, group and private lessons, locker rooms with showers, and a pro shop. Court fees: winter non-resident $27/hour/court, resident $21/summer non-resident $15/hour/court, resident $10.

**GATES TENNIS CENTER**
100 S. Adams, Denver
303/355-4461  CD
Gates Tennis Center, owned by the Gates Foundation, is one of the nicest public tennis facilities in the area. The Center has 20 well-maintained outdoor tennis courts, a large backboard wall, ball machine, clubhouse, locker rooms, and tennis instruction. Players can reserve courts one day in advance, and lessons up to a week in advance. Gates also hosts the summer Colorado State Open and the Boys 5A State Championship. Court fees: Singles $4/hour, doubles $5/hour. Hours: Summer daily 7 a.m.–10 p.m., winter daily 9–5.

**HOLLY TENNIS CENTER**
6651 S. Krameria Way, Englewood
303/771-3654  SD
Tennis players can reserve one of the six outdoor, lighted Holly Tennis Center courts April to October. The courts are all in excellent condition. Non-residents can reserve courts three days in advance. Court fees: Non-residents $5/hour/court, residents $4. Hours: April 9–6, May–Sept 7:30 a.m.–10 p.m.

## SPECTATOR SPORTS

*Auto Racing*

**BANDIMERE SPEEDWAY**
3051 S. Rooney Rd., Morrison
303/697-6001 or 303/697-4870
(24-hour hotline)  WD

*Coors Field, home of the Colorado Rockies*

The sound of race cars revving their engines emanates from the quarter-mile Bandimere Speedway track April to October. Bandimere holds weekly National Hot Rod Association sanctioned races during its six-month season. The July Mopar Parts Mile-High Nationals caps the speedway's summer season. More than 100,000 fans converge from around the country for the four-day event. Bandimere is visible from C-470. Take the Morrison Road Exit and follow signs to the speedway.

## Greyhound Racing

**MILE HIGH GREYHOUND PARK**
**6200 Dahlia St., Commerce City**
**303/288-1591          ND**
Live Greyhound racing at the Mile High Greyhound Park has been a Denver tradition since 1949. The lightning-fast dogs appear in alternating 1 p.m. and 7:30 p.m. races Monday through Saturday during summer, fall, and winter. Call for the seasonal schedule.

Bets are placed at any ticket window in the park, or from off-track betting facilities such as Denver's Red & Jerry's restaurant. Mile High also shows year-round horse racing in simulcasts in the clubhouse. Admission: $1 general admission, $3 clubhouse.

## Professional Sports

**COLORADO AVALANCHE**
**McNichols Sports Arena**
**1635 Clay St., Denver**
**303/830-8497 (ticket office)          DD**
Sports-minded Denverites will be forever indebted to the Colorado Avalanche for bringing the city its first national championship. In the team's first season in Denver, the Avalanche (formerly the Quebec Nordiques) won the 1996 Stanley Cup Final by sweeping the Florida Panthers in just four games. While locals were slow to catch professional hockey fever, the Avalanche logo is clearly the most popular in town. COMSAT Entertainment Group, a global communications and entertainment company, owns the Avalanche. After moving the team to Denver, COMSAT endeared itself to

local hockey fans by allowing them to name the team. Denver voted for the Avalanche, and COMSAT designed the logo—a hockey puck circling a large burgundy A symbolizing the Rocky Mountains. Tickets available through the Avalanche ticket office and TicketMaster outlets.

**COLORADO RAPIDS**
**555 17th St., Denver**
**303/299-1599 (tickets)          DD**
The Colorado Rapids, one of ten teams to compete in the newly formed U.S. Major League Soccer division, made its 1996 debut in Mile High Stadium. The Rapids, a Western Conference team, play 16 home and 16 away games each season. ESPN and ESPN2 will broadcast most of the matches. Jorge Campos will play for the Rapids, and the MLS hopes to attract fans with other soccer stars such as Alexi Lalas, the U.S. soccer male athlete of the year. Tickets are available through the Rapids ticket hotline.

**COLORADO ROCKIES**
**2001 Blake St., Denver**
**303/292-0200          DD**
The Rockies played their first season in the newly finished Coors Field ballpark in 1995. The high Coors Field home run factor, attributed to the mile-high altitude and outfield size, makes every game exciting. Coors Field seats 50,200, including the economy-priced Rockpile section located in centerfield. Tickets available through Rocky Mountain Teleseats and the Coors Field box office. Ticket prices range from $1 to $26. Game day parking spaces within five blocks of the ballpark run about $10. Another option is the 16th Street Mall bus, located four blocks south of Coors Field.

**COLORADO XPLOSION**
**800 Grant St. #410**
**Denver**
**303/832-2225          DD**
The Xplosion, Colorado's women's professional basketball team, takes on opponents in the Denver Coliseum and the McNichols Sports Arena. The American Basketball League team plays 22 home games during the five-month season—November to March. Debbie Black, a member of the 1998 U.S. World Cup championship team, and Alissa Burras, drafted from Texas Tech, are set to lead the team into an exciting 1998–99 season. Tickets range from $10 to $38, and season packages are available.

## The Pepsi Center

*The Pepsi Center has saddled up alongside the new Elitch Gardens and future Ocean Journey to virtually fill in the Central Platte Valley. The 650,000-square-foot sports facility will house the Denver Nuggets basketball team and the Colorado Avalanche Hockey team, in addition to hosting concerts, ice shows, the circus, and other family events. The facility is set to open in October 1999.*

*Mile High Stadium, home of the Denver Broncos*

## DENVER BRONCOS
**Denver Mile High Stadium**
**1900 Eliot St., Denver**
**303/433-7466 (ticket office)    DD**

The love this city has for its professional football team was never clearer than when 600,000 fans packed Civic Center Park to celebrate the Broncos' 1998 Super Bowl win over the Green Bay Packers. It took four trips to the championship game to bring home a win, but the wait made the trophy oh so sweet. The Broncos, who were led to the 1998 championship by quarterback John Elway and running back Terrell Davis, have played in Mile High Stadium since 1970 and have sold out more than 200 consecutive home games. In November 1998, taxpayers vote on whether to support the construction of a new facility. If you can track down a ticket, park in the outlying lots around the Auraria campus and follow the Sports Fan walk to Mile High. Contact the stadium ticket office for tickets.

## DENVER NUGGETS
**1635 Clay St., Denver**
**303/893-3865 (ticket office)    DD**

The NBA Denver Nuggets have played in McNichols Sports Arena since 1976. The team has received more support and interest from Denver sports fans since the Nuggets reached the 1994 NBA playoffs. The arena, also home to the Colorado Avalanche, seats 17,000 for basketball games and 16,000 for hockey games. COMSAT Entertainment Group, the Nuggets and Avalanche owners, plan to build the Pepsi Center, an ultra-modern sports arena, to house the two teams by October 1999.

# 11

# PERFORMING ARTS

The Denver performing arts scene is thriving—just like everything else around the city. Innovative venues like Opera Colorado's opera-in-the-round lure artists from New York and Europe to the Rocky Mountains. Placido Domingo is prominent among the famous to have graced the Boettcher stage. Musical groups love to play beneath the stars at the unique Red Rocks Amphitheater in Morrison. The Colorado Symphony Orchestra (the only musician-owned symphony in the country) accompanies Opera Colorado and Colorado Ballet performances throughout the year. Internationally recognized local dance companies like Cleo Parker Robinson and David Taylor entertain Denver audiences with imaginative modern dance performances between worldwide tours. The local Denver Center for the Performing Arts offers unique theater performances in the Denver Performing Arts Complex every season. Garner Attractions brings popular Broadway hits like Cats and Phantom of the Opera through town. Beyond the major performing arts groups, many smaller theaters around Denver present local talent and experimental production to Denver theater buffs. Relatively low ticket prices make Denver performing arts accessible to almost everyone.

## THEATER

For a relatively small city, Denver supports a large number of local theater companies. In addition to the listings that follow, these small theater companies should not be overlooked: Changing Scene, 1527 1/2 Champa, 303/893-5775; Avenue Theatre, 2119 E. 17th Avenue, 303/321-5925; Jack's Theatre, 1553 Platte, 303/433-8082; and Rivertree Theatre, 1124 Santa Fe Drive, 825-8150.

## ARVADA CENTER FOR THE ARTS AND HUMANITIES
**6901 Wadsworth Blvd., Arvada**
**303/431-3939　　　　　　ND**

The huge brown brick Arvada Center structure houses everything from professional theater, dance, and music concerts to historical exhibits and art classes. The 500-seat main theater hosts year-round Broadway musical and theater productions as well as the local David Taylor Dance Company. Summer theatergoers will enjoy the 1,200-seat outdoor amphitheater. The Arvada Center would like to lure loyal DCPA theatergoers to Arvada's lighter-fare theater with reasonably priced season ticket packages. The ample free parking situation beats busy downtown theater nights. Center hours: Mon–Fri 9–6, Sat 9–5, Sun 1–5. Wheelchair-accessible.

## DENVER CIVIC THEATRE
**721 Santa Fe Dr., Denver**
**303/595-3800　　　　　　CD**

Denver theater baron Henry Lowenstein founded the Denver Civic Theatre in 1985 after the closing of his Bonfils Theatre on East Colfax. Lowenstein passed on the Civic Theatre baton to Christopher Selbie and Mark Connely in 1996. The Compass and Industrial Arts Theatre Companies perform out of the 250-seat proscenium mainstage and the intimate 104-seat Dorie theaters. Compass Theatre performs classics such as *Cyrano de Bergerac* and *Henry VI*, and has world rights to the world premiere of *I, Claudius*. Industrial Theatre is the contemporary component of the theater, performing plays such as *All My Sons* and *The Madwoman of Chaillot*. Free parking is available next to the theater.

*Helen Bonfils*

## DENVER PERFORMING ARTS COMPLEX
**1245 Champa St., Denver**
**303/893-4000 or 303/893-4100**
**(box office)　　　　　　DD**

The story goes that Denver businessman Donald Seawell was walking downtown on 14th Street with a New York friend when he pulled out an envelope and sketched out his dream: a state-of-the-art performing arts complex. The Denver Performing Arts Complex, the second largest in the country, follows Seawell's initial sketch to a tee. A high glass arch covers the complex in a trumpet-like swoop. Electronic kiosks and red-coated ushers direct visitors through the windowed complex. With nine theaters, activity always abounds in the Plex. Architect Roche Dinkloo built the complex around the original 1900 Auditorium Theatre. This 2,100-seat proscenium theater presents smaller dance and theatrical performances. The Denver Center for the Performing Arts performs a mixture of 12 classical and contemporary shows from September to June in the

During busy winter months when most theaters are in use, it's hard to find parking in the 1,700-space Denver Performing Arts Complex garage or anywhere near it. Many veteran theater-goers plan to arrive early and eat dinner at the Theatre Cafe in the complex or another downtown eatery. Otherwise, drivers should seriously consider using public transportation. Park in the light rail lot at I-25 and Broadway and take the train to the 14th and Stout station. If you park in lots outside downtown, the 16th Street Mall bus stops within two blocks of DCPA. The #10 RTD bus stops near 15th and Stout Streets, as does the #15 RTD from Colfax. If all else fails, additional parking may be found in the Executive Tower Inn lot on 14th and Arapahoe or on the Auraria campus lots across Speer Boulevard. For more information, call the parking and traffic hotline at 303/640-7275.

Helen Bonfils Theatre Complex. Opera Colorado and the Colorado Symphony perform in the 2,700-seat theater-in-the-round Boettcher Concert Hall. Colorado Ballet and touring Broadway shows perform in the 1993 Temple Buell Theatre, the newest in the complex. The 215-seat Garner Galleria Theatre offers lighter cabaret-style productions.

### EL CENTRO SU TEATRO
**4725 High St., Denver**
**303/296-0219                   CD**

El Centro Su Teatro is a multicultural art institution located in the north Denver Globeville neighborhood. The theater company, which developed out of a 1971 university class, presents six bilingual plays a year. *Joaquin's Christmas*, Anthony Garcia's adaptation of *A Christmas Carol*, is a seasonal favorite. El Centro moved to its present location in the old Elyria Elementary School in 1989. El Centro is an important resource for the largely Hispanic Globeville community. The company holds the Chicano Music Festival as well as a free outdoor film festival for the neighborhood in the summer. The theater seats about 100 people. Reservations are recommended. Ticket prices range from $3 to $15.

### EULIPIONS, INC.
**1770 Sherman St., Denver**
**303/295-6814                   DD**

Jo Bunton Keel founded Eulipions, an African American theater company, in 1982. The year-round company presents African American works by national playwrights; Langston Hughes' *Black Nativity* is the company's trademark production.

Since its conception, Eulipions has performed out of a large high-ceilinged room in an old building on 24th and Welton. But in 1995 Keel formed an arts coalition to buy the historic El Jebel Shrine Temple at 1770 Sherman. The company moved into the five-story 1906 building in November 1996. They opened their first season in the 550-seat theater with *Black Nativity*. Reservations are recommended for all Eulipions productions.

## Bonfils' Bounty

*The name Helen Bonfils is associated with numerous important Denver institutions. The controlling* Denver Post *stockholder for 35 years, Ms. Helen, as she is still called by colleagues, built the Bonfils Theatre, founded the Belle Bonfils Blood Bank, the Bonfils Tumor Clinic, the Denver Clinic, and the CU School of Nursing. She also made substantial contributions to the Denver Museum of Natural History, the Denver Art Museum, and Central City Opera. While all of these philanthropic causes were an important part of Ms. Helen's life, the Bonfils Theatre was perhaps closest to her heart. She built the theater, located on the corner of Colfax and Elizabeth Streets, in 1953 to bring high-quality theater to the Denver community. Ms. Helen herself acted on Broadway early in her career, and later performed roles, including Regina Giddens in Lillian Helman's* The Little Foxes, *in the Bonfils Theatre. Her dream was to turn Bonfils into a professional repertory company. Unfortunately, her dream didn't materialize during her lifetime. Shortly before her death, Ms. Helen told her close friend and business partner Donald Seawell she wished she could build a "real" theater for Denver. Seawell, Ms. Helen's appointed* Denver Post *successor, fulfilled his dear friend's dying wish with gusto. With funding from the Helen Bonfils Foundation, Seawell started construction on the Denver Performing Arts Complex, and helped form the Denver Center for Performing Arts theater company. Seawell is currently chairman of the DCPA and manages the Bonfils Foundation. Today, the DCPA, one of the wealthiest theater companies in the country thanks to the Bonfils endowment, performs in the Helen Bonfils Theatre Complex. The DCPA is the largest professional resident theater company in the Rocky Mountain region, with an ensemble of more than 40 artists.*

**GERMINAL STAGE THEATER**
**44th Ave. and Alcott St., Denver**
**303/455-7108**  CD

The Germinal Stage program masthead reads "presenting plays of substance in an exciting and intimate atmosphere." Local critics usually praise the company's sometimes eccentric interpretations and performances. Founded by five local actors in 1974, Germinal Stage is one of the oldest continuously running Denver theaters. Ed Baierlein, one of the original founders and a major figure in Denver theater, lists the company's favorite playwrights as Eugene O'Neill and George Bernard Shaw. All Germinal Stage plays are performed in the theater company's 100-seat north Denver theater. Local actors present more than 100 performances of five plays during the October to July season. Ticket prices range $10.75 to $12.75. Economy previews of a play's first three performances cost $8.

### THEATRE ON BROADWAY
**13 S. Broadway, Denver**
**303/860-9360** CD

Theatre on Broadway brings regional premieres of New York Broadway productions to Denver's South Broadway Street year-round. Formerly Lakewood Players, Theatre on Broadway has entertained the Denver area with never-before-seen-in-Denver premieres since 1987. Each performance runs six to eight weeks in the 120-seat theater. Ticket prices range $8 to $16. Free parking is available next to the theater.

## CLASSICAL MUSIC AND OPERA

### CENTRAL CITY OPERA
**621 17th St., Denver**
**303/292-6700 (box office)** DD

While much of Central City has changed since gambling invaded the once sleepy mining town, Central City Opera has retained its historic 65-year-old charm. The renowned opera company, the longest running summer opera festival in the country, presents two classic operas and one operetta each summer in the 1878 Victorian Teller House. The Teller House, made from all native Colorado materials, was built by Welsh and Cornish miners intent on adding culture to their spartan lives. Today, city opera-goers can ride to Central City in chartered buses, or drive the 60-

*Central City Opera*

mile trip. Shuttles transport drivers from outlying parking lots to the Teller House doors. Matinees and evening shows run Tuesday to Sunday. Ticket prices start at $22.

**COLORADO SYMPHONY ORCHESTRA**
1013 13th St., Denver
303/986-8742
or 98-MUSIC (box office)     DD

The Colorado Symphony Orchestra, previously the Denver Symphony Orchestra, is the country's only musician-owned symphony. Under the youthful directorship of Marin Alsop, the revived symphony has met with rave reviews. Alsop, the only woman to direct an orchestra of CSO's size, has brought new accessibility and energy into the organization. The orchestra performs 104 traditional and contemporary symphonies during its September to May season. The CSO performs in the Boettcher Concert Hall as well as at free summer concerts in Washington, City, and Red Rocks Parks. Reduced priced Blue Jean and Family Series make the symphony accessible to a broader audience. Ticket prices range from $4 to $35. The best Boettcher seats are directly facing the orchestra.

**FRIENDS OF CHAMBER MUSIC**
458 Grape St., Denver
303/388-9839     CD

This group of local chamber music lovers puts together a series of five concerts performed by international and national orchestras between October and April. All concerts are in the Houston Fine Arts Center in northeast Denver. Single tickets are available. The series package is $75.

**OPERA COLORADO**
1315 Curtis St., Denver
303/986-874     DD

Internationally acclaimed director Nathaniel Merrill dreamed of establishing a grand opera company of the highest caliber in the western United States. In 1981 he founded Opera Colorado, an innovative grand opera company. Today, Opera Colorado is the only company in the nation to perform operas in-the-round. The in-the-round staging presents challenges to directors and performers, and a more multidimensional stage view to audiences. Since its founding, Opera Colorado has attracted stars such as Placido Domingo and Sherrill Milnes to perform in the Boettcher Concert Hall productions. The company has received national acclaim from opera buffs and critics alike, for its productions of *Carmen*, *La Bohème*, *Faust*, and *Madame Butterfly*, to name a few. The Colorado Symphony Orchestra performs with Opera Colorado throughout the four-month spring season. Advance reservations are recommended. Ticket prices range from $17 to $118. Season packages are also available.

## DANCE

**CLEO PARKER ROBINSON DANCE ENSEMBLE**
119 Park Ave. West, Denver
303/295-1759     CD

The internationally acclaimed Cleo Parker Robinson Dance Ensemble has graced Denver's dance community with storytelling performances since 1970. The modern dance company, which also participates annually in the American Dance Festival, performs historic dances by black pioneer and contemporary choreographers. Strong, fluid movements and rhythms characterize the innovative, high-energy company. Cleo Parker holds three spring, fall, and winter concerts in the company's 300-seat theater and at other local venues. Free parking is available next to the theater and in the Safeway lot across the street.

**COLORADO BALLET COMPANY**
**1278 Lincoln St., Denver**
**303/837-8888** DD
The 35-year-old Colorado Ballet is Denver's premier classical ballet company. Under the leadership of Martin Fredmann, an internationally accomplished director, choreographer, and teacher, the company performs four major concerts during the fall-to-spring season, in addition to its national and international tours. Many of the 23-member troupe trained in the company's own academy. In addition to the annual *Nutcracker*, the company performs classics such as *Swan Lake* and *Cinderella*. All performances are held in the Buell or Auditorium Theatres in the Denver Performing Arts Complex. Ticket prices range from $12 to $48.

## CONCERT VENUES

**FIDDLER'S GREEN AMPHITHEATRE**
**6350 Greenwood Plaza Blvd.**
**Englewood**
**303/220-7000** SD
Fiddler's Green Amphitheatre opened in 1988 as a larger outdoor alternative to Red Rocks. Soon after its debut, however, the concert venue became embroiled in controversy as neighbors bombarded the amphitheater with noise complaints. The final compromise: end concerts by 10:30 p.m. Fiddler's Green offers general

### Preserving the Paramount

*Fearing financial disaster during the Depression, the Paramount Theatre's original owner, Joseph Gould, tried to cancel his Wurlitzer organ order. Luckily for theater lovers, his effort failed. The organ is the main reason the Paramount isn't a parking lot today. When the Paramount faced potential demolition during the office building craze in the 1980s, the American Theatre Organ Society helped organize a coalition to save the historic theater. The Historic Paramount Foundation formed in 1981 to preserve the "grand dame of downtown Denver." Many Denverites felt the Paramount was essential to revitalizing downtown Denver with increased nighttime activity. The foundation restored the original art deco theater features and started holding concerts and events to raise money. Finally, in 1988, former Denver Mayor Federico Peña designated the Paramount a national landmark. Today, the primary function of the foundation is the preservation of the theater.*

*Paramount Theatre*

admission seating on the green and reserved seating on benches in front of the stage. The amphitheater is no Red Rocks, but it does hold popular concerts such as the annual reggae Sunsplash. Arrive early to avoid the top rows on the green, where visibility is limited.

**MAMMOTH EVENTS CENTER**
**1510 Clarkson St., Denver**
**303/860-7181 or 303/860-1333**
**for events information          CD**
Mammoth Events Center looks out of place among neighboring buildings in this East Colfax location. Its palatial facade, lead windows, and ornate towers contrast sharply with the drab Gold Nugget Disco across the street. The building originally opened as Mammoth Skating Rink in 1907, and has undergone continuous changes to bring it to its current status as an events center. The 35,000-square-foot building hosts music concerts, banquets, balls, and sports events. For concerts, Mammoth seats up to 2,900 people, with a 130-foot-long dance floor. The band Tesla is among those to have passed through Mammoth.

**McNICHOLS SPORTS ARENA**
**1635 Bryant St., Denver**
**303/640-7300          CD**
During basketball and hockey season, McNichols Sports Arena is busy switching from an ice to wood playing surface. In its spare time, it serves as a concert venue for the large, big-name shows that come to Denver. The arena seats up to 18,000 people and opened in 1975 with a sold-out Lawrence Welk concert. Since then, groups like Metallica and ACDC have packed the arena. Custom full-range speakers hang from the ceiling, bringing loud sound to every seat in the arena.

**OGDEN THEATRE**
**935 E. Colfax Ave., Denver**
**303/831-9448          CD**
The Ogden Theatre opened in 1917 as a vaudeville theater, and remained

PERFORMING ARTS

a local favorite for art films until it closed in 1990. Concert promoter Doug Kaufman bought the theater (now listed in the National Register of Historic Places) in 1993 and converted it into a 1,110-seat concert venue for his company Nobody in Particular Presents. Today, the Ogden books alternative rock bands. Kaufman renovated the entire theater, from the 45-foot oak stage to the gold leaf detail and stencil paintings on the wall. There is some on-street parking near the theater in addition to Hall and Hall Auto Parks on Pearl Street. Take precautions walking around Colfax at night.

### PARAMOUNT THEATRE
**1631 Glenarm Pl., Denver**
**303/534-8336 (box office)**
**or 303/892-7016 (events)    DD**
Denver architect Temple Buell designed the art deco Paramount Theatre as a silent film movie palace in 1930. The theater still houses one of the only two functioning Wurlitzer twin console organs in the country (the other is in New York's Radio City Music Hall). The Historic Paramount Foundation, formed in 1981 to save the theater from demolition, restored the original terra cotta facade, hand-painted tapestries, and cherry red plush seats. The theater, which accommodates over 2,000 people in orchestra and balcony seating, is a classy, sit-down concert venue featuring acts from Big Head Todd to the Colorado Symphony Orchestra. Parking is available in lots around the 16th Street Mall. The light rail and 16th Street Mall bus also stop nearby.

### RED ROCKS AMPHITHEATER
**12700 West Alameda Pkwy.**
**Morrison**
**303/697-8801 or 303/640-7300    WD**
From the breathtaking 250-million year-old sandstone monoliths surrounding the stage to the perfect natural acoustics, Red Rocks is the premier outdoor concert venue. The amphitheater, which seats up to 9,000, is located within the 640-acre Red Rocks Park. Sixty-nine rows of

*Red Rocks Amphitheater*

> ## Buying Tickets
>
> *TicketMaster sells tickets for local music, theater, and sports events by phone (303/830-TIXS) or in person at Blockbuster Music, Foley's department stores, and Budget Tapes and CDs stores. The Ticket Bus (303/623-1905), a red 1946 British transit bus located on 16th and Curtis Streets downtown, also serves as a TicketMaster outlet (cash only).*
>
> *For tickets to a Rockies game, call Rocky Mountain Teleseats at 800/388-ROCK. Rocky Mountain also sells tickets to Nobody in Particular Presents performances and other local events; call 800/444-SEAT.*
>
> *And if you're looking for premium seats at popular or sold-out concerts, sporting events, or theater productions, try a ticket-finding service such as Ticket Connection (303/758-1999) or Colorado Ticket Company (303/649-9999).*

red rock bench seating lead down to the stage nestled at the foot of the 300-foot-high Creation Rock and Ship Rock monoliths. During the annual Fourth of July shows, concert-goers watch fireworks illuminate the Denver sky. For open seating tickets, arrive at the gate by mid-afternoon, and make sure you're armed with plenty of water and sunscreen. Glass and aluminum containers are strictly prohibited.

# 12
# NIGHTLIFE

To the surprise of twenty-somethings who grew up in Denver, the recent downtown revitalization has brought a hopping nightlife scene to the city. Whereas the 16th Street Mall was sleepy and lifeless in the early 1980s, it's now teeming with after-dusk activity. Nightclubs and bars have sprouted throughout lower downtown, and countless jazz, blues, rock, and alternative music clubs provide live entertainment every night of the week. While this book is intended to cover the Metro Denver region, the nightlife section focuses on central Denver, as most people from the surrounding counties come to downtown Denver when they're ready for a night on the town. The weekly Westword *"Backbeat"* section is a good source for current happenings.

## DANCE CLUBS

**BUTTERFIELD EIGHT**
2850 E. Second Ave.
Denver
303/394-9499                    CD
Butterfield Eight is a sophisticated dance club for the over-30 set. Located in the heart of Cherry Creek about ten minutes from downtown Denver, the cabaret-style club brings in live and DJ music three nights a week. A dress code is enforced. Hours: Wed & Sat opens at 9 p.m., Fri at 5 p.m.

**I-BEAM**
1427 Larimer St., Denver
303/534-2326                    DD
Huge picture windows from the second-story I-Beam dance club afford great Larimer Square people-watching for wallflowers and dancers catching their breath. Most need a break after a few minutes on the hard wood dance floor. The DJ plays only high-energy top 40 dance music with at least 140 beats per minute. Special dance floor effects include strobe lights and fog. Hours: Wed–Sun 8 p.m.–2 a.m. Admission: free–$4.

## Top Ten Places to Dance in Metro Denver

by Mattie Springfield, owner of Mattie Springfield's School of Performing Arts

1. I-Beam, 1427 Larimer St.
2. Spruce Street East, 7800 E. Colfax Ave.
3. Pierre's Supper Club, 2157 Downing
4. Maximilian's, 2151 Lawrence St.
5. Club Spice, 4470 Peoria St.
6. Ebony Rose II, 3940 York St.
7. Park Hill Golf Club, 4141 E. 35th Ave.
8. Mercury Cafe, 2129 California St.
9. Taylor Court, 1490 Lafayette
10. Club Mixx, 11249 E. Colfax Ave.

**LOS CABOS II**
**15 Curtis St., Denver**
**303/571-0007**      **CD**

It's easy to feel you've left the U.S. when you come to this Latin dance club and Peruvian restaurant. Spanish replaces English, Peruvian weavings and paintings hang on the walls, and the dance style clearly isn't Coloradan. For the benefit of Latin dance neophytes, "the Salsa Palace" offers salsa lessons Fridays 7 to 8 p.m. before open dancing starts. Call Nelsa at 303/685-9005 for more information. To get there, take the Bryant Street Exit off the 6th Avenue highway. Dance hours: Fri & Sat 9 p.m.–2 a.m. Cover: $3 for DJ, $6 for live bands.

**9TH AVENUE WEST**
**99 W. Ninth Ave., Denver**
**303/572-8006**      **DD**

Swing, Latin rhythms, and acid jazz are but a few of the many musical styles offered at this snazzy night spot. A different band plays each night, and the Friday martini happy hours are hot. Appetizers and entrees are offered, and there are free dance lessons most nights. Tue 9 p.m.–2 a.m., Wed–Sat 7 p.m.–2 a.m., Sun 7 p.m.–midnight. No cover.

**ROCK ISLAND**
**1614 15th St., Denver**
**303/572-7625**      **DD**

This alternative dance club set up shop in a lower downtown warehouse in 1985, long before LoDo had any night scene to speak of. On most weekends, lines of young people trail from Wazee Street to the dark tunnel-like entrance. Inside, dancers can boogie on platforms built around the dance floor, or play pool in the basement bar. DJs keep the dance energy high with alternative and house music. The club holds weekly 16 and over nights for the younger set. Cover: $3–$7. Hours: Wed–Sat, opens at 9 p.m.

## TRIVIA

During a 1992 presidential campaign stop, Bill Clinton told supporters he was going to El Chapultepec to see what it was all about. News traveled fast, and so many people showed up that the man who would be president was forced to stay in his car.

## JAZZ CLUBS

**CASINO CABARET**
2637 Welton St.
Denver
303/292-2626　　　　　　DD
The historic Casino Cabaret, located in the heart of the newly thriving Five Points business center, adds a wide variety of weekly jazz acts to the Denver music scene. The club's logo, "ain't nothin' but a jazz thing," says it all. The club features big-name Latin jazz artists like the 11-piece Conjunto Cespedes and the firey pianist Eddie Palmer. Chuck Mangione also made an impressive appearance as part of the club's 1998 summer line-up. Tickets are available at the door or through TicketMaster (303/830-TIXS).

**EL CHAPULTEPEC**
1962 Market St., Denver
303/295-9126　　　　　　DD
El Chapultepec is the reigning queen of Denver jazz clubs. While other clubs have come and gone in an eyeblink, the Pec has thrilled the Denver jazz community with local and national acts since 1980. People endure the stuffy, smoke-filled space to hear famous jazz musicians such as Eddie "Lockjaw" Davis and Tony Bennett, whose photographs line the side wall. Despite its national reputation and fame, the Pec has stayed in the same modest space on the corner of 20th and Market since 1933. Bands start at 8:30 p.m. There is a one drink minimum per set. Hours: 7 a.m.–2 a.m.

**HERB'S HIDEOUT**
2057 Larimer St., Denver
303/299-9555　　　　　　DD
The bar's dingy front entrance looks anything but inviting, and, in fact, it's not. Bar-goers must enter through the friendlier blue-lighted alley entrance. Owners remodeled the once-shabby hang-out spot in 1995 and turned it into a cozy piano bar. Local jazz bands play in the intimate space Wednesday nights. Other nights the bar is hopping with karaoke and Roaring Twenties theme nights; weekends feature a piano bar. Cover: $2 for jazz. Hours: 8 p.m.–2 a.m.

**PARK HILL GOLF CLUB**
4141 E. 35th Ave., Denver
303/333-5414 or 303/333-2940
for reservations　　　　　　CD
National and international jazz legends travel to Denver to take part in the Park Hill Golf Club's live jazz series. Old-time performers such as Bob Wilber and Peanuts Hucko have graced the small north Park Hill stage since local jazz pianist Ralph Sutton helped organize the series in 1994. The casual clubhouse series allows concert-goers to mingle with musicians and buy CDs after the performance. The cabaret-style clubhouse seats up to 300, and concert-goers can order dinner from the special bistro menu between 5:30 p.m. and 9 p.m.

Reservations are required. Hours: Music sets run 7–10:30. Ticket prices: Concert only $30; dinners, add $6–$14.

**VARTAN'S JAZZ CLUB AND RESTAURANT**
**1800 Glenarm Place, Denver**

**303/399-1111 reservations and 24-hour jazz line**     **DD**

When Vartan Jazz opened in Cherry Creek in 1995, it became the city's premier sit-down jazz club, and when it moved downtown in 1998 and added an excellent eatery, the crowd followed. Vartan attracts

---

## History of Jazz in Denver
### by Greg Heartman, editor for Microsoft's Denver Sidewalk

*New Orleans, Kansas City, Chicago, and, of course, New York come to mind when we think of the history of jazz. In these cities the first truly unique American art form held court in street bands, smoky clubs, and grand ballrooms. But walk along Welton Street between 26th and 30th Avenues in Denver and you'll find yourself in the heart of this same history. After World War II, Five Points—so called by the old Denver Tramway Co. because the intersection of Welton, Washington, and 27th Streets and E. 26th Avenue met to form a five-pointed star—jumped with the musical talents of the nation's top jazz players.*

*In a time where other venues around the city restricted their audiences to whites only, "the Points" stood out as a haven of tolerance. The Casino Ballroom, the Voters' Club, and The Rossonian's Blue Room were filled with players and audiences of every skin color and economic background. After-hour clubs, where music played from 5 p.m. to 7 a.m., were prime spots for young local players to test their chops with the best the tradition had to offer.*

*Duke Ellington, Charlie Parker, Dizzy Gillespie, Billy Holliday, Nat King Cole, and others would show up for impromptu jam sessions at Knock-out Brown's, Lil's, The Hole, the Voters' Club, and Mr. Green's. Although the history created by such local jazz legends as Beatty "B.C." Hobbs, Charlotte Cowens, Shelly "The Professor" Rhym, Cedar Walton, Paul Quinichette, and the like isn't well known, it's worth noting. Some of these musicians still play around the area (although you might have to do some poking around to find them) and they still offer some of the best music in the country.*

> **TRIVIA**
>
> Denver nightlife was a different animal in the 1860s, according to traveler William Dixon: "As you wander about these hot and dirty streets you seem to be walking in a city of demons. Every fifth house appears to be a bar, a whiskey-shop, a lager-beer saloon; every tenth house appears to be either a brothel or a gambling house; very often both in one. In these horrible dens a man's life is of no more worth than a dog's."

crowds with weekly live national and international acts, such as Freddy Cole and the Hal Galper Trio, as well as the local Joel Kaye Neophonic Big Band. When national acts appear, the club is more expensive than other local venues, but makes up for it with a comfortable, spacious setting. Open Monday through Saturday; hours vary. Tickets start at $3.

**YORK STREET CAFE AND BAR**
2239 E. Colfax Ave., Denver
303/331-0533                          CD
York Street features local fusion jazz bands such as Dotsero and Nelson Rangell in an intimate cafe setting. Located in the old Capitol Hill State Bank building on the corner of Colfax and York, York Street feels like an English pub. Heavy oak booths, a mirrored bar, and paneled walls provide finishing touches. Jazz bands play Thursday, Friday, and Saturday nights. A $6 minimum purchase per person is required.

## BLUES CLUBS

**BRENDAN'S**
1624 Market St., Denver
303/595-0609                          DD
Brendan's, Denver's self-acclaimed "home of the blues," is where the twenty-something and up crowd goes to listen to live local and national blues acts. The club is beneath the 16th and Market Street restaurant and gallery complex. The large space allows room to dance or to sit and sip a drink around the perimeter. Bands start at 9:30. Cover: $1–$5.

**RED FISH LOOZIANA ROADHOUSE**
1701 Wynkoop St., Denver
303/595-0443                          DD
This off-the-wall New Orleans–style restaurant also offers a Voodoo Lounge scene Thursday through Sunday, with local and national blues acts. The Bayou atmosphere adds to the experience, and the raw oyster bar and regular menu of Cajun favorites makes Red Fish a happening place to be in LoDo. Mon–Wed 11:30–10, Fri 11:30–midnight, Sat 4–midnight, Sun 4–9. No cover.

## OTHER MUSIC CLUBS

**BLUEBIRD THEATRE**
3317 E. Colfax Ave.
Denver
303/322-2308                          CD
Two native Denverites, Chris Swank and Evan Dechman, transformed this 1913 silent movie theater-turned-porn house into a local concert venue in 1994. After painstaking

renovations, original frescoes now stand out on both sides of the stage and laughing faces line the walls. The Bluebird features an eclectic mix of weekly live jazz, rock, punk, and country bands. The intimate cabaret-style theater seats up to 325 and has a full liquor and coffee bar. Parking is available across the street. East Colfax attracts sketchy characters, so try not to walk alone at night. Tickets: $3–$14.

### HERMAN'S HIDEAWAY
**1578 S. Broadway, Denver**
**303/777-5840**                    **CD**
Herman's has been a South Broadway bar since the 1960s. The bar owners decided to add live music and dancing to its repertoire in the late 1980s. The club primarily books original local and some national rock and alternative bands. The 500-capacity club has a band stage, dance floor, and two bars. Bands play Tuesday through Saturday nights starting at 9:30. Tickets available at TicketMaster or Herman's box office. Free valet parking is available. Tickets: $3–$15.

### LITTLE BEAR
**28075 Hwy. 74, Evergreen**
**303/674-9991**                    **WD**
A trip to Evergreen's Little Bear combines getting out of the city with listening to good local rock music. The club plays on its mountain-town environs with log cabin walls and a heavy wood bar in the middle of the room. City folk, Harley Davidson bikers, and locals mix here. Hours: Daily 11 a.m.–12:30 a.m. Cover: $5–$10.

### MERCURY CAFE
**2199 California St., Denver**
**303/294-9281**                    **DD**
The Mercury Cafe is a venue for a variety of stage performances. The cafe hosts bluegrass jam sessions, jazz, poetry readings, and open stage nights in addition to local alternative, rock, and reggae concerts. Some shows admit 18 and over. Make dinner reservations to coordinate with shows. Hours vary. Tickets start at $3.

### SLOAN'S LAKE EVENT AND CONFERENCE CENTER
**2045 Sheridan Blvd., Denver**
**303/232-2425**                    **WD**

> **TRIVIA**
>
> For another perspective on Denver nightlife, head to Colfax Avenue, the longest commercial strip in the country. Neon-infested East Colfax Avenue is lined with dark lounges, seedy strip joints, and tattoo parlors, as well as classy antique book stores, quaint cafes, and the State Capitol.

*Mayan Theater, p. 206*

The Events Center opened in June 1995 in the renovated Sloan's Lake Bowling Alley. The new owners preserved the original bowling lanes—wood panels, line-up arrows, and all—and turned them into a dance floor. Located in west Denver's Edgewater neighborhood across from Sloan's Lake Park, the 21-and-over club features jazz performers during happy hour Wednesday through Friday, 5 p.m. to 8 p.m. Crossover II, a salsa band, plays 8:30 p.m. to 1 a.m. Fridays. Call the club for information about monthly national jazz acts. Hours: Tues–Sun 4 p.m.–1:30 a.m.

## COUNTRY AND WESTERN CLUBS

### GRIZZLY ROSE
5450 N. Valley Hwy., Denver
303/295-1330  ND

The Grizzly Rose is the closest you get to real country in Metro Denver. In addition to having one of Colorado's largest dance floors, the club features live music nightly, with six national acts per week. National stars including Jerry Jeff Walker, Conway Twitty, and Garth Brooks have appeared here. Bill and Cathy's Country Dance School gives free line-dancing lessons Mondays, Wednesdays, and Fridays, 7 p.m. to 8 p.m. Thursday is 18-and-over night, Sunday is family night. Hours: Mon–Fri 11 a.m.–2 a.m., Sat 5 p.m.–2 a.m., Sun 3 p.m.–2 a.m. Cover charge varies.

### STAMPEDE MESQUITE GRILL AND DANCE EMPORIUM
2430 S. Havana, Aurora
303/696-7686  ED

Some of Metro Denver's best country dancers strut their stuff at the popular Stampede dance club. Others just come to watch them. Eager would-be dancers pack the dance floor for free weekly lessons. The popular lessons, Tuesday through Thursday and Saturday and Sunday nights, teach everything from the cha cha to line dancing. The two-story main room has six bars, a restaurant, boot shining service, and

*Fadó Irish Pub, p. 202*

Fadó Irish Pub

## Top "Down Home" Denver Bars
by Terrance Kelly, attorney at law
and "down home" connoisseur

These are not the trendy, "see-and-be-seen" bars. These are down home bars frequented by hard-drinking, no-frills, working people who typically live within walking distance of these neighborhood establishments.

- Lookin' Good Restaurant and Lounge, 66 Sheridan Blvd.
- It'll Do Lounge, 2001 W. 48th Ave.
- Mozart Lounge, 1417 Krameria St.
- PS Lounge, 3416 E. Colfax Ave.
- Satire Restaurant and Lounge, 1920 E. Colfax Ave.
- Red Ram, 5026 E. Colfax Ave.
- Charlie Brown's Bar and Grill, 980 Grant St.
- Campus Lounge, 701 S. University
- Don's Mixed Drink's, 723 E. 6th Ave.

an old-fashioned photo booth. Hours: Tues–Sun. 5 p.m.–2 a.m. Cover: $1–$3, no cover Sundays.

## PUBS AND BARS

### CHARLIE BROWN'S
**980 Grant St., Denver**
**303/860-1655**      **CD**

Paul Lopez is the best part of this 35-year-old neighborhood bar. The local piano player bellows out show tunes from behind his corner piano. Charlie Brown's is open Tuesday through Saturday, 6 p.m. to 1 a.m. Regulars gather around the piano gleefully joining Lopez in his melodious rounds while newcomers tap their toes from the bar. Hours: 7 a.m. to 2 a.m.

### CHERRY CRICKET
**2641 E. 2nd Ave., Denver**
**303/322-7666**      **CD**

If you grew up in Denver, you go to the Cricket to see old friends. If you didn't, you go for the casual, friendly neighborhood atmosphere and extensive beer selection. Non-smokers beware: the small space has little, if any, ventilation. Pinball machines, two pool tables, and a few booths pack the back room, while the front room has sit-down space—if you're lucky. Hours: 11 a.m.–2 a.m.

### CRUISE ROOM
**1659 Wazee, Denver**
**303/825-1107**      **DD**

The Cruise Room, located in the historic Oxford Hotel, opened on December 5, 1933, the day Prohibition was repealed. Denver architect Charles Jaka modeled the narrow art deco bar after the lounge on the *Queen Mary* cruise ship. Subtle red lights create a lounge atmosphere and highlight the wall carvings, each

> ## Sports Bars
>
> *When Coors Field opened in the spring of 1995, sports bars sprouted up one by one on all of the surrounding blocks. With such tough competition, it remains to be seen how many will survive even the first off-season. There's no point describing each separately since they're all, well, basically the same: your typical large-screen-TV-sportin' sports bar. Anyway, here's a list of those more highly recommended.*
>
> *__The Sports Column__ (1930 Blake St., 303/296-1930), one of the more popular downtown sports bars, reportedly serves the best bar food. __LoDo's Bar and Grill__ (1946 Market St., 303/293-8555) is notable for its location. Two notorious Denver madames, Jennie Rogers and then Mattie Silk, ran the renowned House of Mirrors brothel in this building. __Stars Sports Garden__ (1860 Blake St., 303/295-7827) is owned by local and national professional athletes, including the Denver Bronco's wide receiver Mike Pritchard, Bruce Riffin of the Colorado Rockies, and former Boston Celtics star Jay Humphries.*

representing an international toast. The Cruise Room is listed in the National Register of Historic Places. Hours: Sun–Thur 4:30 p.m.–midnight, Fri & Sat 4:30 p.m.–2 a.m.

**FADÓ IRISH PUB**
**1735 19th St., Denver**
**303/297-0066**  DD
Irish and American businessmen joined together to bring an authentic taste of Ireland to Denver's famed LoDo area. Right next to Coors Field, Fadó offers a mishmash of contemporary and traditional Irish pub settings, comfortable seating, and the perfect pint of Guinness. The updated Irish food is fairly consistent, and the pub hires musicians to host "impromptu" jams of Celtic favorites. Mon–Sun 11:30 a.m.–2 a.m.

**GIGGLING GRIZZLY**
**1320 20th St., Denver**
**303/297-8300**  DD
Pine walls, heavy wood tables, and stuffed animal heads on the walls give the Giggling Grizzly a mountain-town feel. The Grizzly, next door to El Chapultepec, is usually quieter than other downtown bars. There's plenty of space for big groups, the juke box has a wide song selection, and the beers are served very cold in tall glasses. Hours: Sun–Tues 11 a.m.–5 p.m., Wed–Sat 11 a.m.–2 a.m.

**MY BROTHER'S BAR**
**2376 15th St., Denver**
**303/455-9991**  CD
This former stagecoach stop has been a Denver fixture since the original owner bought the first post-Prohibition beer keg in Denver from

*Pints Pub*

the Tivoli Brewery. Writers Jack Kerouac and Neal Cassady spent hours at the bar in the 1960s. Today, paintings of Beethoven, Mozart, and the first chair violinist from the first Denver Symphony line the front room wall. Classical music floats in the background as people from all walks of life chat, drink, and eat. Live classical music plays Saturday nights from 9 p.m. to midnight. Hours: Mon–Sat 10 a.m.–1:30 a.m. Closed Sunday.

### PINTS PUB
**221 W. 13th Ave., Denver**
**303/534-7543** DD
An authentic red British phone booth stands in front of this Denver pub, silently declaring to customers that this is the real thing. Inside, a photograph of Queen Elizabeth sits next to the front door, British flags hang from the corners, and heavy wood tables fill the smoking and non-smoking rooms. The bar offers a two-page scotch whiskey menu and the kitchen serves British-style pub food. Hours: Mon–Sat 11–11, Sun 11–8. Happy hour: Mon–Sat 3:30–6:30.

### SHAKESPEARE'S
**2375 15th St., Denver**
**303/433-6000** DD
The Bard probably wouldn't complain that his name had been given to this Denver pool hall. Shakespeare's made its home in this former restaurant equipment warehouse near Confluence Park in January 1995. The large open space houses 19 pool, two snooker, and four billiard tables. Table fees are $3.75 per player/hour; three or more pay a flat fee of $11. The full-service bar has daily happy hours 4 p.m. to 7 p.m. Hours: Daily 11 a.m.–2 a.m.

### TRIOS ENOTECA
**1730 Wynkoop St., Denver**
**303/293-2887** DD
The cigar room at the back of this swank lower downtown bar feels like a dated men's club—although it's open to any cigar smoker. Leather

NIGHTLIFE

lounge chairs, an oriental rug, and a TV decorate the homey room. Luckily for non-smokers, a ventilator pushes the cigar smoke out of the bar and into the alley. The rest of the bar is equally comfortable. Couches, booths, and sitting chairs fill the front and back room. Davidoff, Griffin, and Zino cigar prices range from $6 to $18. The bar also has a selection of 60 wines available by the glass, cognacs, scotch, sherry, you name it. Hours: Sun–Tues 4 p.m.–midnight, Wed–Sat 4 p.m.–2 a.m.

**WYNKOOP BREWING COMPANY**
**1634 18th St., Denver**
**303/297-2700              DD**
The Wynkoop, founded in 1988, is Colorado's oldest brewpub. With a full-service restaurant, 22 pool tables, and upstairs and downstairs bars, it's also one of the biggest. The bar's LoDo location attracts downtown business people, young and old. The brewery brews its special recipes from huge basement and first-floor vats. Try the Railyard Ale, Patty's Chili Pepper, or Tiger Root Beer. Hours: Mon–Sat 11 a.m.–2 a.m., Sun 10 a.m.–midnight.

## COMEDY CLUBS

**COMEDY SPORTS**
**1634 18th St., Lower Level, Denver**
**303/297-2111              DD**
The "actletes" (actor-athletes) at Comedy Sports present high-energy comedy shows as if they were sporting events. The audience serves as the show's judges as the actletes compete for points. A referee officiates the improvisational skits. The cabaret-style Comedy Sports lounge is located in the basement of the Wynkoop Brewing Co.

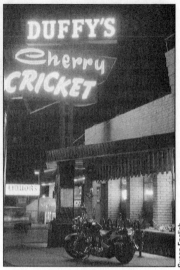

*Cherry Cricket, p. 201*

Show times: Thur 8 p.m., Fri & Sat 7:30 and 9:45 p.m. Tickets: $9–12.

**COMEDY WORKS INC.**
**1226 15th St., Denver**
**303/595-3637              DD**
Roseanne, Jay Leno, Jerry Seinfeld, and Tim Allen are a few of the nationally known comedy stars that performed on the Comedy Works stage early in their careers. Comedy Works has showcased national comedic talent in the historic Larimer Square Granite Building since 1982. All shows in the cabaret-style basement are 21 and over, and some are non-smoking. Show times: Tues–Thur 8 p.m., Fri 8 and 10 p.m., Sat 6:45, 8:45, and 10:45 p.m., Sun 8 p.m. Tickets: $7–$16, plus a two item (food or drink) per person minimum.

## DINNER THEATER

**COUNTRY DINNER PLAYHOUSE**
**6875 S. Clinton St., Englewood**

**303/799-1410**                  **SD**

The Country Dinner Playhouse has won national acclaim for its production of Broadway shows. Award-winning director Bill McHale has produced all-time favorites like *Crazy for You*, *Fiddler on the Roof*, *The King and I*, and *South Pacific*. Actors perform on a theater-in-the-round stage so everyone has a good view. The playhouse restaurant serves an all-you-can-eat buffet. Performances: Tues–Sat buffet 6–7:15, pre-show 7:15, performance 8. Sat & Sun matinees: buffet 12–1:15, pre-show 1:15, performance 1:45. Tickets: $21–$26.

## MOVIE HOUSES

In the first half of this century, Denver abounded with old-time movie palaces. Theaters with names such as the Egyptian, Oriental, Isis, and Vogue brought silent films and other Hollywood entertainment to the local communities. Unfortunately for historians and architects, most of the theaters were destroyed under heavy pressure to build modern office spaces and big parking lots. The Ogden, Bluebird, and Paramount theaters, each built as movie palaces, survived demolition and now serve as concert venues. Below are the most interesting, funky theaters in Metro Denver.

**BLUEBIRD THEATER**
**3317 E. Colfax Ave., Denver**
**303/322-2308**                  **CD**

The Bluebird featured silent movies when it first opened on East Colfax in 1913. After a brief stint as an art house in the 1960s, the Bluebird marred the already seedy Colfax Avenue with yet another porn house from 1974 to 1987. The theater sat

---

## Denver International Film Festival

*The Denver Film Society showcases the new geniuses of the silver screen at its annual Denver International Film Festival held in the downtown Tivoli Theaters. Artists from around the world are invited to submit recent works in categories including new international features, animation, independently produced fiction and documentaries, and children's programs. Prior to the festival, a Program Committee and an International Program Advisory Board select films to feature in the eight-day festival. More than 100 films are featured on six screens during the October event. The festival also gives the John Cassavetes Award to an individual making an outstanding contribution to American independent filmmaking. For ticket, date, and location information, contact the film festival at 1430 Larimer Square, Suite 201, Denver, CO 80202, 303/595-3456.*

empty and run-down until two young locals, Chris Swank and Evan Dechtman, re-opened the renovated theater in October 1994 as a concert venue and movie theater. The Bluebird shows classics such as *Scarface* and *Citizen Kane* at 6 on Sunday nights. Tickets: $5.

**ESQUIRE THEATRE**
**590 Downing St., Denver**
**303/733-5757** CD

The Esquire has been a Denver Landmark since the 1950s. In the theater's early days, neighborhood children packed the two-room theater every Saturday morning to watch cartoons. Today, movie-goers seeking other-than-Hollywood films line Downing Street to view one of the popular featured films. Owned by Landmark Theatres, the Esquire also shows *The Rocky Horror Picture Show* Saturdays at midnight. Limited free parking is available in the south lot and the surrounding streets. Purchase tickets early for popular films.

**MAYAN THEATER**
**110 Broadway, Denver**
**303/744-6796** CD

At dawn of opening day for the new Mayan Theatre, a group of Santa Clara Indians performed an exorcism of evil spirits on the theater's rooftop. Since a raging 1929 fire burned down the original theater, the ceremony was intended to prevent subsequent mishaps. Local architect Montana Fallis designed the Mayan, with its terra cotta facade and rubied Mayan goddess. The theater remains one of Denver's best venues for foreign and art-house films. Landmark Theatres, the current owner, refurbished the Mayan in 1986 and created two additional 110-seat theaters by splitting the balcony. The old seats, while refurbished, are still uncomfortable; bring back support if needed.

# 13

# DAY TRIPS FROM DENVER

## Day Trip: Boreas Pass Scenic Drive

**Trip time:** *The trip from Denver to Breckenridge will take between three and four hours depending on the amount of time spent sightseeing at the suggested stops. Consider spending the night in Breckenridge and returning to Denver on I-70.*

**Denver, South Park and Pacific Railroad** completed its Denver-to-Breckenridge line in August 1882. The much-anticipated service replaced stagecoaches to connect the thriving Breckenridge mining camps with Denver buyers and suppliers. The train service was a lifesaver for the camps, transporting food, mail, and luxury supplies to the camps and then returning to Denver weighed down by the valuable gold and silver ore shipments. The rail line, called the highest narrow-gauge highway in the country, had its own difficulties, however. Chief among them was forging the high winds, heavy snows, steep grades, and hairpin turns on 11,482-foot Boreas Pass. Passengers and Breckenridge miners often had to painstakingly hand-shovel snow off the buried tracks.

Today, travelers can follow the same historic, breathtaking route by car. The scenic drive begins on Highway 285 traveling west from Denver. Drive approximately 50 miles to the small town of **Como**, where the DSP&P trains switched from the main route, to ascend the High Line track over the 21-mile Boreas Pass. The original 19-stall roundhouse still stands proud in sleepy Como. Local historical societies have erected a commemorative plaque in front of the century-old structure. After passing through Como, the Boreas Pass road quickly steepens. An early rail passenger described the initial Boreas ascent: "As our train followed a groove in the mountain

# DENVER REGION

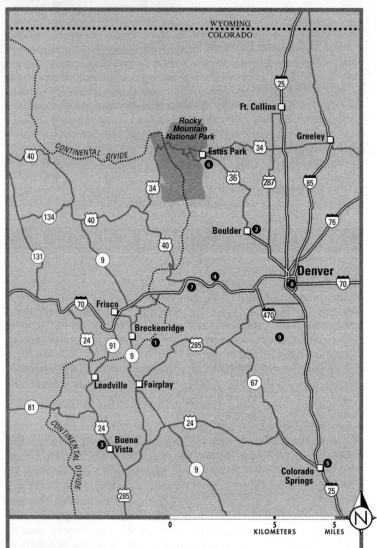

### Denver Region

1 Boreas Pass
2 Boulder
3 Buena Vista
4 Central City
5 Colorado Springs
6 Estes Park/Rocky Mountain National Park
7 Georgetown
8 Rocky Mountain Arsenal National Wildlife Refuge
9 Roxborough State Park

side, we looked down upon a green exquisite little valley.... The mountain sides were all aglow with rainbow tinted flowers, and it seemed that we were being literally 'carried to the skies on flowery beds of ease.'" After maneuvering the switchbacks to the summit, stretch your legs while exploring the remains of the original summit train station. Trains used to stop here to unload mail at the highest post office in the country. During the summer months the mountainside is filled with colorful wildflowers and softly whistling aspen trees. **Quandry Peak** and the **Ten-Mile Range** stand out to the west.

Continue over the pass to Breckenridge. The former mining town has now exploded into an internationally renowned year-round resort. Rather than panning for gold, the major pastimes are skiing down one of the world-class ski slopes, biking across mountain trails, fishing the **Blue River**, or careening down the **Alpine Slide**. Replacing assaying stops and trading stores, t-shirt shops, restaurants, condos, and ski stores now line busy Main Street. However, the town has retained some of its historic Victorian charm. Original Victorian houses still stand on some side streets, and many of the area's surrounding hiking trails lead to abandoned mine shafts. If you plan to spend time in Breckenridge, try eating at the **Breckenridge Brewery** or **Adams Street Cafe** on Main Street. Hotels and condos abound in Breckenridge. For a more out-of-the-way alternative, try the **High Country Lodge**, located about ten minutes from the town on Peak 7. This B&B style lodge looks out over pine forests and surrounding peaks. An open-air Jacuzzi sits on the deck. Call 970/453-9843. For more lodging options, call 800/221-1091.

# Day Trip: Boulder

**Trip time:** *40 minutes from Denver*
The 30-mile drive to Boulder takes travelers into a world much different from neighboring Denver. The New Age college town is renowned for having a population of free-thinkers. In the past, voters have approved ordinances such as no smoking in public areas, sound level limits on the Pearl Street Mall, and anti-growth initiatives. Boulderites are manic about exercise. Mountain bikes, rollerblades, unicycles, and feet have remained the preferred modes of transportation for those not commuting to Denver. The entire population seems physically fit. Boulder is also home to the Buddhist Naropa Institute, which attracts hundreds of people seeking spiritual advising each year.

Scenic also describes Boulder well. Nederland and the Flatirons wrap the town up in their respective arms while the entire Front Range looms nearby. The city originally put its name on the map as home to the **University of Colorado at Boulder**. The university brings more than 30,000 graduate and undergraduate students to the town each academic year. Miles of open green lawn weave between the old, architecturally impressive buildings. CU holds the outdoor **Colorado Shakespeare Festival** in the university's amphitheater during the summer. Call 303/492-0554 for information. To explore the campus, follow Highway 36 until it turns into 28. Take a left on University and the campus looms large to your right.

Boulder is probably best known for the **Pearl Street Mall**, which extends from 9th Street to 16th Street on Pearl. Everything abounds on Pearl Street. Mysterious magicians, bouncing acrobats, bellowing musicians, and white-faced mimes entertain crowds on warm days throughout the year. Children love to climb on the boulders and sculptures on the east side of the mall. Denverites bored with the local shopping selection flock to Boulder's Pearl Street. Stand-out favorites are **Knit Wit** off Pearl on Broadway and **Applause**. After you shop until you drop, rest assured you can eat until you burst. Fine cafes, ice cream shops, and fast food stops fill the mall with delectable aromas. Students flock to Pearl Street for the nightlife. Local and touring concerts perform nightly at the **Boulder Theatre** on 14th. Bars line both sides of the mall, and spread out to the south and north as well.

Hiking and picnic spots make **Chatauqua Park** on Baseline Road a good place to relax an afternoon away. The Gregory Canyon trail, which starts at the picnic grounds, is an easy 5-mile hike that affords panoramic views of the Continental Divide. The Boulder Philharmonic Orchestra performs summer concerts in Chatauqua. To reach the park, follow the Baseline Road Exit off Highway 36 straight to Chatauqua. Rock climbers find popular and challenging climbing routes in the Flatirons while the nearby Nederlands brim with a variety of mountain trails.

*Aerial view of Boulder*

> **TIP**
>
> Boreas Pass lights up with brilliant reds, oranges, and yellows starting in mid-September, when the aspens start changing colors.

## Day Trip: Rafting at Buena Vista

**Trip time:** *2½ hours*

The **Arkansas River** makes its way through Colorado in alternating torrents of rapids and smooth waters. The section that passes through Buena Vista is one of the most popular stretches for water-sports enthusiasts. Hordes of rafting companies have sprouted up along the river to capitalize on the growing interest. Companies offer a variety of half-day, full-day, and overnight trips. The most popular trips are the half-day rides down 15 miles of the **Brown's Canyon**. Rafters will scream, laugh, and get soaked as this stretch of river travels through the Pinball, Zoomflume, Big Drop, Staircase, Widow Maker, and other breathtaking rapids.

All-day trips generally continue an extra 7 miles through the canyon to catch foreboding rapids like Siedell's Suckhole and Twin Falls, and they also include lunch or dinner. Most Buena Vista raft companies take trips down the Arkansas seven days a week throughout the summer season, usually May 1 to Labor Day. With so many companies competing for business, the rates vary little. Most charge $25 to $30 for a half-day adult trip, $60 for a full-day trip. Some companies offer group discounts, so it's worth calling around. Reservations are always encouraged. Here are a few recommendations: **Buffalo Joe River Trips**, 800/356-7984; **American Adventure Expeditions**, 800/288-0675; and **Dvorak's Kayak and Rafting**, 800/824-3795.

If you plan to spend a few days in the area, you'll find plenty of ways to fill your time on and off the river. Buena Vista is nestled in a beautiful mountain valley at the foot of the Collegiate Peaks. The small town has many hotels, restaurants, art galleries, and stores to visit. Outdoor enthusiasts can explore the area on mountain bikes in the summer and by snowmobile or cross-country skis in the winter. There are hot springs and golf and tennis facilities nearby. Here are a few lodging options: **The Blue Sky Inn**, 719/395-8862; **Streamside Bed and Breakfast**, 719/395-2553; and the **Alpine Lodge**, 719/395-2415. Visitors can also call the Buena Vista Chamber of Commerce at 719/395-6612.

**From downtown Denver:** Take Broadway south to Hampden Avenue. Turn right (west) and follow Hampden until it turns into 285. Follow the highway 120 miles to Buena Vista. One suggested detour along the way is to stop in historic **Fairplay** to visit the South Park Historic Foundation's museum village, **South Park City**. Using donated mining artifacts and buildings relocated from nearby towns, the historic foundation re-created a true nineteenth-century Colorado mining town. With a little help from the imagination, visitors can step back in time to visit the local drug store, drop by the barber shop for a trim, or order a drink from the saloon bar. Volunteers moved the original stagecoach from the Mosquito Pass summit to the village, as well as the first Fairplay ranger station. Hours: May 15–Oct 15 the village opens at 9. Between Memorial and Labor Days, the village closes at 7. All other times it closes at 5. Admission: $5 adults, $4 seniors 62 and over, $2 children 6–12, children under 6 free.

## Day Trip: Central City

**Trip Time:** *45 minutes*
Early prospectors tried to make their fortunes gold mining in Central City. Today, fortune seekers try a different lady luck: pushing coins through slot machines or trying their hand at the blackjack table. In the 1980s voters approved legislation allowing gambling in several Colorado mountain towns. While gambling has brought new vitality into the once-sleepy towns of Central City, Black Hawk, and Cripple Creek, it has also stripped them of much historic charm. Developers chipped into the surrounding mountains to build casinos in Black Hawk and parking areas in Central City. Long charter buses from Denver struggle through the narrow Central City streets dropping gamblers off at the casino doorsteps. In the face of this adversity, however, Central City has maintained some of its history.

Central City was first noticed in 1859 when John Gregory discovered the Gregory Lode. News of the gold jackpot slipped out fast and within a few months 20,000 prospectors pitched tents and started digging in the area. Welsh and Cornish miners paid Robert Roeschlaub to build an opera house in 1878. Roeschlaub used only materials native to Colorado to complete the building. **Central City Opera** took up residence in the opera house in 1932. Today it claims the longest running summer opera festival in the United States. The Teller House next door leads tours through the opera house year-round. Although ticket sales plummeted after gambling hit town, Central City fills the house for most summer shows. Call 303/292-6700 for reservations.

If you plan on seeing an opera, consider arriving early to enjoy a picnic overlooking the city's original cemetery. Follow the main street past the opera house and out of town. The road will wind around until it's on the hill above the opera house. Pull off to the side of the road and enjoy a preshow picnic.

Next door to the opera house is the **Teller House** where Herndon Davis painted the famous "Face on the Barroom Floor." Victorian artifacts and furniture once belonging to the mysterious Baby Doe Tabor and Governor John Evans make the Teller House a living museum. Head to the Teller House after the opera for a drink and people-watching. Some of the night's cast members typically fraternize in the bar following the performance.

**TRIVIA**

Breckinridge (spelled with an "i" instead of an "e") was named after U.S. Vice President John Cabell Breckinridge. General George E. Spencer, one of the original settlers, named the town for the vice president in his effort to have a U.S. post office established in the mining town. Citizens switched the name to Breckenridge with an "e" after learning Breckinridge had joined the Confederate army during the Civil War.

**Central City** and **Black Hawk** gamblers have 35 casinos to choose from. Depending on the casino, players will find blackjack, video gaming machines, poker, and slots throughout both towns. If drinking will play a part in your gambling night, or you don't like mountain driving, consider a Denver-Central City shuttle rather than maneuvering the winding Highway 119. The first shuttles leave Denver at 6:30 a.m., and the last return at 2:30 a.m. People's Choice at 303/936-1117 and Ace Express at 303/421-2780 are two options.

**From downtown Denver:** Take Highway 6 west to Highway 119. Highway 119 heads north to Black Hawk and Central City.

## Day Trip: Colorado Springs

**Trip time:** *75 minutes*

Colorado Springs, located 60 miles south of Denver, is a major urban center set in the shadow of 14,110-foot-high Pikes Peak. Although an economic boom has increased the city's population and size in recent years, it's still possible to reach a remote mountain trail or lake within 15 minutes.

Many competing factors shape Colorado Springs into the diverse area it is. The United States Air Force Academy and Fort Carson bring a military focus to the city. Right-wing Christian groups such as Colorado for Family Values and Focus on the Family both have their headquarters in the Springs. Wide open farmlands surround the city creating a large agricultural interest group, and students from local colleges give parts of town a youthful feel. Spending an evening at Cowboys bar on Academy Boulevard is a cultural experience. The country western bar attracts urban cowboys, air force cadets, and liberal Colorado College students. Beyond the political environment, the Colorado Springs area has many natural and man-made sites worth a visit.

The following is a suggested itinerary for a day in the Springs. The **Air Force Academy** is located off I-25, north of the Colorado Springs city limits. Visitors are welcome to explore the massive facility. Take the north entrance exit to the visitor center. The next stop is majestic **Garden of the Gods**, again accessible directly off I-25, Exit 146. A rock garden of 300-million-year-old red sandstone formations seemingly sprouts out of nowhere.

Students often hole up with books in one of the garden's secret nooks. Climbers scale many of the formations and walkers wind in and out of the rocks on paved trails. Those more inclined to drive can cruise through the garden on the roads.

After working up an appetite, jump back on I-25 south to the Uintah Street Colorado College Exit. Turn left on Uintah Street and then right on Cascade. Cascade runs through the **Colorado College** campus. Park on the street and explore the two-block campus. For lunch, continue on Cascade, turn left on Cache la Poudre, and make an immediate right onto Tejon to find Wooglin's Deli on the left-hand side of the street. The deli is a popular student hang-out serving excellent sandwiches and salads.

Next stop is the historic **Broadmoor Hotel**. Turn right on Cache la Poudre to Nevada Street. Turn right on Nevada and continue for about 5 miles to the Broadmoor Exit. After following signs to the hotel, the majestic pink facade will rise out of the distance. Park on one of the surrounding side streets and enter through the front doors. Walk through the hotel to the pond at the west doors and enjoy a quiet walk around the trail. The **Cheyenne Mountain Zoo** is worth a stop if you still have energy. Follow the road around the Broadmoor to El Pomar Road. Turn left on Penrose Boulevard and right on Zoo Road. The zoo, which sits at 6,800 feet, has more than 500 diverse species in outdoor and indoor exhibits.

Before heading back to Denver, stop at **Manitou Springs** for some shopping or dinner. Take I-25 north to Exit 141. Turn left and continue to Manitou Springs. The city is rumored to have the biggest practicing witch population per capita in the United States, and is filled with historic Colorado row houses, cafes, and Native American and silver jewelry stores.

**From downtown Denver:** I-25 south runs directly to Colorado Springs.

*Colorado Springs skyline*

# Day Trip: Estes Park and Rocky Mountain National Park

**Trip time:** *90 minutes*

The Colorado Mountain Club pushed forward a vocal campaign in the 1910s to designate the hundreds of acres outside Estes Park as national park land. The CMC enlisted the help of several Northern Arapaho elders living on the Wyoming Wind River Reservation to name the major landmarks in the area. The Arapahos, who remembered growing up on the land, accompanied CMC members on a trek through the park. Never Summer Range, Big Meadow, Tonahutu Creek, and Lumpy Ridge each derived from the expedition. The CMC also learned from the trip that the Arapahos had ascended Longs Peak long before the first white man's ascent, in 1868. Congress dedicated Rocky Mountain National Park in the fall of 1915.

Today the Estes Park/Rocky Mountain National Park area is a primary Colorado attraction. Visitors will find all the modern amenities—from modest to plush—in the mountain village of Estes Park bordering the park. More than 300 shops, restaurants, and lodging options fill the mountain village, and nightly theater and club acts give the town an interesting nightlife. Those wanting to bask in the town's serenity can explore the playgrounds, picnic areas, and river walks. An 18-hole golf course sprawls out in the valley below Longs Peak. Two lodging options are **Aspen Winds**, 800/399-6010, and **Trappers Inn**, 800/552-2833. Call the **Estes Park Visitors Center** at 800/443-7837 for more information.

The town of Estes Park serves as one entry point into Rocky Mountain National Park. The park can feel as busy as the Grand Canyon in the summer when visitors flood the area, but if you're adventuresome and patient, park staff can recommend places to avoid the crowds. A $5 pass is required to enter the park. Stop by the Visitor Center Headquarters for maps and information before starting a trip.

Different elevations throughout Rocky Mountain support a variety of ecosystems. Ponderosa and lodgepole pine, juniper, and aspen grow at lower levels while subalpine fir and brilliant wildflowers characterize the middle elevations. Near the mountaintops, the trees disappear and the landscape turns to alpine tundra plants. During the warm months, typically April to October, hikers forge the 355 miles of trails to reach remote park areas. **Longs Peak**, standing high at 14,255 feet, is one of the more famous, and more technical, of the hikes. If you do plan on climbing Longs, stop at the Longs Peak Ranger Station before starting the ascent. A more leisurely hike is the trail to **Bierstadt Lake**. Park in the Bear Lake lot and begin walking right on the Bear Lake loop. A quarter of the way around the lake you will spot the Bierstadt Lake trailhead.

The park maintains drive-in campsites open year-round, and campers may purchase a permit to use the backcountry campsites. Reservations are required at some of the sites, and most fill up fast in summertime.

*Rocky Mountain National Park*

In snowy winter months, cross-country skiers and snowshoers can access most of the closed-off park trails. **Wild Basin**, a mile north of the Allenspark entrance off Highway 7, is a beautiful winter trail. Local outfitters take guided horseback tours through the park in the summer. The **Cache La Poudre River** touts some of the best trout fishing in the state. Photographers and sightseers consistently view elk, Rocky Mountain bighorn sheep, river otters, coyotes, various songbirds, and eagles in the Estes Valley and the national park. If you don't feel like getting out of your car but want to enjoy the scenery, drive the **Trail Ridge Road**—the highest continuous paved highway in the U.S.—to Grand Lake. The road is open May through September.

**From downtown Denver:** Highway 36 is the fastest route to Estes Park from Denver. However, the **Peak-to-Peak Scenic Byway**, which passes through Black Hawk and Nederland, is worth the extra time. Take Highway 6 west out of Denver to the Highway 119 north junction. Highway 119 turns into Highway 72 past Boulder, and then Highway 7 past Allenspark to Estes. To take the quicker route, take I-25 north to Highway 36, which continues to Estes Park.

## Day Trip: Georgetown

**Trip time:** *45 minutes*
More silver poured out of the Georgetown mines in the 1880s than anywhere else in the world, a fact that earned the town its nickname, "Silver Queen of the Rockies." The Denver, South Park and Platte Railroad made Georgetown

*Georgetown Loop Railroad*

easily accessible from Denver and other mining towns. Within a few years, 5,000 people moved to the quaint mountain town tucked in the valley.

Today, Georgetown still looks like a nineteenth-century mining town. More than 200 of the town's original Victorian homes and buildings are still intact, and remnants of mining days long past fill the outlying area. Visitors will find much to do throughout the historic Georgetown area. Consider touring the Old Town Business District. Visit the restored 1880 **Hamill House**, Louis Dupuy's posh **Hotel de Paris**, or the old 1860 **jailhouse**. Or shop for souvenirs on the narrow restaurant- and shop-lined streets.

Georgetown and neighboring Silver Plume mining camps were connected by the 4½-mile **Georgetown Loop Railroad**. The two town's are actually only 2 miles apart, but the track had to wind back and forth to gain 600 feet of elevation. Today, visitors can re-create the trek on the original railroad. The steam locomotive travels across the 100-foot-high Devil's Gate Bridge and through the scenic pine forests and aspen groves lining the south side of the valley. Visitors can board the 80-minute train trip either at the Silver Plume (#226) or Georgetown (#228) Exits. Trips run from the end of May to October.

The scenic 22-mile **Guanella Pass** road connects Georgetown to Grant and Highway 285. Early developers constructed the road in 1880, so logging companies and nearby gold mines could ship goods from the pass to Grant. The road passes through a number of vegetation and geologic variations as it changes elevations. From Georgetown, the windy road parallels Clear Creek, passing through beaver-populated wetland areas. Beyond the wetlands, the road continues to the summit where 14,060-foot Mt. Bierstadt looms in the east. Several hiking trails are accessible from Guanella Pass.

The very adventurous and fit might brave the **Mt. Bierstadt** challenge. Day hikers can also access the more moderate **Rosalie Trail** and **Scott Gomer Trail** from the summit. Cross-country skiers use these trails in the wintertime. After continuing over the pass, the road heads through the **Geneva Basin** where four-wheel-drive vehicles and mountain bikes can access the **Geneva City Townsite**. An old miner's cabin marks the spot of the mining town. Continuing toward Grant, **Falls Hill** will appear to the left, where Scott Gomer Creek pours over a garden of large boulders. Grant lies about 4½ miles north of Falls Hill. The former supply town now supports one restaurant, a county store, and a lodge. Only the Grant to the Guanella Pass summit portion is maintained year-round for vehicle travel. Once you've continued south on the pass and reached Grant, continue east to Denver on U.S. 285.

**From downtown Denver:** Take I-25 north to the I-70 junction. Take I-70 west about 45 miles to the Georgetown Exit.

## Day Trip: Rocky Mountain Arsenal National Wildlife Area

**Trip time:** *25 minutes*

With the Rocky Mountains looming so prominently to the west, most Denver visitors and residents alike forget that they are on the outskirts of a great plain. This day trip featrues the other side of Denver's landscape.

In 1942 the U.S. Army bought a chunk of undeveloped Colorado prairie land to make chemical and incendiary weapons for World War II. The land was eventually called the **Rocky Mountain Arsenal**, and weapons were made there until the 1960s. The army never used weapons produced at the arsenal, and instead used a buffered zone within the site's central core area as a weapons destruction location site until the 1980s. Unaware of its ugly neighbor, a large animal population gradually settled throughout the protected buffer area. Later, the army chose Rocky Mountain Arsenal as a military and industrial wastes disposal area. Shell Oil Company added to the environmentally dangerous setting by producing agricultural pesticides in Arsenal facilities until 1982. Some of the land and, subsequently, the animal population, was contaminated by toxic waste burial, wind dispersal, and accidental spills. The Army initiated a major environmental clean-up plan in the mid-1980s, still underway today.

Now for the good part: The U.S. Fish and Wildlife Service took interest in the Arsenal after discovering a bald eagle roost on the land in the winter of 1986. The eagles apparently nested in the Arsenal to feed on the abundant prairie dog population. The Service conducted numerous surveys and discovered other large animal populations, some endangered species, inhabiting the Arsenal lands. In 1992 congress declared the Arsenal a national wildlife refuge; official designation will come once the clean-up project is completed.

The current wildlife status is fascinating, given the Arsenal's history,

> **TRIVIA**
> 
> English explorer and writer Isabella Bird climbed Longs Peak with Rocky Mountain Jim in 1873. Bird, the fourth woman to climb Longs, described her adventure: "Longs Peak turned red with the afterglow of the sun and before it a big half-moon hung out of the heavens, shining through the silver blue foliage of the pines on the frigid background of snow, and turning the whole into fairyland." For more reading about women in the Rockies read *The Magnificent Mountain Women* by Janet Robertson.

and promising considering its proximity to urban Denver and its 2 million inhabitants. Bird-watchers head to the Arsenal during the winter when the bald eagles, golden eagles, and ferruginous hawks are seen flying overhead or perched on top of high poles. Even great horned owls have been spotted in the bare fall trees. In the spring, songbirds such as the oriole, warbler, and finch sing from the woodlands while great blue herons wade in the Arsenal's lakes. The summer months bring out the lark bunting, American white pelican, and rare ground-burrowing owls. A diverse duck population makes the Arsenal a pit-stop during the fall migration.

Today, the Rocky Mountain Arsenal National Wildlife Area brings visitors to the site for free guided weekend tours and educational nature programs. Access to the site is heavily controlled, so all visits are guided and reservations are required. The bald eagle watch runs from December through mid-March. Visitors can access the site on the east side of the Arsenal daily from 3 p.m. to dusk. For more information, call 303/289-0232.

**From downtown Denver:** Take I-25 north to I-70 east. Take the Quebec Street Exit off I-70. Turn left and continue to the parking lot on 72nd Ave.

## Day Trip: Roxborough State Park

**Trip time:** *40 minutes*
Golden eagles soar above Roxborough State Park, reminding visitors that this is natural wildlife habitat. Rattlesnakes, coyotes, mule deer, and an occasional bear or bobcat also prowl the area—sometimes close enough to spot. And to make a good thing even better, this complex wildlife system exists only 30 miles from Metro Denver.

Hiking through Roxborough State Park is a lesson in geologic and natural history. The Fountain Formation, the red, dark orange, and salmon pink rocks jutting out of the ground, started forming 300 million years ago when sand and gravel eroded from the surrounding Rocky Mountains. As the earth shifted, the formations were slowly but surely pushed out of the ground, the result of which we see today. In front of the foothills and on the edge of the plains, this spectacular field of rocks seems to appear out of nowhere. In fact, the Roxborough Formations are the southern continuation of the same formations found in Red Rocks Park near Morrison.

Because Roxborough Park is located in a transition point where plains meet mountains, the area supports a unique mix of vegetation. Desert yucca and cactus plants grow relatively close to wild roses and aspen trees. Oak brush grows on the hillsides while cottonwoods thrive along the Little Willow Creek banks. The deep green of the Ponderosa pine and Douglas fir growing on ridge tops contrasts strikingly with the red rock formations.

The State of Colorado bought Roxborough in the early 1970s as part of the state park system. Today, hikers can explore Roxborough's wonders through a variety of trails. The **South Rim Loop** is a 3-mile moderate to difficult trail that climbs across ridges, old stagecoach routes, and low brush in the southern part of the park. Hikers can climb to the highest point in Roxborough via the strenuous 6-mile **Carpenter Peak Trail**. The park summit provides expansive views of the surrounding mountains to the west and the flat plains to the east. Hikers seeking more leisurely trails will enjoy the relatively flat Fountain Valley and Willow Creek loops. Watch for rattlesnakes sunning on the lower trails. The snakes probably won't strike unless they are bothered, so keep your cool and your distance. Cross-country skiers can access the moderate trails in the winter. Visitors must purchase a $3 per vehicle day pass at the park entrance. Park maps are available from the visitor center. Park hours: Daily 8–5.

**From downtown Denver:** Drive south on Highway 85 (Santa Fe Drive) to Titan Road. Turn right and continue to Roxborough Park Road. Follow signs to the park.

# APPENDIX: CITY·SMART BASICS

## IMPORTANT PHONE NUMBERS

### EMERGENCY
Ambulance, 911
Fire Department, 911
Police Department, 911

### MAJOR HOSPITALS
Children's Hospital, 303/861-8888
Denver General Hospital, 303/436-6000
National Jewish Hospital, 303/388-4461
Porter Memorial Hospital, 303/778-1955
Rose Medical Center, 303/320-2121
St. Anthony Hospital, 303/629-3511
St. Joseph Hospital, 303/837-7111
Swedish Medical Center, 303/788-5000
University Health Science Center, 303/399-1211

### EMERGENCY CENTERS
Drug Abuse Hotline, 800/222-0828
Rape Crisis Hotline, 303/322-7273
Rocky Mountain Poison Control Center, 303/629-1123

### VISITOR INFORMATION
Denver Metro Chamber of Commerce, 303/534-8500
Denver Metro Convention and Visitors Bureau, 303/892-1505

### METRO DENVER TIME AND TEMPERATURE
303/976-1311

## CITY MEDIA

### NEWSPAPERS
*Denver Business Journal*
*Denver Post*
*La Voz*
*Rocky Mountain News*
*Westword*

### MAGAZINES
*Colorado Homes and Lifestyles*
*5280: Denver's Mile High Magazine*

### COMMERICAL TV STATIONS
Channel 2/WB2
Channel 4/CBS
Channel 6/PBS
Channel 7/ABC
Channel 9/NBC
Channel 12/PBS
Channel 31/FOX

### RADIO STATIONS
KBCO FM 97.3/rock, folk
KBPI FM 105.9/rock
KCFR FM 90.1/Colorado Public Radio
KDKO AM 1510/soul, hip hop
KHIH FM 95.7/jazz
KOA AM 85/news, sports
KOSI FM 101/easy listening
KTLK AM 760/talk
KUVO 89.3 FM/jazz
KVOD FM 99.5/classical
KXPK FM 96.5/rock
KYGO FM 98.5/country

## CITY TOURS

### COLORADO STATE CAPITOL
Broadway and Colfax
303/866-2604

### COORS FIELD
20th and Blake Sts.
303/762-5437

### CULTURAL CONNECTION TROLLEY
303/299-6000

**DENVER PUBLIC LIBRARY**
1357 Broadway
303/640-6206

**GRAY LINE OF DENVER**
P.O. Box 17527
Denver, CO 80217
303/289-2841

**LOWER DOWNTOWN DISTRICT, INC.**
1616 17th Street #372
Denver, CO 80202
303/628-5428

**VICTORIAN HOUSE TOUR**
303/331-0621

## CAR RENTAL

**AVIS**
800/831-2847.

**BUDGET**
800/527-0700.

**DOLLAR RENT-A-CAR**
800/800-4000.

**ENTERPRISE RENT-A-CAR**
303/660-0690.

**HERTZ**
800/654-3131

## BANKING

**BANKONE**
1125 17th Street
303/759-0111

**COLORADO STATE BANK**
1600 Broadway
303/861-2111

**FIRSTBANK**
370 17th St.
303/623-2000

**UMB BANK COLORADO**
1670 Broadway
303/839-1300

**US BANK**
918 17th St.
303/585-5000

**WELLS FARGO**
1740 Broadway
303/861-8811

**WOMEN'S BANK**
821 17th Street
303/293-2265

## CHURCHES/SYNAGOGUES

*Baptist*

**GETHSEMANE BAPTIST CHURCH**
2567 W. Iliff Ave.
Denver, CO 80219
303/922-7931

**MACEDONIA BAPTIST CHURCH**
3240 Adams St.
Denver, CO 80205
303/377-8821

*Catholic*

**CATHEDRAL IMMACULATE CONCEPTION**
1530 Logan St.
Denver, CO 80203
303/831-7010

**HOLY GHOST CATHOLIC CHURCH**
1900 California St.
Denver, CO 80202
303/292-1556

## Christian Science
**SIXTH CHURCH**
2701 S. University Blvd.
Denver, CO
303/777-0489

## Episcopal
**CHURCH OF THE ASCENSION**
600 Gilpin St.
Denver, CO 80218
303/388-5978

**ST. JOHN'S EPISCOPAL CATHEDRAL**
1313 Clarkson St.
Denver, CO 80206
303/831-7115

## Greek Orthodox
**ASSUMPTION GREEK ORTHODOX CATHEDRAL**
4610 E. Alameda Ave.
Denver, CO 80222
303/388-9314

## Lutheran
**MESSIAH LUTHERAN CHURCH**
1750 Colorado Blvd.
Denver, CO 80220
303/355-4471

## Methodist
**SHORTER COMMUNITY A M E CHURCH**
3100 Richard Allen Ct.
Denver, CO 80205
303/320-1712

**TRINITY UNITED METHODIST CHURCH**
1820 Broadway
Denver, CO 80202
303/839-1493

## Presbyterian
**MONTVIEW BOULEVARD PRESBYTERIAN CHURCH**
1980 Dahlia St.
Denver, CO 80207
303/355-1651

## Synagogues
**TEMPLE EMANUEL**
51 Grape St.
Denver, CO 80222
303/388-4013

**TEMPLE MICAH**
2600 Leyden St.
Denver, CO 80207
303/388-4239

# POST OFFICES

Post offices are located in every Metro Denver neighborhood. The main branch is located downtown.

**DOWNTOWN ANNEX STATION**
1595 Wynkoop St.
Denver, CO
303/294-4100

**DENVER DOWNTOWN STATION**
2012 Curtis St.
Denver, CO 80205
303/297-6000

# BABYSITTING AND CHILD CARE

**COLORADO CHILD CARE ASSOCIATION**
1665 Grant St., Denver
303/860-7174

**KID'S CORNER DAY CARE AND LEARNING CENTER**
2601 York St., Denver
303/296-3596

**THIRD AVE. DAY SCHOOL**
300 Garfield, Denver
303/322-6659

## DISABLED ACCESS INFORMATION

**ADVOCATE SERVICES FOR THE DISABLED**
1424 Madison St.
Denver, CO 80206
303/355-8403

## MULTICULTURAL RESOURCES

**ARTS MONTAGE: THE MULTI-CULTURAL CALENDAR OF EVENTS**
Mayor's Office of Art
280 14th St., Denver
303/640-1037

**ASIAN AMERICAN CHAMBER OF COMMERCE**
930 W. 7th Ave., Denver
303/595-9737

**COLORADO BLACK CHAMBER OF COMMERCE**
1564 Elmira St., Aurora
303/341-1296

**DENVER INDIAN CENTER**
4407 Morrison Rd., Denver
303/936-2688

**EULIPIONS INC.**
2425 Welton St., Denver
303/295-6814

**GAY, LESBIAN, AND BISEXUAL COMMUNITY CENTER OF COLORADO**
1245 E. Colfax Ave. #125
Denver
303/831-6268

**HISPANIC CHAMBER OF COMMERCE**
930 W. 7th Ave., Denver
303/534-7783

**HUE-MAN EXPERIENCE BOOKSTORE**
911 Park Ave. West, Denver
303/293-2665

# INDEX

accommodations, 35–60
Alamo-Placita Park, 119
altitude, 17
Arvada Center for the Arts and Humanities, 185
Auraria Higher Education Center, 97
Aurora Reservoir, 145, 167
auto racing, 180–181

Barr Lake, 119
Belleview Park, 120
Buerger Brothers Building, 97
biking, 27–28, 165–166
bird-watching, 171
Black American West Museum and Heritage Center, 132, 133
boating, 166–168
Bonfils, Helen, 187
Boreas Pass Scenic Drive, 207, 209
Boulder, 209–210
bowling, 168
Bronco Buster statue, 97
Brown, Molly, 107, 108
Brown Palace Hotel, 37–39
Buckhorn Exchange, 74, 75
Buena Vista, 211–212
Buffalo Bill Memorial Museum and Grave, 114
Butterfly Pavilion and Insect Center, 120
Byers-Evans House, 97

camping, 168
Carr, Ralph, 13
Cathedral of the Immaculate Conception, 98
Celestial Seasonings Tour of Tea, 118

Central City, 212–213
Central City Opera, 188–189
Chatfield Reservoir, 167–168
Chatfield State Park, 145–146
Cheesman-Evans-Boettcher Mansion, 108–109
Cheesman Park, 140
Cherokee Ranch and Castle, 115
Cherry Creek Reservoir, 168
Cherry Creek State Park, 146
Cherry Creek Trail, 28
Children's Museum, 122
City and County Building, 98
City Ditch, 145
City Park, 110, 111, 120–121, 140–141, 143
Cleo Parker Robinson Dance Ensemble, 189
Colorado Avalanche, 181–182
Colorado Ballet Company, 190
Colorado Rapids, 182
Colorado Rockies, 182
Colorado History Museum, 133
Colorado Springs, 213–214
Colorado Symphony Orchestra, 140, 189
*Colorado Wildflowers*, 98
Colorado Xplosion, 182
comedy clubs, 204
Confluence Park, 98–99
Coors Brewery Company Tours, 115, 117
Coors Field, 99
Corona-Dora Moore School, 111
Cranmer Park, 141

Cultural Connection Trolley, 24

Daniels and Fisher Tower, 99–100
Denver Art Museum, 123, 130
Denver Botanic Gardens, 121, 143
Denver Broncos, 183
Denver Buffalo Company, 67
Denver Civic Center, 100
Denver Civic Theatre, 185
Denver Firefighters Museum, 123
Denver Gas and Electric Building, 100
Denver International Airport, 28–31
Denver International Film Festival, 205
Denver Museum of Natural History, 124, 134
Denver Nuggets, 183
Denver Performing Arts Complex, 185–186
Denver Public Library, 100–101, 124–125
Denver Puppet Theater, 125
Denver U.S. Mint, 101
Denver Victorian Playhouse, 125–126
Denver Zoo, 121–122
dinner theater, 204–205

El Centro Su Teatro, 186
Elitch Gardens Amusement Park, 127
Elitch, John and Mary, 126
Emmanuel-Sherith Israel Chapel, 101–102
Estes Park, 215–216
Eulipions, 186

225

Fiddler's Green Amphitheatre, 190–191
fishing, 170, 172
fitness clubs, 172–173
Ford, Barney, 163
Ford, Justina, 133
Forney Transportation Museum, 102
The Fort, 90–91
Four Mile Historic Park, 113
Friends of Chamber Music, 189

galleries, 135–138
Genesee Park, 141–142
Georgetown, 216–218
Germinal Stage Theater, 187–188
golfing, 173–174
Grant-Humphries Mansion, 111
Greek Theater, 102
greyhound racing, 181

hiking, 168–170
horseback riding, 174–175
House of Mirrors, 102–103
Hudson Gardens, 144
hunting, 175

Ice House, 103, 105
in-line skating, 175, 176

kayaking, 175–176
Kerouac, Jack, 103

Lakeside Amusement Park, 127
Larimer Square, 105
Littleton Historical Museum, 125
Lumber Baron Inn, 47, 48
McNichols Sports Arena, 191
Mammoth Events Center, 191
Melbourne Hotel and Hostel, 45, 47

Mizel Museum of Judaica, 131
Molly Brown House, 108
Mother Cabrini Shrine, 114–115
movie theaters, 205–206
Museo de las Americas, 132

Newton, Quigg, 4
night clubs, 194–204
Ninth Street Historic Park, 105

Observatory Park, 122
Ocean Journey, 99
Ogden Theatre, 191–192
Old Prospector statue, 105
Opera Colorado, 189
Oxford Hotel, 42, 43

Paramount Theatre, 190, 192
The Park People, 146
Peña, Federico, 5, 11
Pioneer Monument, 105
Plains Conservation Center, 113
public art, 136, 138

Red Rocks Amphitheater, 118, 192–193
restaurants, 61–94, 129
Richtoffen Castle, 114
Rocky Mountain Arsenal National Wildlife Area, 218–219
Rocky Mountain National Park, 215–216
Rocky Mountain Quilt Museum, 132
Roxborough State Park, 219–220
RTD Light Rail, 21, 23–24, 25

St. Cajetan's Church, 105–106

St. Elizabeth's Church, 106
St. John's Episcopal Cathedral, 111–112
scuba diving, 176
shopping, 127–129, 147–164
skating, 176
skiing, 177–180
Ski Train, 33
SkyRide, 24–25
sledding, 180
Sloan's Lake Park, 142
Speer, Robert, 2
Stapleton, Benjamin, 3
State Capitol, 106

Tabor, A. W., 44
Tattered Cover, 157
tennis, 180
Theatre on Broadway, 188
Tivoli Brewery, 106–107
Trinity United Methodist Church, 108

Union Station, 32, 108

Washington Park, 122, 142
weather, 13–14
Webb, Wellington, 5, 11–12
Westin Hotel Tabor Center, 44, 45
Windsor Hotel, 41
Wings Over the Rockies Aviation and Space Museum, 134
Wynkoop, Edward W., 72

# You'll Feel like a Local When You Travel with Guides from John Muir Publications

## CiTY·SMaRT™ GUIDEBOOKS

Pick one for your favorite city: *Albuquerque, Anchorage, Austin, Calgary, Cincinnati, Cleveland, Denver, Indianapolis, Kansas City, Memphis, Milwaukee, Minneapolis/St. Paul, Nashville, Portland, Richmond, San Antonio, St. Louis, Tampa/St. Petersburg, Tucson*

Guides for kids 6 to 10 years old about what to do, where to go, and how to have fun in: *Atlanta, Austin, Boston, Chicago, Cleveland, Denver, Indianapolis, Kansas City, Miami, Milwaukee, Minneapolis/St. Paul, Nashville, Portland, San Francisco, Seattle, Washington D.C.*

## TRAVEL✦SMART®

Trip planners with select recommendations to: *Alaska, American Southwest, Carolinas, Colorado, Deep South, Eastern Canada, Florida Gulf Coast, Hawaii, Kentucky/Tennessee, Michigan, Minnesota/Wisconsin, Montana/Wyoming/Idaho, New England, New York State, Northern California, Ohio, Pacific Northwest, South Florida and the Keys, Southern California, Texas, Western Canada*

## *Rick Steves'* GUIDES

See *Europe Through the Back Door* and take along country guides to: *France, Belgium & the Netherlands; Germany, Austria & Switzerland; Great Britain & Ireland; Italy; Russia & the Baltics; Scandinavia; Spain & Portugal;* or the *Best of Europe*

## ADVENTURES IN NATURE

Plan your next adventure in: *Alaska, Belize, Costa Rica, Guatemala, Honduras, Mexico*

**JMP travel guides are available at your favorite bookstores. For a FREE catalog or to place a mail order, call: 800-888-7504.**

John Muir Publications ✦ P.O. Box 613 ✦ Santa Fe, NM 87504

# Cater to Your Interests on Your Next Vacation

**The 100 Best Small Art Towns in America
3rd edition**
Discover Creative Communities, Fresh Air, and Affordable Living
U.S. $16.95, Canada $24.95

**The Big Book of Adventure Travel
2nd edition**
Profiles more than 400 great escapes to all corners of the world
U.S. $17.95, Canada $25.50

**Cross-Country Ski Vacations**
A Guide to the Best Resorts, Lodges, and Groomed Trails in North America
U.S. $15.95, Canada $22.50

**Gene Kilgore's Ranch Vacations, 4th edition**
The Complete Guide to Guest Resorts, Fly-Fishing, and Cross-Country Skiing Ranches
U.S. $22.95, Canada $32.50

**Indian America, 4th edition**
A traveler's companion to more than 300 Indian tribes in the United States
U.S. $18.95, Canada $26.75

**Saddle Up!**
A Guide to Planning the Perfect Horseback Vacation
U.S. $14.95, Canada $20.95

**Watch It Made in the U.S.A., 2nd edition**
A Visitor's Guide to the Companies That Make Your Favorite Products
U.S. $17.95, Canada $25.50

**The World Awaits**
A Comprehensive Guide to Extended Backpack Travel
U.S. $16.95, Canada $23.95

**JMP travel guides are available at your favorite bookstores.
For a FREE catalog or to place a mail order, call: 800-888-7504.**

**John Muir Publications • P.O. Box 613 • Santa Fe, NM 87504**

## ABOUT THE AUTHORS

The authors of this book—a mother-daughter team—have lived in Denver's Park Hill neighborhood for more than 24 years. **Georgia Garnsey**, a former editor at *Colorado Homes and Lifestyles* magazine, has also written for *Denver* magazine and other local publications. She is a graduate of Stanford University and a member of the Denver Women's Press Club. Georgia and her husband, Woody, have two daughters, Megan and Hilary.

**Hilary Garnsey** holds a bachelor's degree from Colorado College and has studied journalism at the University of California at Berkeley. Hilary's articles have appeared in *Colorado Homes and Lifestyles*, the *Aurora Sentinel*, the *Berkeley Voice*, and other publications. Hilary currently lives in Guadalajara, Mexico.

**Kyle Wagner**, author of the dining chapter, is the food writer at *Westword*, Denver's news and arts weekly.

**JOHN MUIR PUBLICATIONS** and its City·Smart Guidebook authors are dedicated to building community awareness within City·Smart cities.

We are proud to work with the Colorado Center for the Book as we publish this guide to Denver.

The **Colorado Center for the Book** is a nonprofit organization dedicated to instilling a lifelong love of reading in Colorado residents. The center's purpose is to promote reading and writing and to encourage all people to develop the skills necessary to be responsive, creative, and culturally literate citizens. Highly visible community projects include the Rocky Mountain Book Festival, the Colorado Book Awards, the Rocky Mountain Children's Book Festival, and the Colorado State Library Summer Reading Program.

**For more information, please contact:**
Colorado Center for the Book
2123 Downing Street
Denver, CO 80205
303/839-8320

**Colorado Center for the Book**